Human Monsters

An Illustrated Encyclopedia of the World's Most Vicious Murderers

DAVID EVERITT

D1378320

CB

CONTEMPORARY BOOKS

Library of Congress Cataloging-in-Publication Data

Everitt, David, 1952–
      Human monsters : an illustrated encyclopedia of the world's
  most vicious murderers / David Everitt.
            p.   cm.
      Includes bibliographical references and index.
      ISBN 0-8092-3994-9
          1. Murderers—Biography—Encyclopedias.   1. Mass
  murder—History—Encyclopedias.   I. Title.
  HV6245.E84   1993
  364.1'523'0922—dc20   92-41188
                                                            CIP

Front cover photographs:
Clockwise from upper left © Bettman, © Bettman, © Bettman, © AP/Wide World.
Center, left to right © Culver Pictures, © Bettman.

Published by Contemporary Books
A division of NTC/Contemporary Publishing Group, Inc.
4255 West Touhy Avenue, Lincolnwood (Chicago), Illinois 60712-1975 U.S.A.
Copyright © 1993 by David Everitt
Printed in the United States of America
International Standard Book Number: 0-8092-3994-9

  8 9 10 11 12 13 14 15 16 VRS/VRS 05 04 03 02

ILLUSTRATION CREDITS

CONTENTS

FOREWORD

by Harold Schechter

Though words, not oils, are his medium, David Everitt has painted one hundred portraits of humanity's ghastliest members and assembled them for public contemplation. Operating in a dual capacity—both as creator and curator—he has put together a collection that displays, in every gruesome detail, the many faces of human evil.

Welcome to the Gallery of Gore.

Like all museums, this one offers the visitor a variety of lessons. Though our time is often defined by its scientific achievements—the Computer Age, the Video Age, the Age of High Technology—it is also, as criminologists never tire of telling us, the Age of the Serial Killer. This terrifying figure, the psychopathic night prowler who hunts humans for his sick, sadistic pleasure, has come to haunt the dreams of America. And it is true that serial slaughter has reached, if not epidemic, then certainly unsettling proportions in our country. According to Robert Ressler, cofounder of the FBI's psychological-profiling program (and the prototype for author Thomas Harris's heroic agent, Jack Crawford), there were more than 170 serial killers in America in 1991. Thirty-five years earlier, there had been one.

To many, the proliferation of these creatures—real-life Jekyll-and-Hydes whose monstrous appetites are generally masked by normal facades—is a symptom of large-scale social pathology, of the impending collapse of modern civilization. There is just enough truth in this charge to make it seem plausible. No doubt, certain contemporary conditions—the breakdown of the family, the loss of religious faith, the frenetic mobility of our culture—are conducive to the sort of rootlessness, alienation, and emotional dysfunction that can lead to sociopathic violence.

But the first lesson that David Everitt teaches is that the capacity for perversion and savagery is no modern phenomenon. To take a tour through Everitt's Museum of Murder is to discover that bloodlust is one of humankind's most primal—and ineradicable—drives. A medieval butcher such as Gilles de Rais makes today's serial killer seem relatively tame. Trolling the streets of Chicago, John Wayne Gacy collected thirty-three male victims over the course of six years. In roughly the same time span, Gilles tortured and dismembered at least 140 young boys—and he never had to leave his castle. When he hungered for blood, he simply sent out the servants, ordering in fresh bodies the way you or I might have a Chinese meal or pizza delivered to our door.

There are plenty of other premodern monsters on exhibit here: Peter Stubbe, the sixteenth-century German werewolf who killed and cannibalized more than a dozen children; Joseph Vacher, the "French Ripper" of the late 1800s who butchered and disemboweled at least eleven women; Jesse Pomeroy, the nineteenth-century American socio-path who had slaughtered two playmates by the time he was fourteen; and many more. By giving us a historical overview of homicidal mad-ness, Everitt offers one grim consolation at least: our age is not uniquely pathological in its production of horror.

It is not unique in its *consumption* of horror, either. To tongue-clucking moralists the contemporary taste for true-crime literature is another sign that our world is plunging into a new age of darkness. And there is no denying the popular appeal of these gory stories. Today's serial killer is tomorrow's media celebrity. At times it seems as though the victim's blood has barely dried before the book contracts are signed and the movie rights optioned.

The fact is, however, that human beings have always possessed a keen appetite for real-life stories of gruesome crimes—and the bloodier the better. In preliterate times sensational killings were immortalized in "murder ballads," which transformed mayhem into folk poetry. The true-crime genre itself was born in the early 1700s with the publication of *The Newgate Calendar*, which offered accounts of England's most notorious murderers and thieves. A century later, British readers gobbled up the grisly morsels dished out in tabloids like *The Illustrated Police News* and made best-sellers of books like Borrow's *Celebrated Trials* (1825) and Pelham's *Chronicles of Crime* (1841). In America Matthew Worth Pinkerton's *Murder in All Ages* (1898), Thomas Duke's *Celebrated Criminal Cases of America* (1910), and H. B. Irving's *A Book of Remarkable Criminals* (1918) became early classics of the genre.

Not content with simply reading about lurid crimes, the public has often demanded—and been treated to—simulated re-creations. In the days before the TV miniseries, showmen catered to this craving in various inventive ways. In turn-of-the-century Chicago, for example, spectators could view the savageries of Dr. H. H. Holmes—"America's first serial killer"—reproduced in a downtown dime museum. A half century later, Midwestern fair-goers could fork over a quarter for a gander at the "death car" (complete with fake dismembered corpses) of Edward Gein, "the original 'Psycho.'"

Clearly, then, David Everitt's work is part of a centuries-old tradition growing out of a basic human fascination with gruesome crime. The question that needs to be answered, of course, is, What is the source of this grim fascination?

Part of the answer lies in the title Everitt has chosen for his collection—*Human Monsters*. At a glance the phrase seems paradoxical, a contradiction in terms. Monsters, after all, are wholly alien beings, the hulking embodiments of the *nonhuman*. The very word conjures up not the seamy realities of everyday homicide, but the fantasy realm of folklore, myth, and dream. In childhood (and in societies still in the grip of archaic belief), people fear the dark because it is full of monsters. Werewolves and vampires, zombies and ghouls, witches and cannibal ogres—these are the night dwellers, prowling the shadow land beyond the borders of daylight.

As we outgrow superstition and come to see the world through "enlightened," scientific eyes, we perceive that such demons do not *truly* exist. And so it is a shock to encounter the beings in this book—to learn that the world really does contain creatures like Fritz Haarmann, "the Vampire of Hanover"; Theo Durrant, "the Demon of the Belfry"; Earle Nelson, "the Gorilla Man"; the French werewolf, Gilles Garnier; and Gertrude Baniszewski, an ogress who seems to have stepped from the pages of "Hansel and Gretel."

These and other subjects of David Everitt's research are literally living nightmares, folklore creatures in the flesh. (Indeed, a number of them are the real-life prototypes for such fabled monsters as Bluebeard, Dracula, and Norman Bates.) There is a "Believe It or Not" quality to the profiles in this collection. We read them with a mixture of consternation and awe, transformed once again into wonderstruck children. We are both horrified *and* amazed—appalled but also enthralled.

Everitt's title offers another clue to the peculiar fascination that these criminal fiends exert. By stressing not only their monstrousness but their humanness as well, he reminds us that these deviant personalities are not quite as alien from ourselves as we would like to believe. And in fact, we would not be so deeply drawn to these graphic accounts of violently aberrant behavior unless there were a part of ourselves that took pleasure in them. This part is perhaps best summed up in the title of a novel by the cult crime writer Jim Thompson: *The Killer Inside Me.*

This is not to say, of course, that the average reader of crime literature is a potential murderer. Quite the contrary. The mass audience for best-sellers like *Fatal Vision* or movies like *The Silence of the Lambs* is clearly not made up of psycho-killers, but of the great American middle class. To claim that crime books inspire criminal behavior is equivalent to arguing that paperback romances cause housewives to abscond with Barbary pirates, or that readers of Anne Rice's vampire novels might be tempted to join the ranks of the undead.

Conversely, it is demonstrably true that homicidal maniacs do not require crime books to feed their madness. The blood spree orchestrated by Charles Manson, for example, was set off by the lyrics of the Beatles' *White Album.* And amid the charnel wreckage of Jeffrey Dahmer's horror house, the police uncovered a ghastly collection of human bones and body parts—but not much in the way of reading matter.

Nevertheless, our desire to learn every gory detail of Dahmer's crimes—along with the atrocities of the ninety-nine other sadists, sociopaths, and psychotics whose case histories Everitt presents—clearly reflects that on some deep, dark, largely unacknowledged level, we share certain common impulses with these "human monsters." Dimly, even shamefully, we sense that they function as the living incarnations of a secret self—what psychologists call the Shadow, the feral Mr. Hyde that lurks deep beneath the law-abiding realities of our waking lives.

In short, though we are generally disinclined to admit it, these prodigies of horror reveal something important about the rest of us, who regard ourselves as paragons of normalcy. They show us not what we were capable of *doing,* but what all of us are capable of *dreaming.* This revelatory function is implied in the very word *monster,* which derives etymologically from the Latin word *monstrare,* meaning to show forth. The novelist Carson McCullers captures this quality in her book *A Member of the Wedding,* when, in the murk of a carnival sideshow, her heroine confronts a different sort of living monstrosity, a half-male/half-female "morphodite," who looks at her "as though to say, *We know you. We are you!*" The great American poet, Emily Dickinson, puts the same thought somewhat differently:

Ourself behind ourself, concealed—
Should startle most—
Assassin hid in our Apartment
Be Horror's least.

"Ourself behind ourself, concealed." It is precisely this hidden personality, the dark side of our daily selves, that derives such enjoyment from the ghastly and forbidden.

And so the time has come to step into the murder museum. It is a murky and mazelike place, hung with one hundred grisly portraits, one more nightmarish than the next. And if you stare at them long enough, a peculiar sensation may begin to overtake you—a dizzying sense that you are looking not into the face of a terrifying stranger, but into a dark, distorted mirror.

Indeed, you may find yourself believing that the features staring back at you bear a mocking, monstrous resemblance to your own.

—Harold Schechter
Professor of American literature and culture at Queens College, The City University of New York, and the author of the true-crime books *Deviant* and *Deranged*

ACKNOWLEDGMENTS

I wish to express thanks to my agent, Harold Schmidt, and my editor, Stacy Prince, as well as to Gary Hertz for his assistance in researching this book, and to Reid Rossman at the Bettmann Archive, Bill Fitzgerald at AP/Wide World Photos, Allen Reuben at Culver Pictures, and Charlotte Otten. Special thanks go to Harold Schechter for all his help in making this book possible.

INTRODUCTION

The selection of one hundred gruesome murderers is a difficult process. To be more precise, the process of *narrowing down* the selection to one hundred is difficult. Humanity has never suffered from a scarcity of men and women willing to kill other human beings in the most reprehensible manners, and any collection of a hundred such people is going to comprise only a fraction of the grisly grand total. Any list of this kind is bound to exclude infamous criminals that some true-crime buffs believe should be included. Knowing that I couldn't compile a list that would be absolutely complete, I have done my best to make it a fair, if unsettling, representation.

What qualifies someone to be included among humanity's grisliest murderers? Obviously, no single, purely objective method exists for answering this question, but I have tried to keep certain considerations in mind. One criterion for selection is the killer's number of victims. But alone, this body-count method, concentrating only on those with the highest, most-appalling totals, would leave out some of the most fascinating cases. The Lizzie Borden case, for instance, involved two killings, a total that has been surpassed by countless other murderers, but it continues to intrigue people a hundred years after the crimes were committed, both because of the ghastly nature of the two murders and the mystery and controversy that still surround them.

Another factor that I have considered is the degree to which a murderer inspired fear or shock at the time of the killings. The shooting deaths carried out by David Berkowitz in the mid-1970s in New York City, for example, were not nearly as sadistic as crimes committed by some other recent serial murderers, but his series of random killings were unnerving enough to terrorize one of the great cities for over a year. Similarly, in 1984 teenager Ricky Kasso committed just one murder, but the satanic trappings of this killing, along with the incongruous fact that it occurred in an unusually idyllic community, succeeded in shocking the entire nation. In other instances I've chosen cases for what could only be called their sheer bizarreness. Perhaps the best example would be Texan innkeeper Joe Ball, who made a habit of feeding his waitresses to a pet alligator.

Above all, what I've tried to do in my selection is to convey the idea that grisly murder has taken on many faces over the years. Although sadistic serial murder is often thought of as a recent phenomenon—and it certainly has become alarmingly common in the last twenty years— it is not anything new (especially vivid cases in point: fifteenth-century serial cannibal Sawney Beane and seventeenth-century torturer-murderer Elizabeth Brownrigg). Furthermore, gruesome murder is not confined to any particular country, and consequently the profiles you'll find here include killers from England, Hungary, Ecuador, France, and Russia. You won't, however, find any here from Africa or the Far East; language and cultural differences make it difficult to find any reliable information on many killers from these regions. Last, I have also tried to illustrate the scope of infamous murder, including those killings committed in the ruthless pursuit of money, those committed for the twisted pleasure of inflicting pain and death, as well as those motivated by impulses that are barely comprehensible, the acting out of some hidden obsessions.

The collection here offers such obvious choices as Ted Bundy and John Wayne Gacy, as well as relatively obscure murderers like Vasili Komaroff (the so-called "Wolf of Moscow"), Vincenz Verzeni (the Italian disemboweler and vampire), and Thomas Piper (the Baptist sexton turned rapist-murderer). From around the world and across five centuries, here are a hundred faces of homicidal mania.

SAWNEY BEANE

?–1435

Cannibalism was not unheard of in Scotland. In the days of the Roman Empire, St. Jerome wrote of Scottish man-eating as late as the fourth century. By the fifteenth century, however, cannibalism was considered to be something buried in the country's distant, tribal past. But old ways die hard, and newfangled, civilized taboos do not always hold sway. During medieval times Scotland was haunted by several instances of human throwbacks who succumbed to some primitive, ferocious instinct to consume their own kind.

The most notorious of these was a man named Sawney Beane. For twenty-five years he and his feral, inbred clan waylaid travelers and feasted on their flesh. They may have preyed upon as many as a thousand victims.

Sawney Beane was born into a farmer's family outside Edinburgh, near Scotland's east coast, sometime in the late 1300s. It is believed his penchant for brutality was apparent at an early age. For some reason he left his home district as a young man, taking a young woman with him, and began a trek that eventually took him to the opposite side of the country. The home he and his woman finally settled on was at the base of a seaside cliff along the southwestern coast of Galloway. The entrance was little more than a fissure in a wall of rock that led to a dark, winding passageway, which in turn led to a cave. The cavern that served as home for Beane and his common-law wife was a mile from the seaside entrance. Further setting apart the Beane domicile from the outside world was the incoming tide that flooded the passageway twice a day. Beane had found the perfect hideaway for a primitive man who intended to live on plunder.

At first Beane's subsistence was derived from the money belts worn by travelers that he killed along the barren highland roads. But this turned out to be a meager existence, especially as he and his wife spawned a brood of offspring, fourteen children in all. The need for food, fresh meat in particular, then accelerated when the Beane boys and girls began to mate among themselves and produced yet another set of mouths to feed. The solution was simple. The Beanes' traveler victims carried not only coins and jewels on their person but also meat on their bones. Sawney Beane and his clan developed a taste for human flesh.

For twenty-five years travelers disappeared among the rocky reaches of Galloway. Apparently there was not even safety to be found in numbers; not only lone travelers but parties of a half-dozen people were known to vanish. The only trace left of the victims was an occasional body part washed ashore along the Galloway coast. For a while the popular theory was that packs of man-eating wolves were prowling the highland roads; then, as the number of disappearances grew, the explanations became more desperate: perhaps Galloway was plagued by werewolves or demons. The official response was not much more rational. An investigation commissioned by Scotland's King James I resulted in the hanging of anyone who was in any way suspicious. If these arbitrary executions were meant to strike fear into the hearts of evildoers, the effect was lost on the hungry Beane clan. The disappearances continued.

No one in the southwestern corner of Scotland had any idea who the real demons in their midst were until a group of Galloway travelers happened to witness the unspeakable butchery firsthand. A party of thirty people, returning home from a day at a local village fair, heard a commotion up ahead along the winding, coastal road. When they reached the site of the commotion, they could do nothing at first but stare. Before them, a man defended himself with pistol and cutlass against a band of savage-looking attackers; nearby, the man's wife was lying on the ground, disemboweled; some of the attackers were ripping off chunks of her flesh and eating them raw. In another moment the thirty travelers were able to shake off their astonishment and rush the cannibals.

The Beanes fled into the hills, out of reach, but now, finally, there were witnesses to testify to the clan's atrocities. The surviving husband's horror story was relayed through official channels to King James, and before long, the king himself was in Galloway. With him were four-hundred troops and a pack of bloodhounds.

The dogs eventually led the pursuers to the opening at the bottom of the cliff. The king's men followed the long zigzag passageway to the cavern that Sawney Beane called home. Huddled there were forty-eight people: Beane and his wife, their fourteen children, and their thirty-two incest-spawned grandchildren. Suspended above them were human arms, legs, and torsos. Some of the meat was pickled for the lean months ahead. After a brief scuffle the well-armed soldiers subdued the killer clan.

With considerable justification, King James classified Sawney Beane and his family as nothing more than wild beasts. As such, the cannibalistic Beanes did not, the king ruled, deserve a trial. They were, however, entitled to long and painful executions. The procedure began with the dismemberment of Sawney and the twenty-six other Beane men. The agonizing process of bleeding to death was watched by the twenty-one Beane women, whose own end then came in the blaze of three roaring bonfires. According to a contemporary account, the Beanes, killers and devourers of hundreds of people, "continued cursing and venting the most dreadful imprecations to the very last gasp of life."

GILLES DE RAIS
1404–1440

"The Original Bluebeard"

The first man to be associated with the name Bluebeard had, in fact, very little to do with the Bluebeard legend. Unlike the fairy-tale villain popularized by Charles Perrault in the seventeenth century, Gilles de Rais, who lived and died in the first half of the fifteenth century, was not a wife-killer. He was, however, worthy of the dread attached to the Bluebeard name: he was a deranged French aristocrat guilty of crimes so terrible that they are difficult to contemplate—he was the torturer, murderer, and mutilator of well over a hundred children. As is suggested in Leonard Wolf's biography of Rais, the transmutation of the original Bluebeard into the wife-killer of folk tales may have been a way

for the popular mind to make the real Bluebeard horrors more palatable.

The great irony about Gilles de Rais's life was that he was one of France's greatest heroes before he became its most despicable villain. Brought up to be a knight, he was a soldier in the closing phases of France's Hundred Years' War with England and was allied with that most revered of deliverers, Joan of Arc. He was Joan's most trusted lieutenant in her divinely inspired quest to drive the English out of France, and played a crucial part in her greatest victories. He was so appreciated by King Charles VII that, at the age of twenty-five, he was named marshal of France. And it wasn't only in military efforts that Rais shared Joan of Arc's mission; he was devoutly religious and a true believer in the holiness of her cause.

But even in these heroic years, Rais occasionally exhibited part of his dark side, which would horrify Europe years later. He was known, for instance, to authorize the wholesale killing of prisoners of war.

In 1431, after Joan of Arc's capture and execution, as well as his own final victory at Lagny, Rais left the battlefield behind and returned to his aristocratic family's far-flung estates in Brittany. He then waged another war, against the children in his domain.

Rais was one of medieval Europe's great patrons of the arts, spending huge sums of money to sponsor the creation of music, literature, and plays, all with a religiously inspirational theme. At the same time, he was sending out servants to lure children to his castle. His homicidal preference was for boys. Typically, he would sodomize his victims, then kill them either by slitting their throats or by complete decapitation (sometimes he had his servants do the killing while he watched). The victim would then be cut open and Rais would masturbate over the entrails.

The murders went on for eight years. Since Rais was a baron and lord of all he surveyed, there was no one to stop him, even if anyone was interested in finding out why so many children in the area were disappearing. The only people interested in that were the parents of the missing children, but they were common people and therefore didn't matter.

As he decimated the youthful population of his region, Rais also became involved in the occult. All the money he spent on the arts and on his own luxury depleted his financial resources, and he recruited magicians to replenish his wealth through alchemy. Rais's flirtation with magic soon involved the summoning of demons. In 1439 one of his child victims became part of a ritual sacrifice.

According to tradition Gilles de Rais acquired the Bluebeard nickname because of a conspicuous jet-black beard that contrasted sharply with the blond hair on his head—and that supposedly took on a bluish sheen under a certain light. In the 1430s that blue-black beard might have inspired curiosity and wonder, but when the full truth about Rais came out in 1440, it became a symbol of terror.

Ultimately, it wasn't Rais's sadism that attracted the attention of the law—it was his arrogance. And it wasn't any sense of moral duty that initiated his prosecution—it was greed. In the summer of 1440, Rais decided to renege on the sale of one of his castles, and believing he was above any law, he set out to forcibly retake the property. This entailed having his soldiers beat up the man who held the keys for the disputed castle. It didn't matter to Rais that the man was a priest.

This arrogant violation of the sanctity of the church was considered an outrage. The duke of Brittany, who coveted Rais's lands, took the offense to heart. Seeing an opportunity to strip Rais of his possessions and claim them for himself, he filed charges against Rais with the bishop of Nantes.

The only reason Rais's abominable mass murders finally came to light was that the duke of Brittany was not content with merely prosecuting Rais for religious violations. If he could find something more against the man—perhaps even something to do with those missing children that the peasants had been complaining about for so long—

then the duke could be even surer of complete victory over the marshal of France. For this reason the duke ordered a search of Rais's castle. The mutilated bodies of about fifty children were found in one of the towers. Other evidence indicated that many more had been cremated.

Faced with the prospect of both excommunication and torture, Rais confessed to torturing and killing 140 children, although chroniclers of the case have speculated that the total might have been as high as 200 or 300. He was condemned by an ecclesiastical tribunal for the heresy of engaging in black magic and was convicted by a civil court of murder.

On October 26, 1440, Rais was led to his execution, where he was to be simultaneously hanged and burned. A bonfire's flames scorched his body as he was strangled by the hangman's noose, but some of his relatives were able to rescue his corpse before it was completely destroyed by the blaze. The two servants who were convicted as Rais's accomplices in unspeakable murder did not enjoy any such royal privileges. They were simply burned alive.

VLAD THE IMPALER
1431–1477
"Dracula"

The real-life Dracula was not a vampire. That may be the only good thing that could be said about him. Although he didn't indulge in the drinking of human blood, his life was otherwise a catalog of horrors, colossal in scale and infinitely sadistic. When novelist Bram Stoker used the name and invoked images of this historical figure in his world-famous vampire story, he chose a fittingly evil background for his bloodthirsty and thoroughly irredeemable archvillain.

For years scholars remembered Dracula, if at all, as only a little-known participant in early Romanian history. His life was finally brought to more widespread attention in the early 1970s by Raymond T. McNally and Radu Florescu in their book *In Search of Dracula*. Their revelations were a lesson in human nature's potential for cruelty.

Dracula, or Vlad III, as he was more properly known, was a member of an aristocratic family of Walachia, a Romanian state bordered on the north by Moldavia and the much mythicized Transylvania. His father, Vlad II, had acquired the name Dracul, meaning dragon or devil. Dracula, in turn, means son of Dracul. The younger Vlad was born into a time of immense uncertainty and tumult for his homeland. Pressured from the north by the more powerful Hungarians and from the south by the Turks, Walachia survived only by playing one side against the other, often changing allegiance to whichever

empire seemed to have the upper hand at the time. In this, Vlad II, Dracula's father and prince of Walachia, was something of an expert. His ability to switch sides, however, did not always inspire trust in the people he was trying to appease. For this reason his sons had to spend four years in a Turkish prison.

The sultan took the sons hostage as insurance against further double-dealing by the Walachian prince. Dracula was in captivity between the ages of thirteen and seventeen. It's not clear how instinctively cruel he may have been before this term in prison or how much his mind was twisted by his captivity. In any case, when he was released upon his father's death in 1448, most of his efforts were devoted to the sort of allegiance hopping that would have made his father proud. First, he was an officer in the Turkish army, then he was aligned with Moldavia, then he was a military leader for Transylvania. Finally, in 1456, he found his way clear to take the Walachian throne. As prince and absolute ruler of his country, he was free to begin his reign of atrocity.

Dracula became known as Vlad the Impaler because of his preferred means of inflicting agony and death. He would often impale his victims upon stakes, sometimes through the heart or navel, often through the anus or, in the case of women, the vagina. Many times, he used this hideous practice for mass executions. On one occasion Vlad impaled five hundred Walachian noblemen who, in his mind, were not sufficiently impressed with his claim to power. In another instance, in the city of Brasov in 1459, he ordered the impalement of thousands of Saxons; he witnessed their sickeningly slow deaths while he dined a few feet away.

The impalements could be carried out for demented political reasons, as in the case of the five hundred noblemen, or as a way of destroying the populations of enemy towns in times of war, or they could simply be a result of a perverted whim. Vlad's female subjects often bore the brunt of this sadism. Prince Vlad considered himself a righteous man and would not tolerate any sexual indiscretions—if they were committed by women. Impalement and such punishments as being skinned alive were meted out to female adulterers and women who had sex before marriage. Sometimes the indiscretion did not have to be that overt. Once Vlad impaled a woman for the crime of bad tailoring: Dracula discovered one day that one of his male subjects was wearing a shirt and pair of pants that the man's wife had made too short; after impaling the wife for this lapse in her duties, Vlad then supplied the widower with a new spouse.

Among Vlad's other grotesque punishments were blinding, dismemberment, scalping, and boiling alive. Once, he filled one of his castle halls with beggars invited to a sumptuous feast. After the meal he asked if the beggars wished to live without care. When they replied that they would, Vlad had the hall set ablaze and all the beggars burned alive.

Vlad the Impaler's unspeakable reign began to collapse when he provoked war with the Turks by refusing to pay tribute. Early on, his troops penetrated Turkish territory, but they were eventually routed. The key to Vlad's defeat was the refusal of other Christian leaders in the region to side with him in his war. Considering Vlad's ghastly reputation, this refusal was understandable. When the sultan's soldiers came upon what has been described as a forest of impaled victims that Vlad had left in his wake, they temporarily slowed their advance in horror and dismay, but by 1462 they had prevailed and Vlad was forced to leave his Walachian throne behind. In his six-year reign he may have been responsible for 100,000 torturous deaths.

Vlad the Impaler was in exile for fourteen years. For four years he was in a Hungarian prison, where he made a practice of impaling small animals, and then the Hungarian military called him into service as an officer in yet another war with the Turks. His victories led him back to Walachia and its throne, but only for two months. In January 1477 he was killed near Budapest in a battle against the Turks. His head was taken back to Constantinople.

ELIZABETH BATHORY

1560–1614

"The Blood Countess"

When novelist Bram Stoker created his legendary vampire, he based the monstrous character on a historical figure named Vlad the Impaler, also called Dracula, or Son of the Devil, a Romanian prince of unimaginable cruelty. But some experts believe that there was another historical inspiration for Stoker's nightmare creation. They point to another

medieval aristocrat, a mad countess known to be a real-life vampire—Elizabeth Bathory. If Stoker did indeed draw upon this woman's life for his classic tale of terror, he could not have picked a more apt inspiration, for little elaboration is necessary to make Countess Bathory's exploits read like a scenario for an old-fashioned gothic horror story.

Elizabeth Bathory slipped into the role of depraved villainess very easily, and at an early age, as if evil were her birthright. Even as the teenaged bride of one of Hungary's celebrated war heroes, she was constantly devising ways to get even with those who displeased her. If the offending persons were far away, she practiced supernatural curses designed to punish them from afar. For those close at hand, those living with her in Castle Csejthe, the retribution was more immediate—and infinitely more painful.

Servant girls were a special target of Bathory's. Those deemed insolent by the countess were likely to be bound and stripped naked, then have their genitals burned with the flame of a candle. When one of these girls struck her mistress as being too noisy, Bathory ensured the girl's silence by having her mouth sewn shut.

For years Countess Bathory reigned in this way over her personal domain, making her home as horrific as any dark, sinister castle found in fairy tales. But she was really only getting started.

Her descent into vampirism began after her husband died in 1600. Starting to feel the march of time, the forty-year-old countess was haunted by the prospect of losing her beauty. Given her past proclivities, it was only natural that her solution to the problem involved a combination of black magic and sadism. As the story goes, Bathory accidentally drew blood one day while beating one of her servant girls, and a spot of the young woman's blood happened to fly onto the countess's hand. Most of the punishments administered to helpless female servants simply gave the countess cruel pleasure, but this one was different. It was a revelation. Bathory was convinced that the flesh of her hand, touched by the servant girl's blood, looked miraculously younger, magically rejuvenated. Her mind jolted with a sudden leap of diabolical faith.

Not wanting to waste any time, she had two of her male servants butcher the girl and fill a tub with her blood. Countess Bathory then immersed herself in the bloodbath, certain that she had finally found the elixir of youth.

If the authorities heard rumors about all the young women who subsequently disappeared in the vicinity of Castle Csejthe, they paid little attention. As later developments would indicate, members of the Hungarian royalty, as was the case with royalty everywhere, were inclined to allow each other a great deal of latitude. In the meantime Elizabeth Bathory unleashed a wave of unspeakable horrors.

One young woman after another was brought to Castle Csejthe and was taxed in blood, the currency that paid for Countess Bathory's mad preoccupation with eternal youth. There is some uncertainty about how many women Bathory actually drained to death in her ten years of blood bathing. According to one version, the total was forty. But another account maintains that Bathory kept a ledger of her atrocities indicating as many as six hundred victims. What we do know is that many were tortured in addition to being killed. Some of the women were forced to eat strips of their own flesh.

When troops finally arrived at Castle Csejthe—in response to shocking testimony from a young woman who had barely escaped Bathory's clutches—there was no doubt as to the validity of the horrific allegations: a blood-draining orgy was in progress at the time. In the face of such evidence, justice was swift and terrible, at least for some people. The servants who carried out Bathory's vile orders bore the brunt of Hungary's outrage: some were beheaded, others dismembered, all were put to the torch. But not Countess Bathory. After all, royalty— even unconscionably deranged royalty—has its privileges.

Bathory's connections included a cousin who was prime minister. He persuaded the king that a unique jurisprudential concept known as an indefinitely delayed sentence would be the most appropriate, if incredibly subtle, punishment for hideous crimes past imagining. What this amounted to was house arrest. Bathory spent the last three-and-a-half years of her life in her castle of horrors, walled up in her bedchamber. She was found dead on the floor on August 21, 1614.

GILLES GARNIER
?–1573

There was a crime problem in the rural areas of France in the sixteenth and seventeenth centuries. Periodically, vicious multiple murderers preyed upon the populace. Today, we would call these criminals serial killers. In those days, though, they were called werewolves.

In France at that time—as well as in other parts of Europe, a werewolf was not considered to be merely some fictional creature. The lycanthrope, a man turned into a ravenous wild beast, was an urgent social concern. Outside the French cities provincial parliaments were so troubled by the phenomenon that they were known to authorize procla-

A 16th-century wood-cut of a werewolf attack.

mations on the subject; the resolutions would outline the sort of vigilant procedures to be followed in the detection and arrest of werewolves, as well as the proper punishments to be administered to them. There was also a lively debate in print about the true nature of lycanthropy, arguments about the precise way in which Satan inflicted this plague upon society.

As one might expect, no convincing documentation has been handed down to us about the existence of actual supernatural were-wolves in those days, but many men who were accused of lycanthropy believed they truly were demonic canine predators. And their offenses were easily as ferocious as any committed by fictional werewolves in gothic novels or horror films.

One of the men who helped inspire French concerns about the outbreak of lycanthropy was Gilles Garnier, a hermit who lived outside Dole in the eastern province of Franche-Comte. Modern knowledge of the case is based primarily upon a pamphlet about Garnier published in 1574.

Garnier was supposed to have turned toward evil one night while taking a walk through the woods near his home. Accustomed for years to living completely on his own, he had recently found a woman to marry. Since she had come to live with him in his isolated house, he had found it difficult to supply enough food for both himself and his wife. In this state of discontent, he was tempted by a phantom, who made promises of a better life. Garnier's bargain with dark forces was sealed when he accepted a black-magic ointment that would enable him to change shape.

Convinced of his ability to become a devil-spawned wolf, Garnier began to stalk local children.

Around the beginning of October 1572, Garnier trapped a ten-year-old girl in a vineyard outside Dole. Pouncing on her like the wild beast he thought he was, he throttled her to death while at the same time tearing into her with his teeth. Then he ripped off her clothes and began to eat the flesh of her thighs and arms. Some of the flesh he took home to his wife. A month later he killed another girl in the same way but was scared off by some passersby before he could cannibalize the body. The possibility of being discovered again was not enough, however, to slow down his flesh-eating mania.

In only two weeks' time Garnier struck once more, this time strangling and cannibalizing a ten-year-old boy. He killed one other boy but was once more run off by people who happened upon the scene before he could finish his depraved ritual. The pamphlet on Garnier's crimes makes the curious comment that he would have eaten the boy's flesh if he hadn't been interrupted, "notwithstanding that it was a Friday," as if cannibalism might have been less heinous if enacted on a day when Catholics were allowed to eat meat.

Having been seen during two of his attacks, Garnier was tracked down by local authorities and was placed under arrest as the latest manifestation of the region's werewolf menace. His confession bore out the official supernatural interpretation of the hideous child murders. He was convicted of "crimes of lycanthropy and witchcraft" and delivered to the master executioner of high justice. Garnier was burned alive on January 18, 1573.

PETER STUBBE
?–1589

While the bloody exploits of reputed werewolf Gilles Garnier were becoming the shocking sensation of sixteenth-century France, another bestial marauder was sharpening fears in Germany about wolfmen on the loose along the Rhine River. Perhaps the most infamous convicted werewolf of his time, Peter Stubbe terrorized the countryside surrounding Cologne for some twenty-five years. According to a pamphlet published a year after his execution, Stubbe could change into a beast with "eyes great and large, which in the night sparkled like brands of fire; mouth great and wide, with most sharp and cruel teeth; a huge body and mighty claws." Stubbe's crimes against men, women, and children certainly seemed to warrant the monstrous reputation.

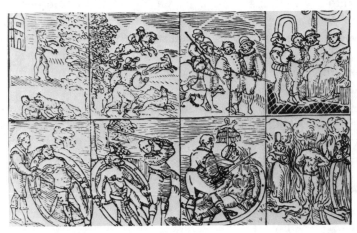

A picture chronicle of the "damnable life and death" of convicted werewolf Peter Stubbe, taken from a 1590 pamphlet.

The magic power that enabled Stubbe to change into a wolf was supposed to have been derived from an enchanted belt, bestowed upon him by the devil. A modern, psychological explanation might suggest that Stubbe, known to be an evil character at an early age, deluded himself into believing Satan had endowed him with evil powers, thereby giving himself license to commit the most heinous atrocities. In any case, he played the part of a lycanthrope to terrifying extremes. He preyed upon anyone who had slighted him in any way; many times he merely singled out those people who arbitrarily appealed to him in some twisted fashion. He seemed to have a preference for those who were defenseless, namely children. Among his catalog of horrors were rape, the ripping out of throats, and cannibalism.

In many cases Stubbe would simply pounce upon his victims as soon as he found them alone in an isolated field or forest. Other times he would exercise animallike cunning. Once, he spotted two young men and a young woman, all of whom he knew, walking down a country road. Running up ahead, he found a place of concealment along the edge of some woods and waited for the threesome to reach him. He called out to one of the young men, as if he were a friend beckoning him over for the purpose of playing some mischievous trick. When the young man drew near, Stubbe grabbed him and killed his prey so quickly and quietly that the others didn't realize what had happened. He then waited for the second young man to come see what was going on and killed him too. Now alarmed, the young woman ran away. But the possessed Stubbe was too fast for her. Since her body was never found, the authorities believed her corpse was completely eaten.

Perhaps Stubbe's most depraved and sickening crime was one of his child murders; the child in this case was his own son. After he tore the boy apart, he cracked open his son's skull and ate his brains.

As for his daughter, Beell, Stubbe had other plans. He repeatedly committed incest with her and eventually enlisted her aid as an accomplice in his crimes. Her part in the murders was not spelled out in the 1590 pamphlet on Stubbe; neither was it made clear whether she was a willing accomplice. The same was true of Stubbe's other accomplice, an extramarital lover named Katherine Trompin.

Stubbe was finally run to ground by one of the many hunting parties that, for many years, had been trying to track down the area's elusive fiend. According to the contemporary account the hunters chanced upon Stubbe in his demonic wolf form, and the party's pack of dogs chased him across the countryside. Eventually conceding that he couldn't outrun his pursuers any longer, Stubbe came to a stop and allowed himself to be caught, but not before he took off the magic belt and tossed it aside, which, according to the beliefs of the time, allowed him to return to human form.

After the culprit was caught, he was brought before the local magistrates in the town of Bedburg, and the interrogation process began—that is, Stubbe was put on the rack. Predictably, he confessed to his crimes as a werewolf. When he said that he had discarded the enchanted belt along the route of pursuit, a search party was sent to retrieve it, but the belt couldn't be found. The explanation: the devil had already taken it back.

Stubbe stood trial, along with Katherine Trompin and his daughter Beell, and they were all three convicted on October 28, 1589. Stubbe was said to have slaughtered fifteen people, thirteen of which were children.

The punishment meted out in this case suggests a striking difference in the relative severity of German and French judicial systems in the sixteenth century. The punishment given notorious French werewolf Gilles Garnier—being burned alive—was adjudged lenient enough for Stubbe's two accomplices, but for Stubbe himself, the main culprit, something more stringent was required. While he was strapped to a wheel, red hot pincers were used to tear away his flesh in ten places, then his arms and legs were crushed with the head of an axe. The hideous process was completed with decapitation and the burning of the body. In case their feelings still weren't quite clear, the authorities then instituted a symbolic warning to illustrate the dim view they took of devil worship in their jurisdiction: they erected a pole in a public place, on which was lashed the torture wheel and a picture of a wolf, while at the very top was perched Stubbe's decapitated head.

ELIZABETH BROWNRIGG
1720–1767

In eighteenth-century England, apprenticeship could be a way out of hopeless poverty. Children whose parents could not support them and who had to live in public workhouses could be sent to live with and work for local tradespersons, and after a number of years, they could acquire a livelihood that would maintain them the rest of their lives. But while apprenticed, they were also under what amounted to their benefactor's absolute power. Under a cruel tradesperson, a young apprentice might have to endure a great deal of mistreatment. Sometimes it could be much worse than mistreatment. In London in the mid-1760s, three teenaged girls apprenticed to a midwife were forced to endure months of unspeakable torture.

In 1765, when the authorities of St. Dunstan's Parish assigned fourteen-year-old Mary Mitchell to the home of Elizabeth Brownrigg,

they had no reason to think that
the girl's mistress would do anything improper. Brownrigg,
forty-five at the time, had raised
a family of her own and had
since established herself as the
district's most respected midwife. The care and skill she had
shown in bringing children into
the world was certainly a strong
recommendation for her ability
to supervise and tutor a young
apprentice, not much more than
a child herself. Brownrigg's husband, James, was a plumber with
a good business and was also a
respectable member of the com-

munity. The confidence the parish overseers had shown in the Brownriggs was justified in Mary Mitchell's successful and uneventful first
month of service. Before long, as Elizabeth's midwifery practice required more assistance, a second apprentice by the name of Mary Jones
was also put in the woman's care. Then things changed.

As some madness took hold of her, Elizabeth Brownrigg began to
punish the girls' slightest infractions with the severest of measures.
Quickly, the punishments escalated until they were no longer punishments at all—they became pure, unbridled acts of sadism. Whippings
and beatings were the order of the day. During those times when
Elizabeth was particularly out of control, she would lay Mary Jones
across two chairs and whip every part of the girl's body until she was
so exhausted she couldn't raise the whip anymore. Finding some reserve of energy, she would then fill a pail of water, splash the blood off
the girl's body, and, for good measure, force the apprentice's head into
the water until the girl practically drowned.

Early one morning, Mary Jones managed to escape and, with one
eye blinded, somehow made her way to the foundling hospital that had
released her to the Brownrigg household. Her horrendous physical
condition prompted authorities to act—but not very forcefully. They
had a lawyer's letter sent to the Brownriggs, demanding an explanation

for Jones's treatment. They received no response and pursued the matter no further.

Indicative of the societal lack of concern for the welfare of poor children, yet another girl was apprenticed to Elizabeth Brownrigg. Fourteen-year-old Mary Clifford, along with Mary Mitchell, who was still trapped in the Brownrigg house, was subjected to brutality that made Jones's ordeal pale in comparison.

Elizabeth, with the cooperation of her husband and her son, John, would force the girls to work naked for days at a time, leaving their flesh exposed to constant thrashings with canes and horsewhips. The midwife would sometimes underscore the apprentices' position as beasts of burden by securing each with a chain, one end nailed to a door, the other wrapped around the neck in a sort of choke collar. At night Mary Clifford underwent a special torture designed especially for her. When Elizabeth discovered one day that the girl had wet her bed, she had the girl sleep in the cellar's bitterly cold coal bin, with just a bare mattress and no blankets.

Elizabeth was constantly devising new ways to savage her charges. Eventually, her preferred means of punishment was to tie her victim's hands together, sling the loose end of the rope through a hook screwed into a ceiling beam, and hoist the girl off her feet; then she would bring out the horsewhip and start thrashing. She no longer let her own exhaustion bring the beatings to an end. When she was too tired to whip, she would bring in her son to spell her.

According to the eighteenth-century volume *The Newgate Calendar*, the heads and shoulders of both girls "appeared as one general sore." Mary Clifford's condition was especially horrible: by the summer of 1767, gangrene had invaded her wounds.

The torture finally came to an end when Clifford's stepmother came to the Brownrigg house. She became suspicious when James Brownrigg told her that there was no Mary Clifford apprenticed there. After a neighbor said she had spotted the girl lying senseless in the Brownriggs' enclosed yard, the stepmother went to the authorities. The police rescued Mitchell and Clifford, but for Clifford it was too late. The grotesquely battered girl died just a few days later.

At the trial, held in September 1767, Elizabeth Brownrigg, alongside her husband and son, stood accused of the murder of Mary Clifford. The eye-witness testimony of Mary Mitchell was devastating. Elizabeth was convicted and sentenced to die, but James and John, clearly willing accomplices, received remarkably soft prison sentences of six months apiece. Elizabeth Brownrigg was hanged on September 14, 1767.

ANDREAS BICHEL

1770–1808

"The Bavarian Ripper"

Despite an occasional inability to keep his hands off things that did not belong to him, Andreas Bichel was not considered to be a dangerous man. It was true that he sometimes pilfered vegetables from neighbors' gardens, and once, while working at an inn, he was caught trying to sneak away with some of the hay from his employer's barn, but in the early nineteenth century, in the Bavarian town of Regendorf, he was still considered to be a harmless enough fellow. He certainly kept up a respectable front: he had a wife, children, and a home and was able to support all three. In the now quaint language of Major Arthur Griffiths, an 1898 chronicler of the man's life, Bichel was "not a drunkard, nor a gambler, nor quarrelsome."

In order to support his family, Bichel was willing to try unorthodox

vocations. After he wore out his welcome with his innkeeper employer, he went into the business of fortune-telling. He professed to be able to see people's futures through a special "magic mirror," as it was called. What this amounted to was a magnifying glass propped up on a small wooden board, a makeshift device that was supposed to provide a mystical glimpse into things that will be. This fortune-telling gimmick would play a part in the first murder Bichel would commit.

When Barbara Reisinger came to his house in 1807, on a day that his family was not around, Bichel was only interested in the young woman as a prospective housemaid. But then something about her triggered an altogether different idea. Steering the conversation away from her qualifications for employment, he told her about his talent for divination, and the young woman agreed to have her fortune told. But the procedure for seeing the future in this case turned out to be quite unusual, if not outright bizarre.

Bichel had Reisinger sit down, facing the magic mirror placed on an adjacent table. To make sure that she wouldn't touch the special glass—and thus ruin the spell—Bichel insisted that the young woman's hands would have to be tied behind her. She would also have to have her eyes covered. Clearly not the suspicious type, Reisinger went along with this. Once she was bound and blindfolded, Bichel got hold of a knife and plunged it repeatedly into her neck. According to some accounts he severed her spinal cord, then stabbed her in the lungs. Whatever his exact methods, Bichel disposed of the body before his family returned home.

Over the next few months Bichel lured three other young women to his house and tried the same thing, but these women weren't about to have their hands tied. They left his house unharmed. In 1808, though, Bichel found a young woman named Catherine Seidel, who was passing through town and was naive enough to submit to Bichel's peculiar fortune-telling technique. She also agreed to Bichel's request that she come to his house in her best dress and bring three other dresses besides. The young woman ended up like Barbara Reisinger.

A short time later, Catherine Seidel's sister was in Regendorf looking for her missing sibling and chanced upon a discovery in a local tailor's shop. The tailor was in the process of making a waistcoat, and he was using a distinctive corded fabric that looked awfully familiar to

Seidel's sister. It was material that had come from the petticoat worn by Catherine Seidel at the time of her disappearance. The material had been supplied by the person who had ordered the garment—Andreas Bichel.

Catherine Seidel's sister notified the local police, who went to Bichel's house to investigate. Bichel's explanation for Catherine Seidel's disappearance was that she had met a young man at his house and had run off with him to elope. The story didn't impress the police. They searched the house. In a bureau they found a collection of women's clothes, including some that had belonged to Catherine Seidel. They then continued the search, intent upon finding the bodies that went with the garments. They got on the right track when they followed the nose of a police dog that kept sniffing at the Bichel woodshed.

Inside, the police dug under a pile of straw and uncovered a woman's body, cut in half. Nearby, they dug up a human head and another bisected female corpse. The missing Barbara Reisinger and Catherine Seidel were now accounted for.

Despite all the evidence presented against him at his trial, Bichel denied everything. A peculiar practice of nineteenth-century Bavarian jurisprudence then turned things around. Bichel was confronted with the mutilated bodies of the two women he had allegedly murdered. This proved to be too much for him: he collapsed in his chair. Later, in his jail cell, he became so rattled that he confessed to both murders. As for what had triggered his first killing, he gave what would have to be one of the most insipid motives for murder that was ever offered. Bichel, apparently still a petty thief at heart, said he had decided to kill Barbara Reisinger because he had been tempted by her fine clothes.

Some extravagant accounts of the case have attributed as many as fifty murders to Bichel, but more convincing versions keep the total at two. The two bodies, along with the cold-blooded nature of the murders, was more than enough to outrage Bichel's contemporaries. As the judge in this case put it, Bichel was beneath even the dignity of the common criminal, who would at least have the "energy or courage" to "rob on the highway, or break into a house"; only the most loathsome creature, the judge concluded, would "cunningly induce young girls to go to him, and then murder them in cold blood for the sake of their clothes or a few pence."

Bichel was sentenced to be broken on the wheel, the old Germanic method of execution in which the condemned man's bones were methodically clubbed into bits. In an act of mercy, of sorts, the sentence was then commuted to decapitation.

ANNA ZWANZIGER
1760–1811

The life of Bavarian poisoner Anna Zwanziger is a story of mental disintegration. Whatever predisposition she might have had for homicidal madness, her derangement took years to fully develop, nurtured by a series of hardships, until at some point in her forties she became a woman spinning out of control. She was an example of a psychopathic killer who was both monstrous and pathetic.

Life started to go astray for Anna Zwanziger, nee Schonleben, when she got married. Her choice of husband was poor. He spent most of their marriage getting drunk with his friends and spending the money Anna had inherited from her father, a Nuremberg innkeeper.

Nuremburg, where a serial poisoner Anna Zwanziger first descended into madness and where she was finally arrested in 1809.

Her husband's alcoholic ways sent him to an early grave and left Anna saddled with debts, as well as the responsibility of raising their daughter alone. A good part of Frau Zwanziger's life was spent trying to recover from this disaster.

For a while she tried her hand at the celebrated Nuremberg tradition of toymaking, but failure forced her to abandon the enterprise. She went on to one occupation after another, moving from town to town, going wherever she might stand a chance of making a comfortable living. She was always struggling. She was so hard-pressed, in fact, that twice she attempted suicide.

By the time she was forty, Zwanziger was working primarily as a housemaid. It was in this line of work that she first resorted to crime as a way of getting what she felt she deserved: she stole a diamond ring from one of her mistresses. She fled the town and may have continued stealing in other cities as well. This first step away from the law was not to be her last.

A new way to better her position occurred to Zwanziger when she became a maid to a Judge Glaser in Rosendorf. Zwanziger calculated that this well-to-do man might make a fine husband and provider. The problem was that Glaser was still legally married, though he was separated. In order for Zwanziger to realize her ambition of making her old age comfortable, the wife would have to be eliminated. This was impractical, as Frau Glaser was not at hand.

First, Zwanziger engineered a reconciliation between her employer and his wife. Once Frau Glaser returned to the Glaser house, Zwanziger started spiking her mistress's tea with arsenic, increasing the dose with each pot of tea until Frau Glaser went into the agonizing final stages of arsenic-induced sickness. For three days she vomited and vainly tried to quench an unquenchable thirst, all the while tortured by unbearable stomach pains. Since there wasn't any sophisticated means of detecting arsenic poisoning at that time, Frau Glaser's death was attributed to natural causes. As it turned out, Zwanziger was still no closer to attaining her goal because Judge Glaser had no interest in marrying her. But in a way, that almost became irrelevant; the act of poisoning became a twisted end in itself. One evening she also poisoned the food of Judge Glaser's guests, apparently out of insane spite. The guests lived, but not without considerable sickness and pain.

The deranged pattern was now set. Zwanziger moved on to a new maid's position, and once more she cultivated ideas about marrying her employer, this time a man named Grohmann, who happened to be single. But when Grohmann announced his engagement to another woman, Zwanziger went to work preparing him a special bowl of soup. Grohmann soon died an excruciating death. Along the way, Zwanziger tried unsuccessfully to poison two male servants in the house simply because they annoyed her.

Despite all this, she managed to create the impression of being a devoted, industrious servant and was recommended to another judge's household. Here the man of the house, Judge Gebhard, had a wife who was already sickly. If she were to suddenly worsen and die, there would be no reason to suspect foul play. Zwanziger's menu of steadily increasing doses of arsenic did its deadly work. Even though, once more, no marriage was in the offing for Zwanziger, she took satisfaction in killing a woman who had what she herself never could.

Zwanziger might have gotten away with this third murder, but she couldn't resist plying her trade on other members of the household as well. As her madness possessed her, she poisoned and inflicted sickness upon Gebhard's guests, a fellow maid, and a messenger boy. Their sudden illnesses were too suspicious to be tolerated, and Gebhard dismissed her. But Zwanziger still had a parting shot to be fired.

The day she left the Gebhard household, Zwanziger poisoned the servants' coffee, then cuddled Gebhard's baby and fed the infant a biscuit dipped in arsenic-laced milk. The servants and baby got violently ill but survived. Finally, the authorities were brought in to investigate.

Arsenic was discovered in the salt box that Zwanziger had refilled the night before. Then the bodies of Frau Glaser, Judge Grohmann, and Frau Gebhard were exhumed. No definitive tests for isolating arsenic traces in corpses existed at the time, but all three bodies were hardened instead of decomposed, arguably due to arsenic's preservative action. The police had enough evidence now to track down Zwanziger and place her under arrest.

Before they could reach her, Zwanziger sent off some letters to Gebhard. In one of them she told him she was willing to forget his rude dismissal and willing to resume work in his house. In another she sent all her love to the baby she had poisoned, whom she referred to as her "darling child," as if she were clinging to some fantasy of domestic bliss. This unhinged correspondence came to an end when the police caught up to her on October 18, 1809.

A packet of arsenic was found on her at the time of the arrest. According to a contemporary account, she looked at the poison and "trembled with pleasure . . . with eyes beaming with rapture." When Zwanziger later confessed in court, after six months of grueling questioning, she referred to arsenic as her "truest friend." After her confession was finished, she dropped to the courtroom floor, seized by convulsions.

In July 1811 Zwanziger was beheaded. Her body was then lashed to a wheel so the public could gaze upon the consequences of a murderous life.

JOHN WILLIAMS

?–1811

"The Ratcliffe Highway Murderer"

Few things are more unnerving than the idea of a murderous intruder invading the sanctity of one's house in the middle of the night. In London during the early 1800s, the authorities apprehended a man guilty of committing this crime not just once, but two times in the span of just twelve days. In recent years some writers have argued that the man arrested, Irish seaman John Williams, might have been innocent, but the people of London's East End in 1811 did not harbor any such doubts. They considered Williams so irredeemably monstrous that they disposed of his body in a manner reminiscent of the final scene from an old-fashioned gothic horror film.

The East End area surrounding Ratcliffe Highway catered to the sailors who came and went via the nearby docks. With its profusion of taverns and prostitutes, the section was not, by any means, a genteel place, and it most definitely had its share of criminals. But vice and larceny did not prepare the people of Ratcliffe Highway for the events occurring on the night of December 7, 1811. Sometime around midnight, a man entered 29 Ratcliffe Highway, the home of shopkeeper Timothy

FIFTY POUNDS
REWARD.

Horrid Murder!!

WHEREAS,
The Dwelling House of **Mr. TIMOTHY MARR**, 29, Ratcliff Highway, Man's Mercer, was entered this morning between the hours of **Twelve and Two** o'Clock, by some persons unknown, when the said **Mr. MARR, Mrs. CELIA MARR**, his wife, **TIMOTHY** their **INFANT CHILD** in the cradle, and **JAMES BIGGS**, a servant lad, were all of them most inhumanly and barbarously **Murdered!!**

A Ship Carpenter's Pem Maul, broken at the point, and a Bricklayer's long Iron Ripping Chissel about Twenty Inches in length, have been found upon the Premises, with the former of which it is supposed the Murder was committed. Any person having lost such articles, or any Dealer in Old Iron, who has lately Sold or missed such, are earnestly requested to give immediate Information.

The Churchwardens, Overseers, and Trustees, of the Parish of St. George Middlesex, do hereby offer a Reward of FIFTY POUNDS, for the Discovery and Apprehension of the Person or Persons who committed such Murder, to be paid on Conviction.

By Order of the Churchwardens, Overseers, and Trustees,

Ratcliff-highway,   **JOHN CLEMENT,**
SUNDAY, 8th, DECEMBER, 1811.   **VESTRY CLERK.**

SKIRVEN, Printer, Ratcliff Highway, London.

Marr. The intruder massacred the entire household: Marr, his wife, his thirteen-year-old male apprentice, and his baby.

The multiple murder was as senseless as it was brutal. There was no evidence of robbery, but even if there had been, theft would not have been sufficient motive for the horrific carnage. The berserk killer had bashed in the skulls of his four victims with a sledgehammer—left behind at the scene—and, with his bloodthirst still not quenched, proceeded to slash his victims' throats.

The city went into a state of panic. No one, it seemed, was safe in their beds, as long as the murderer walked the streets looking for his next target.

On December 19 a second attack, in the same part of town, justified the widespread fears. Selecting the King's Arms Inn on New Gravel Lane, a Ratcliffe Highway side street, the killer this time found three helpless victims. His methods were just as grisly. He left Mr. Williamson, the inn's owner, on the cellar stairs, his head pulverized by a blunt instrument. In the parlor he smashed the skulls of Mrs. Williamson and the inn's maid, then slit their throats. The horrifying nighttime raid came to an end when an upstairs boarder caught a shadowy glimpse of the murderer and shouted for help before he could become the next victim.

At the sound of alarmed citizens on the way, the killer fled the scene through a rear window and crossed a muddy slope. A short while later, in the Pear Tree Inn off Ratcliffe Highway, sailor John Williams returned to his lodgings. His arrival was conspicuous to the men who shared his room because he made a fuss about one of his roommates' leaving a candle burning. It so happened that in this same inn was a tool chest from which was missing a sledgehammer belonging to a sailor named John Petersen, currently at sea. The police soon accounted for the missing tool when they linked John Petersen's name to the initials "J P" carved into the wooden handle of the sledgehammer used in the Marr murders.

Circumstantial evidence trapped John Williams, and he was arrested on December 23. Not only did he have the opportunity to get his hands on Petersen's hammer, the murder weapon, but police found bloodstains on one of his shirts, on a pair of his pants, and in his coat pocket. They also found a bloody knife in the Pear Tree Inn. As for the mud found encrusted on Williams's shoes, the police surmised that it might have come from the muddy slope along the killer's escape route from the King's Arms attack.

Perhaps it was the weight of this evidence that drove John Williams to hang himself in the Coldbath Fields Prison. In any case, his suicide preempted the need for a trial that might have conclusively established his guilt. For this reason there remains some room for doubt, even if alternative solutions to the case are not completely convincing.

Williams's untimely death did not, however, prevent the people of Ratcliffe Highway from exacting their own sort of justice. To their mind Williams was some evil creature of the night, to be dealt with accordingly. Before burying his body, they hammered a stake through his heart, as if they were suspicious medieval Europeans disposing of a vampire.

WILLIAM BURKE
1792–1829

WILLIAM HARE
1792–?

William Burke and William Hare knew how to take financial advantage of a situation.

In November of 1827, they were both living the life of immigrant lower-class laborers, residing in a squalid boardinghouse in the slums of Edinburgh, Scotland. In addition to the more general problems of desperate poverty, the two relocated Irishmen had a very specific problem to face: an elderly resident at the boardinghouse had just died. The death of another human being was not in itself especially vexing to either Burke or Hare, but Hare in particular had something else to consider. He was running the boardinghouse with his common-law

William Hare

wife, and the old lodger had died owing four pounds in rent. As his friend Burke commiserated with him, Hare wondered how to make up for the four pounds in arrears. He didn't have to wonder for very long. Some people, he knew, were worth a lot more dead than alive.

At this time the demands of medical science had progressed faster than society's willingness to accommodate those demands. This was especially troublesome for anatomists, who were unable to get enough bodies for dissection and research; often they had to pay grave robbers, or Resurrection Men as they were called,

to steal bodies from the cemetery in order to maintain a steady supply. Being a man who knew something about underhanded ways of making money, William Hare saw the opportunity in his situation with the deceased deadbeat lodger. And his friend William Burke did not need much persuading to join the venture.

They took the old lodger's body out of its coffin, weighed the coffin down with bark instead, and smuggled the fresh corpse to the offices of Dr. Robert Knox, a famed anatomist and surgeon at the Medical School of Edinburgh. For their trouble they received seven pounds, ten shillings, considerably more than the rent owed by the old man. What was more, Dr. Knox's staff made it clear that they would be willing to pay good money for more fresh specimens. Burke and Hare could see they were on to a good thing.

One question remained, however: what was the best way to acquire bodies? Digging up recently buried corpses was hard work, and possibly dangerous, too, since outraged citizens had been known to post armed guards at the cemeteries. Once more Burke and Hare seized upon a resourceful solution. From time to time, sickly lodgers roomed at the boardinghouse. Burke and Hare realized they could prevent these people from getting better; one of them could hold the sick person down while the other closed off the nose and mouth. Suffocated in this way, the victim would make a fresh, unbruised specimen for Dr. Knox's dissecting knife.

This method produced two marketable bodies, earning ten pounds apiece, but the remaining lodgers weren't sick at all and couldn't be dispatched in an inconspicuous way. To the minds of Burke and Hare, more aggressive measures were called for. With the aid of Burke's mistress, Nelly McDougal, and Hare's common-law wife, Maggie Laird, they began to rope in people from the streets.

William Burke

As a rule, Burke and Hare persuaded their victims to come with them to their lodging house where the dissection-specimens-to-be were given a steady supply of liquor. Once the victims were thoroughly drunk, suffocation was a fairly easy task.

Burke and Hare tended to prey upon rootless people—prostitutes, beggars, newcomers to town—but they also had no compunction about striking close to home. One of their victims was Nelly McDougal's cousin, another was Burke's washwoman. They became more brazen as they went along, on occasion killing well-known street characters, sometimes murdering two at once. In one case they brought an elderly Irishwoman and her deaf-mute grandson back to their rooms. After the woman was asphyxiated, Burke put the twelve-year-old grandson on his lap and broke the boy's back across his knee. Still not asking any questions, Dr. Knox paid sixteen pounds for the pair of bodies.

Burke and Hare's final victim was an old woman named Mary Docherty, suffocated on Halloween night, 1828. Docherty's body, naked and bound in a doubled-up position, was discovered beneath the straw on Burke's floor by two of the boardinghouse's lodgers, who then took their story to the police. Burke, Hare, and their two women were taken into custody. Still, though, the authorities did not have sufficient evidence for a conviction. But then William Hare, always with an eye for opportunity, put himself at the police's disposal; in exchange for immunity against prosecution for both himself and his wife, he testified against his friend Burke.

Although Burke and Hare, with their female accomplices, murdered sixteen people over the course of nine months, the prosecution was only able to mount a case for the Docherty killing. Burke was convicted and was hanged for the crime on January 28, 1829, to the delight of 25,000 outraged spectators. Burke's mistress, Nelly McDougal, received the peculiarly Scottish verdict of "not proven." From such a verdict one could conclude that the defendant was actually guilty, set free only because of insufficient evidence. And that was clearly the inference drawn by a group of citizens who tried to drag McDougal out of jail so that they could administer their own sentence. To protect her life, the authorities had to sneak her out of the country. As for Hare, who was obviously as guilty as the man who went to the gallows, he wisely made himself scarce, as did his wife, Maggie Laird. There were alleged sightings of Hare over the years, but as far as verifiable fact is concerned, he simply vanished. Dr. Robert Knox, who provided the financial impetus for Burke and Hare's atrocities, was officially cleared of any wrongdoing, but the public was not so lenient. Knox was hounded out of Edinburgh and was not able to practice medicine for years.

HELENE JEGADO
?–1851

Early in her career as a domestic servant, Helene Jegado of Brittany decided to get herself to a nunnery. Life in the secular world, she made it known, was not going well for her. "I am a wretched creature," she bemoaned. "I carry an evil influence with me everywhere. Wherever I

go people die." Always a regular churchgoer, Jegado believed that
housekeeping work in a convent was the logical choice for a servant
with a troubled soul. What she neglected to tell her new ecclesiastical
employers was that people were dying wherever she went for a very
simple reason: she was killing them.

The details of Helene Jegado's early life are scarce, but it is believed that by the time she
started working in a convent she
had already poisoned to death a
household of seven people. One
of those people was supposed to
have been her sister. Not only
that, her lethal cooking may have
decimated another family as
well. As she did throughout her
life, she managed to evade serious suspicion in these cases by
presenting a thoroughly pious
demeanor. Her religious devotion
no doubt helped her land a position in a convent when she decided to leave the worldly life
behind. But it did not keep her
from exercising her murderous
passions.

Over the next few years
Jegado moved from convent to
convent, then to the homes of
clergymen. Accusations of pilfer-
ing dogged her from one employer to the next, particularly
the stealing of liquor. Also cloud-

*The guillotine was the final destination
for housemaid-turned-deranged-poisoner
Helene Jegado.*

ing her path was a succession of deaths following sudden, violent
illnesses. But no matter how many questions were raised about Helene
Jegado, she was still able to find another employer ready to believe her
professed devoutness and willing to give her a job.

This period in Jegado's life came to an end in 1841. After leaving a
job in a house where a child suddenly died and the rest of the family got
violently sick, Jegado abandoned the use of arsenic for a while. Beginning with her next job in the Breton town of Port Louis, she was content

merely to steal. This time of restraint lasted eight years. In 1849, in the city of Rennes, she became homicidal again.

We know more about Jegado's activities in Rennes, which reveal that she didn't murder for profit but out of pathological malice instead. In the home of Monsieur Rabot she was caught stealing wine, and she took offense when her employer gave her notice. Before leaving, she lashed back by mixing arsenic into one of the meals and making four members of the family sick. A similar sequence of events occurred in the next household, except this time Jegado got revenge by murdering a small boy, a death that was ascribed to croup. Then, in the Rennes inn called the World's End, she fatally poisoned a fellow female servant, apparently for no other reason than that Jegado simply didn't like her, and went on to murder her mistress, who had made the mistake of criticizing Jegado, as well.

Jegado's final housekeeping job was with a university professor named Theophile Bidard. Like other employers, Bidard was impressed with Jegado's Christian ways—in particular, her alleged habit of periodically sending money to her family, which included her aged, beloved mother. What Bidard didn't know was that Jegado's mother had been in her grave for some forty years.

Jegado didn't care much for a younger servant in the house named Rose Tessier. She would creep to the girl's door in the middle of the night and, trying to sound like a voice from beyond the grave, call out Tessier's name. When this artificial haunting didn't succeed in driving Tessier out of the house, Jegado fell back on a more decisive method. She began dosing the girl's food with arsenic. Tessier's final thirty-six hours were spent in excruciating pain.

Later, a new servant by the name of Rosalie Sarrazin was hired, and she soon earned Jegado's hatred by assuming household responsibilities more important than those handled by the illiterate Jegado. The slow poisoning of Sarrazin resulted in three weeks of agony before death came on July 1, 1850.

Throughout all this, Bidard, the master of the household, was unable to take decisive action. He gave Jegado notice at one point for verbally abusing fellow employees, an action which probably triggered Jegado's first round of poisonings of Sarrazin; then he about-faced and let the psychopathic housekeeper stay on, after which she succeeded in killing Sarrazin. But after two suspicious deaths in his home, Bidard finally contacted the police. Jegado's overly defensive manner when the authorities arrived heaped further suspicion upon herself.

Traces of arsenic were found not only in the bodies of Jegado's most recent victims but in many of the others as well. The authorities believed Jegado had murdered twenty-three people between 1833 and 1841. Her trial, however, concentrated on the deaths of Rose Tessier, Rosalie Sarrazin, and a victim named Perrotte Mace. Admitting nothing, Jegado said she "never had a thought of injuring a single soul." The one lesson for her to derive from this, she said, was that "it had warned me to avoid sick people. I will nurse no more of them." The court agreed with her on that score. Jegado was convicted of murder and sent to the guillotine.

MARTIN DUMOLLARD
?–1862

In May 1861 an unemployed servant girl by the name of Marie Pichon was approached by a stranger on the streets of Lyon, France. The stranger, a man who had the rough-hewn appearance of a laborer, said that he was the gardener for a wealthy family outside the city. He had come to Lyon for the purpose of finding a new housemaid for his employer, one that was hardworking and honest, and he thought, perhaps, Marie Pichon would be the right young woman for the job. Enticed by the idea of working for a fine family at an elegant chateau, Pichon accepted the offer. Soon she was accompanying the gardener out of the city.

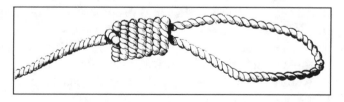

As they walked down a country road, Pichon began to get suspicious. Perhaps, now that she was alone with this man named Martin Dumollard, she took a closer look at his features and decided she didn't much like them: the tumor on his face, the scar on his upper lip, the dim look in his eyes. Or perhaps she sensed that he was leading her on a route that would not take her to a chateau. Whatever the reason, it was this suspicion that saved her life, because she was already on guard when Dumollard produced a rope fashioned into a noose and tried to sling it around her neck. Pichon managed to fight him off, then ran away. She didn't stop running until she reached the safety of a nearby farm.

The next day she told the police about her narrow escape. The authorities didn't waste a moment. They had been aware of deadly foul play in the area for some time. The naked body of a young female servant, stabbed several times in the head, had been found in the woods six years before, but no evidence had been discovered that would have led to the culprit. Other girls had also apparently disappeared. Now the police moved quickly to the cottage where Dumollard and his wife lived.

A search of the premises uncovered a stash of women's clothes that were identified as the property of servant girls who had been reported missing. There were ten sets of clothes in all. Madame Dumollard, who was wearing a shawl belonging to the girl who had most recently disappeared, started to panic. Not about to let the finger of blame be pointed at her, she blurted out the story of her husband's crimes, a string of cold-blooded murders that had been committed over the past twelve years.

Dumollard had found his victims, as he had in the case of near-victim Marie Pichon, by traveling to Lyon in search of servant girls. Usually, he would consult an employment agency and ask that a young woman be sent to his home in the country. (It's possible that Madame Dumollard may have handled these preliminary arrangements for him.) Once the servant was out of the city and walking along a lonely country road, Dumollard would intercept her and drag her into the woods. His method of murder varied: sometimes he would use a knife, other times he would choke the victim with a noose; in still other instances he would crush the woman's skull with a blunt object. In all cases he would strip the body of its clothes and all other possessions. Some were sold, some were worn by his wife.

Madame Dumollard's statement was followed by Martin Dumollard's confession. He directed the authorities to some of the burial sites, but a good number of the corpses would not be found because, as Dumollard explained, they had been dumped in the nearby Rhone River.

While a vengeance-mad crowd cried for his blood, Dumollard was convicted and sentenced to death in January 1862. His wife was convicted as an accessory and was given life in prison.

It is not clear whether Martin Dumollard, the killer of at least ten young women, was a homicidal—perhaps sexually motivated—psychopath or simply a murderer for profit. Writers have advanced both theories. If he was acting out of nothing else but ruthless greed, he didn't seem to have hit upon the most lucrative way of going about it; poor servant girls would not seem to have been the best targets for a man out for plunder. On the other hand, as his early biographer Major Arthur Griffiths pointed out, Dumollard did exit this world in the manner of a man motivated by petty avarice. As he stood on the scaffold, about to be decapitated by the guillotine, Dumollard had one last pressing thought to share with his wife, who was standing close by. He reminded her that a man in their village still owed him twenty-seven francs.

JEAN-BAPTISTE TROPPMANN
1848–1870

Successful brush manufacturer Jean Kinck had two significant things in common with the young man named Jean-Baptiste Troppmann. First, they both hailed from Alsace, that distinctive border region characterized by a mix of German and French influences (at that time, in 1869, under French control). Second, they both had a keen interest in making money. Kinck, middle-aged and the head of a large family, had already succeeded in finding a way to make a comfortable living, but he was still susceptible to financial temptation. As for twenty-one-year-old Troppmann, his lust for money ran deeper. When he first met Kinck, while they both were in Alsace on business, Troppmann was struggling to make a living in the textile business and was always on the lookout for some way to escape his impoverished upbringing. In Kinck he saw an opportunity to realize his goal.

Apparently gifted with a glib tongue, Troppmann was able to interest Kinck in a scheme that promised to be highly lucrative, albeit illegal. Troppmann's idea was to set up a plant for printing counterfeit

money in a remote area of their native Alsace. While their agreement to pursue this scheme demonstrated that the two Alsatians shared a common greed, a huge difference between them was about to emerge: Kinck's avarice was reckless; Troppmann's, on the other hand, was absolutely maniacal.

Late in the summer of 1869, Kinck accompanied Troppmann to Herrenfluch in Alsace, ostensibly to survey the site of their money-printing operation. As they walked together along a country road, Troppmann offered his partner a sip from his flask of wine. Kinck took a drink. Soon after that he was dead, poisoned by the prussic acid Troppmann had mixed with the wine. All Troppman's talk of counterfeiting ended there. He had other ideas about making his fortune.

With the head of the Kinck family out of the way, Troppmann attempted to loot his would-be partner's wealth. He corresponded with Kinck's pregnant wife, Hortense, who had no idea she was now a widow. Claiming to be acting on behalf of her husband, Troppmann instructed Hortense to send a check for fifty-five hundred francs from her home in Roubaix on the Belgian border to Alsace, for the funding of her husband's latest business venture. A trusting woman, Hortense went along with this, but Troppmann, pretending to be Jean Kinck's agent, was not able to collect the money from the post office because he lacked the proper authorization. He then persuaded Hortense Kinck to send her oldest son, Gustave, to Alsace, in the hope that the sixteen-year-old could facilitate the release of the check. Still there were difficulties. Without authorization from Jean Kinck himself, the check could not be picked up. In Troppmann's mind the time had come to expedite matters.

He got Gustave to wire a message to Hortense: she was to bring the money personally to her husband in Paris. Now Gustave was of no further use to Troppmann. He took Gustave to the Pantin Common outside Paris's encircling fortified wall and hacked the boy to death. He stabbed Gustave seven times, shredding his throat in the process, then beat him with a pickax. He returned to Paris in time to greet Jean Kinck's wife.

Hortense brought the fifty-five hundred francs, as instructed, but she also brought her remaining five children: four boys and one girl, ranging in age from two to thirteen. Troppmann didn't want any of them on hand to ask troubling questions about Jean Kinck and how the money was going to be used. On the night of September 19, 1869, he took all six Kincks by cab to the Pantin Common, claiming that he was bringing them to see Jean. First, he got out of the cab with Hortense, her two-year-old daughter, and one of her small boys, saying that this first group would pick up Jean Kinck and then return to the cab. They were gone twenty-five minutes. Then Troppmann came back alone. There was a change of plans, he said. He was to take the remaining three children to their father and dismiss the cab. Troppmann led the children to a deserted spot where he strangled, beat, and slashed the three boys, just as he had done to Hortense and the other two children minutes before. As far as Troppmann was concerned, he was free to live his new, wealthy existence.

But the case began to unravel the next day.

A workman at Pantin chanced upon suspiciously broken ground, which led to the discovery underneath of the mutilated remains of Hortense and the five children. Soon after that, Troppmann was arrested at the northern port of Le Havre as he tried to obtain false exit papers for a getaway to America. The Kinck family documents found in his pockets made him a prime murder suspect.

The list of charges against him grew when Gustave Kinck's body was discovered on September 25 and when Jean's corpse was unearthed two months later. Strengthening the case against Troppmann was the gathering of key witnesses who testified to his comings and goings at the time of the murders, the most important being the cabman who took Troppmann, Hortense, and the five children to Pantin on the night of the mass killings.

Troppmann, the murderer of an entire family of eight—nine if one includes the unborn child inside the pregnant Hortense—was convicted and sentenced to die. He went to the guillotine, at the age of twenty-two, on January 19, 1870.

THE BENDER FAMILY
1871–1873

"The Bloody Benders"

The raw, frontier state of Kansas was no stranger to violence in the years following the Civil War, but cold, calculated mass murder was not something people were accustomed to, even in that time and place. When it was discovered that this particular brand of violence was business as usual at the Bender place in southeastern Kansas, the news shocked not only the region but the entire nation. The details of this case are hard to pin down, clouded through the years by unreliable reminiscences. The brutality of the Benders' crimes, however, is one thing that is beyond question.

The Benders came to Labette County, Kansas, in either 1870 or

A contemporary illustration of the Bender Family murder method.

1871. At the head of the family were two German immigrants: the father, around sixty years old, was generally known as either John or Old Man Bender, and the somewhat younger mother was known simply as Ma Bender. Their son, John, Jr., was in his late twenties. He gave people the impression he was dimwitted, while his younger sister, Katie, was smart enough to be considered the brains of the family. According to some writers John, Jr. was actually a child from his mother's previous marriage. He and his half-sister, the story goes, might have had an incestuous relationship.

The Benders erected a wooden building along one of the county's principal roads. A canvas curtain divided the single-room dwelling into two sections: sleeping quarters for the family in back, and a roadside business up front. The sign above the door read Groceries, but the Benders were also ready to serve travelers hot meals and to provide a bed for the night.

The most colorful, and the most romanticized, of the family was Katie. Claiming to be in touch with the spirit world, she would hold seances and practice faith healing in the front section of the Bender establishment and was known to deliver spiritualist lectures in neighboring towns. Over the years Katie has been described alternately as a red-faced, mannish frontierswoman and as a red-haired beauty. She probably wasn't the prairie temptress that some romanticizers have claimed she was, but she seems to have been the one member of the Bender family who could turn on a certain amount of charm when need be, a key element in the family's most lucrative enterprise: murder for profit.

Once it was determined that a traveler stopping at the Bender place was carrying a large amount of money, Katie was the one who would convince him to stay for dinner, and she was also the one who would persuade him to sit with his back to the canvas curtain. With that done, either the Old Man or John, Jr. could take over. Standing on the other side of the curtain, one of the Bender men would wait until the traveler's head made a clear impression against the canvas. Then he would swing a stone-breaker's sledgehammer and bash in the back of the man's skull. Disposal of the body was efficient. The family members stripped the victim, opened a trapdoor in the rear portion of the house, and dumped the body into the pit below. There one of them slit the victim's throat, just to make sure he was dead. At night, when there was little chance of a passerby noticing anything, the body was taken out back and buried in the orchard.

The Benders' murder inn stayed in business for about a year and a half, in which time, it has been estimated, they stole about ten thousand dollars from their victims. The end finally came when they lured the wrong man to stay for dinner.

A man by the name of Dr. William H. York disappeared on his way from Fort Scott, Kansas, to his home in Independence. A few weeks later, in April 1873, Col. A. M. York, the missing man's brother, formed a search party; he was determined not to let the disappearance go unexplained. Colonel York stopped briefly at the Benders' wayside inn during his quest, then moved on. But something about the family must have nagged at him, because in early May he recruited another search party and returned to the inn. By that time, though, he wasn't the only one who had become suspicious.

A neighboring homesteader had recently discovered that the Benders had abandoned their home in a hurry, even leaving valuable livestock behind to die of hunger and thirst. By the time Colonel York arrived for his second visit, the Bender property was being thoroughly searched by neighbors.

After discovering congealed blood in the pit beneath the house, the search party took a closer look at the Benders' orchard. A recent rain had settled the ground in some places, places that approximated the size and shape of graves. Metal rods were pushed through one of these spots, then withdrawn. Left on the rods were foul-smelling clumps of hair and decomposed flesh. In the first grave the posse discovered the body of Dr. William York. When the search was finally completed, seven graves were dug up, containing eight bodies in all. Seven of the victims were men, all with their skulls crushed and their throats slit. The eighth was an eighteen-month-old girl. The Benders had dispensed with their usual murder method in this case. The child had been buried alive beneath her already dead father.

Vengeance-driven posses searched in vain for the Bloody Benders, as the killers were quickly dubbed by the newspapers of the day. According to one story the murderous family was tracked down and slaughtered before they left Kansas. Other stories placed the fugitives, alive and well, as far north as Michigan and as far south as an outlaw colony in Texas. None of these stories was ever proved. No one can say for sure where the Benders came from before they set up their wayside inn on the Kansas prairie, and after eighteen months of cold-blooded butchery, they simply disappeared without a trace.

VINCENZ VERZENI
1849–?

Italian sex killer Vincenz Verzeni had a simple reason for attacking women: the experience gave him pleasure. In 1861, while other boys his age were coming to terms with their newfound sexuality in more conventional ways, twelve-year-old Verzeni discovered that he felt an indescribable sort of excitement as he wrung the neck of a chicken. For the rest of his years at large, strangulation and sexual stimulation would be linked in Verzeni's mind.

He put his hands to the throat of a woman for the first time at the age of eighteen. In the course of choking the woman, he became so aroused that he achieved orgasm, and seeing no reason to continue the

It was along lonely roads and fields outside 1870s Rome that Vincenz Verzeni prowled for his victims.

attack, he released her before she suffocated. As Dr. Richard von Krafft-Ebing put it in *Psychopathia Sexualis*, "The life of his [Verzeni's] victim hung on the rapid or retarded occurrence of ejaculation."

Two more times he pounced upon women and choked them and let them live. Then his sadistic urges seemed to explode. While Verzeni continued to seek out victims on the outskirts of Rome, his demented satisfaction took longer to achieve. Eventually, not even strangulation would be enough for him.

One morning, he stalked a fourteen-year-old girl named Johanna Motta along a country road. When he caught up to her and dragged her into a nearby field, choking was just the beginning. After the girl was asphyxiated, Verzeni disemboweled her and bit into her thighs until he broke the skin. He later revealed that he "took great delight in drinking Motta's blood." His orgy of atrocities still not over, he sliced off a piece of her calf and carried it, along with her intestines, on his way home. He intended to eat the flesh after roasting it on the family stove, but he had second thoughts—not because of any sudden pang of remorse; he simply didn't want to give his mother any cause for suspicion. So he discarded the flesh, but he continued to carry the intestines for a while, until he had derived what he considered sufficient gratification from their smell and touch.

Verzeni killed again in August 1871, using a thong to strangle a twenty-eight-year-old woman named Frigeni. Once more, he disemboweled his victim. The next day, he turned his sights on one of his own cousins, nineteen-year-old Maria Previtali. He knocked her down while she crossed a field, grabbed her throat, and squeezed. Then he thought he heard someone approaching. As he turned to look, he loosened his grip, giving his cousin a chance both to breathe and to plead for her life. She must have been persuasive because Verzeni let her go. It was her report to the police that prompted Verzeni's arrest.

Verzeni was charged with two murders and three assaults. Dr. Cesare Lombroso, one of Italy's leading psychiatrists, examined the killer and, in the manner of psychiatry in those pre-Freudian days, focused on Verzeni's hereditary traits. Lombroso analyzed such things as Verzeni's oversized upper jaw, the irregular shape of his skull, the large size of his genitals, the poor coordination of his eye muscles. The doctor believed that congenital degeneration played a part in accounting for Verzeni's appalling crimes. At his trial Verzeni fulfilled people's expectations of a born murderer by displaying absolutely no sign of contrition for the horrors he had committed; in his confession, he shocked people further by openly admitting to the sexual pleasure he had experienced while carrying out his crimes. At the age of twenty-four, he was sent to prison for life.

JESSE POMEROY
1860–1932

In the 1870s young Jesse Pomeroy was not analyzed in any way that could be mistaken for modern psychiatric procedure. No one placed great emphasis on discovering emotionally scarring traumas in his early childhood or on searching for any possible brain damage that could have caused uncontrolled violence. Instead, he was simply characterized as a natural-born fiend. Given the nature of his crimes, this interpretation was not unreasonable.

Jesse Pomeroy was raised by his widowed mother, who made a scant living as a dressmaker in South Boston. Not much else is known about his life before he reached the age of eleven. At that age he started torturing other children.

Between the winter of 1871 and the fall of 1872, Pomeroy trapped and attacked seven boys, all younger than he. Pomeroy took each to a secluded spot, where he then stripped his captive and tied him up. The first victims were savagely beaten; then Pomeroy's sadistic violence started to include frenzied cutting with a knife as well. In one case he repeatedly poked pins into a boy's flesh.

With so many victims it was only a matter of time until a composite description of the preteen monster would lead to the culprit's arrest. Pomeroy's appearance made the task easier. Among his unusual characteristics were a harelip and a completely white eye. As a result of his arrest at the end of 1872, he was sent to the West Borough Reform School, where he was to be incarcerated until the age of twenty-one.

Jesse Pomeroy's case is proof that a revolving-door penal system, in which dangerous criminals are released from prison to commit increasingly violent crimes, is not exclusively a late-twentieth-century problem. When he was serving time at the reformatory, Jesse understood very well what the rules were, namely that a well-behaved inmate could win an early probation. Accordingly, he put up a good front for the reform school officials, and after only a year and a half, the serial torturer of seven boys was released, free to carry on in his horribly twisted ways—except now the fourteen-year-old Pomeroy was no longer content with merely inflicting agony. He was homicidal.

In March 1874 he kidnapped Mary Curran, a ten-year-old girl from his neighborhood, and mutilated and killed her. A month later, he snatched a four-year-old boy by the name of Horace Mullen and took him to a stretch of marshland outside the city. Pomeroy slashed him so often and so ferociously that the boy was nearly decapitated.

The first of the bodies to be found was Mullen's. When reviewing their most likely suspects, the police naturally placed Pomeroy, the known sadist, near the top of the list. They picked him up for questioning and found he was carrying a bloodstained knife. Further investigation revealed that the mud on Pomeroy's shoes matched the soggy ground of the murder-scene marsh, and that the soles of his shoes matched the footprints found at the scene. A confession followed when police showed Pomeroy the body of the horribly ravaged Mullen and asked if he had killed the boy. "I suppose I did" was Pomeroy's matter-of-fact response.

The decomposed remains of Mary Curran were found in July after Pomeroy's mother moved out of her house. Laborers assigned by the landlord to do some construction work found the girl buried in the cellar's earthen floor. Now that he had already admitted to one killing, Pomeroy confessed to the Curran murder as well. He was tried and convicted at the end of the year.

At the time of the trial, some moral reformers attempted to bring wider social meaning to Pomeroy's appalling crimes. They argued that Pomeroy's hideous acts were caused by lurid, blood-and-thunder stories found in dime novels—much in the same way that social activists today point to violent videos as instigators of real-life violence. In Pomeroy's case this argument was undermined somewhat by the young murderer's statement that he had never read any dime novels.

Most people in 1874, however, were not interested in explaining Pomeroy's crimes, only in punishing them. The murders were so appalling that the court was willing to ignore Pomeroy's young age and proceeded to sentence the fourteen-year-old "fiend" to death. Subsequently, the sentence was commuted by the governor of Massachusetts, but still with a harsh provision: Pomeroy would serve his lifelong prison sentence in solitary confinement. He ended up serving his term in this way, completely isolated, for forty-one years, at which point he was finally allowed to have some contact with other inmates. He died in captivity in 1932 at the age of seventy-two.

THOMAS PIPER

1849–1876

"The Boston Belfry Murderer"

Thomas Piper killed for the first time on December 5, 1873. That night, the twenty-four-year-old man spotted a young female servant named Bridget Landregan on the streets of Boston and, deciding she was to be the one, followed her to the outskirts of the city. Concealed under his coat was a heavy club he had recently fashioned just for this purpose. Once the young woman had reached a dark, empty stretch of road, Piper attacked.

He smashed her over the head with the club, cracking her skull. Then he dragged her into the nearby woods and started to rip off her clothes. He stopped when he saw a man walking in his direction along the road. Piper had to run away, leaving his victim behind before finishing what he had in mind. As if to make up for the interruption of this assault, Piper moved on to find another victim that same night, a young woman with the last name of Sullivan. This time he not only bludgeoned his victim but raped her as well. Like Landregan, Sullivan would die of her wounds.

The next day, Piper resumed his normal routine. Thomas Piper, maniacal killer of women, was the sexton for the Warren Avenue Baptist Church.

For the next seven months he appeared to be a respectable young Bostonian as he maintained the church property and took responsibility for ringing the church bell. When no one was looking, though, he was not only drinking whiskey, but smoking opium as well. Then, on July 1, 1874, he took up with a prostitute named Mary Tynam. Some time in the night, as she slept beside him in her room, Piper fetched the plumber's hammer he had brought along with him from the church and proceeded to beat her head in. At first it looked like Tynam might survive, even if the trauma of the attack landed her in an insane asylum, but eventually she too would die.

Once more, Piper's bloodthirst seemed to be quenched. But less than a year later, he once again felt compelled to kill. This would be his most atrocious crime. Some time in the spring of 1875, he began to brood about the idea of murdering a child, and on the afternoon of Sunday, May 23, an opportunity presented itself to his increasingly deranged mind. Anticipating that he would find a victim on that day, he brought his cricket bat up into the belfry, while Sunday School was in session. After shooing away some raucous boys playing in the church vestibule, he noticed a small girl walking in his direction, a five-year-old named Mabel Young. He tempted her into accompanying him up to the belfry for the purpose of seeing the pigeons that he kept as pets. As soon as he had her alone in the bell tower, he picked up the cricket bat and clubbed the child over the head. Then he hit her again.

Noises from downstairs told Piper that people were already looking for Mabel. He slipped out of the belfry through a window that was within jumping distance of the ground. A woman named Mrs. Drake saw him at the window just before he climbed out, and a man named F. H. Glover saw him drop to the ground. A few minutes later, after the battered child was discovered in the bell tower, the observations of these two witnesses would prompt the police to arrest the church sexton. When Mabel Young died later in the day, Piper was charged with murder.

None of Piper's crimes before May 23 were known, so the Mabel Young murder would be the only charge for which he would be tried. Piper denied everything. He maintained that the child's death was nothing more than a hideous accident. He claimed that he had propped up the belfry's trapdoor with his cricket bat in order to facilitate the church's ventilation, and the fifty-pound door subsequently fell on Mabel's head as she tried going up to the belfry on her own. The jury did not find this story convincing. After his conviction Piper's lawyers managed to win him a second trial, but the result was the same. He was sentenced to hang.

Piper stuck with his accident story in the hope that his death sentence might be commuted. Soon, though, even one of his lawyers, Edward P. Brown, began to doubt him. During a meeting in Piper's jail cell, Brown confronted him with discrepancies in his various versions of the events of May 23. Piper became confused, and when his lawyer continued to challenge him, Piper finally admitted the lie. Sobbing, he went on to confess not only to the Mabel Young murder, but the killings of Bridget Landregan, Mary Tynam, and the Sullivan girl. Filling in the picture even further, he would later say that his penchant for destruction also included arson, and admitted to burning down Concord Hall a little over a week after the Landregan murder.

Brown was eager to find some explanation for the transformation of a righteous young man into a fiendish murderer. He asked if Piper's thoughts might have been shaped by *Cord and Creese*, a contemporary adventure novel many considered to be lurid. Piper couldn't oblige him there. He said he'd hardly read any of the book. All he could say by way of explanation for his grisly impulses was that he was often under the influence of whiskey and opium. He said he had been drinking and taking drugs to ease the pain he frequently felt in his head.

Piper's lawyers were unable to secure any further appeals or win a commutation of sentence. The "Belfry Murderer" went to the gallows at the Charles Street Jail on May 26, 1876.

Jack the Ripper
1888

Modern serial murder has its beginnings in 1888, the year that Jack the Ripper stalked the East End slums of London. Like the multiple-homicide cases that have become all too common in the past few decades, the unsolved Ripper murders were seemingly random and horribly gruesome. Previously, murders committed for purely sexual reasons, as opposed to murder for profit, had been rare, and even when this sort of crime had been committed, it had not produced the sort of panic associated with the Ripper killings, which were carried out in the middle of a modern, urban setting and succeeded in terrorizing an entire city. The Jack the Ripper case has also proven to be endlessly, if morbidly,

fascinating. It has been so fascinating that even today writers continue to propose solutions to the case, more than a hundred years after the fact, long after any realistic possibility of identifying the culprit has passed.

The facts of the case that can be verified concern the Ripper victims and their ghastly deaths. The victims were all prostitutes plying their trade in the impoverished East End. The method of murder employed in the first attack was savage, but the viciousness of the crimes got drastically worse as the killing spree progressed.

The murders of prostitutes in April and early August 1888 have been designated by some writers as the first Ripper slayings, but the majority opinion excludes these killings from the official count. While these two women, like later victims, died by the knife, they were not subjected to the sort of mutilation that ultimately became the trademark of the Ripper nightmare.

The first definite victim was Mary Ann Nichols, whose body was found at 3:45 A.M. on August 31, 1888. Her throat was slit, and her abdomen was opened with a jagged slash. The abdomen of the second victim, found only eight days later, was also sliced open, but the killer was no longer content with that; he also pulled out the intestines.

The ferocity of the attacks intensified. The bodies of two more prostitutes were discovered on September 30. The killer abandoned the first of that night's victims after slashing her throat—he was probably interrupted by a passerby—but went through the disemboweling ritual with the second victim, Catherine Eddowes. Later the killer sent a letter to the local vigilance committee and enclosed half a human kidney. The organ, it was determined, was afflicted with Bright's disease, which corresponded with Eddowes's known condition. The letter stated that the other half of the kidney had been fried and eaten.

The body of the final victim, Mary Kelly, was subjected to a frenzy of mutilation that went beyond any previous attack. In addition to the customary killing stroke delivered to the throat, the lower torso was ripped open, the entrails yanked out, and the chest and legs were skinned. With this atrocity the Ripper horror came to an end—five women killed in just a little over two months. For all the pressure exerted on the police by a frantic citizenry, the Ripper was never caught. The killings simply stopped.

Over the years amateur sleuths have tried to do the job left unfinished by the London police. One theory after another has been put forward, but none of them has provided a definitive solution.

A reasonable explanation for the sudden end to the Ripper murders is that the killer died soon after savaging Mary Kelly. Perhaps the Ripper committed suicide. This latter notion has led to one of the more popular Ripper theories, that the murderer was a man named Montague John Druitt, who killed himself shortly after the Kelly murder. Brought up in a well-to-do family, Druitt was believed by some people to have gone insane around the time of the East End terror. The argument against Druitt's being the Ripper is that the source of this theory—the written recollections of noted police officer Sir Melville Macnaghten—is not entirely reliable. Macnaghten didn't join the police force until six months after the Ripper killings had ended, and consequently he had to rely on a great deal of secondhand information; his account is also compromised by errors in his presentation of the facts of Druitt's life.

Perhaps the best-known theory, and clearly the most sensational, is that the murders were committed by Edward, the duke of Clarence, heir to the throne of England. Official history attributes Edward's death in 1892 to influenza, but some Ripper theorists (or Ripperologists, as they're sometimes called) maintain that he actually died of syphilis, an affliction that had also, supposedly, disordered Edward's brain and driven him to commit the sadistic East End murders.

One of the problems with this theory is that some of Edward's documented activities in the late 1880s were too rational to have been carried out by a man driven hopelessly insane by venereal disease. Another, larger problem with the duke-of-Clarence hypothesis is that it seems to equate possibility with proof. One would have to concede that it's not completely impossible that Edward committed the Ripper murders, but on the other hand, there is no hard evidence to directly link him to the crimes.

The same can be said of all the other proposed Ripper solutions. It may be possible, as various writers have asserted over the years, that the Ripper was the duke of Clarence, or a deranged, vengeful physician named Dr. Stanley, or upper-class poet James Kenneth Stephen, or notorious poisoner George Chapman, or a Jewish ritual slaughterman, or a demented midwife, or a black magician named D'Onston, or a mysterious lodger named John Hewitt, or even a team of Russian agents who committed the East End murders on behalf of the Czar's secret police. But as respected Ripperologist Donald Rumbelow points out, there are varying degrees of weakness in all these theories, and no real evidence placing any of these suspects at the scenes of the murders. And at this late date there is not much chance that any new, compelling evidence will be uncovered.

Not that any of this will discourage future Ripper theories. Regardless of whatever evidence there may or may not be about the case, Jack the Ripper is a potent figure in modern folklore who probably will always fascinate us, and always haunt our dreams.

LIZZIE BORDEN
1860–1927

Lizzie Borden—ax murderess. That name and that term have become synonymous in American folklore. She may have been found innocent of killing her father and stepmother in a court of law, but in the popular mind Lizzie Borden never fully escaped the shadow of presumed guilt.

Over the years a number of writers have come to her defense. Like the jury that acquitted her, they could not believe that quiet, proper Lizzie Borden was capable of taking a hatchet and hacking away at her stepmother twenty times and her father another nine. They have characterized Borden as a wronged woman. Other writers, however, have continued to argue that she was guilty. In the final analysis, after considering the complete record of evidence and testimony, there seems to be reason to believe that there may be something, after all, to the legend of Lizzie of the bloody hatchet. There may have been something peculiar about this quiet, proper woman, some emotional undercurrent that exploded on the oppressively hot day of August 4, 1892.

Much about the case is obscure, but what we do know is that at around eleven o'clock on Thursday, August 4, Lizzie Borden yelled upstairs to the family maid, who was taking a late-morning nap. "Come quick!" she said. "Father's dead! Somebody came in and killed him!" Her father, Andrew, a wealthy businessman, was on the sitting-room sofa, where he had been asleep when the killer attacked. One side of his face was completely smashed and shredded, his eye slit open. Soon, the body of Abby Borden, Lizzie's step-

mother, was discovered in an upstairs bedroom. She had been on her knees, making the bed, when the murderer approached from behind and repeatedly battered her skull. Further examination revealed that Abby had been killed between nine and nine-thirty, and Andrew, who had returned home from business in town at ten forty-five, had been killed around eleven, approximately an hour and a half after his wife's death.

For a while, Bridget Sullivan, the Borden maid, was suspected, as was Lizzie's Uncle John, who had been staying with the family at the time. But after the inquest it was thirty-two-year-old Lizzie who was arrested, accused of the horrid crime of parricide. Her acquittal a year later, due to insufficient evidence, did not seem to resolve the case in any way; it was merely the beginning of controversy.

Why has Lizzie Borden's acquittal failed to convince so many people? One compelling reason is that Lizzie, who was home on the morning of August 4, seems to have been the only suspect with the opportunity to commit the murders. Her sister, Emma, was away at the time, visiting friends in a nearby town, Uncle John Morse had verifiable alibis for his whereabouts away from the neighborhood, and testimony indicates that Bridget Sullivan was outside the house washing windows at the time of the murders. As for the theory that the killer was an outsider, it is hard to imagine someone sneaking into the small Borden house and hacking Abby to death undetected, then either leaving the house and coming back an hour and a half later to kill Andrew, or managing to hide inside the house for that length of time. Also suspicious is the alibi Lizzie offered for her father's murder. She claimed she was in the loft of the family barn at the time, looking for scrap metal to repair a window screen (no broken screens were found) and a lead weight to use as a fishing sinker (she had no immediate plans to go fishing). For these reasons she spent twenty minutes in the most stifling space on the Borden property on the most sweltering day of the year.

It seems Lizzie had a motive for killing, as well, one having to do with bottled-up tensions in the Borden family. Lizzie hated her stepmother. In particular, she had been profoundly resentful five years before the murders when her father put some property in her stepmother's name. At the time of the killings, Andrew was about to assign another piece of property to his wife, which may have triggered the outburst of violence on August 4. While this could explain the reason for killing her stepmother, what about Lizzie's father, whom she supposedly adored? It turns out that she had reason to harbor feelings other than devotion for her father. An animal lover, Lizzie had kept some pet pigeons in the barn. When some local boys tried to steal some of the birds, Andrew Borden, the hardheaded Yankee, decided to remove temptation. He decapitated Lizzie's pets.

Evidence of a predisposition to murder also exists. Shortly before the double killing, Lizzie attempted to buy poison, in the form of prussic acid, from several druggists; the pharmacists refused to sell it to her because this highly dangerous substance was not considered safe, except in prescribed mixtures.

But then, why would Lizzie, presumably considering poison, suddenly resort to the hatchet? In the book *A Private Disgrace*, author Victoria Lincoln offers an intriguing explanation. Lizzie had been known to have what were called "peculiar spells" three or four times a year. Based upon evaluations by modern psychiatrists, Lincoln believes these spells may have been epileptic seizures of the brain's temporal lobe. In seizures of this kind, a person functions automatically, often doing things that seem completely out of character. Lincoln speculates that Lizzie had succumbed to a seizure before taking a hatchet and going upstairs to see her stepmother.

Two points have typically been raised in Lizzie's defense: First, if she were guilty, the hatchet murders would have left her drenched in blood, but she was later found to be spotless and no bloody dress was found. Second, no murder weapon was ever discovered.

In actuality, as Victoria Lincoln points out, neither point is well founded. At both murder scenes blood was splattered primarily *away* from the killer, most likely leaving the culprit relatively clean. There is also reason to believe that Lizzie destroyed some evidence relating to this point of controversy. Three days after the double murder, and just before a police search of the house, she burned a dress in the kitchen stove. She claimed it had been stained with paint. And as for the murder weapon, police found a hatchet in the basement that had some very suspicious characteristics. The wooden handle had recently been broken off and had apparently been discarded in some way (bloodstains on wood can be impossible to remove), and the blade was covered with ash while other hatchets in the same spot were covered with dust; the blade might have been recently washed, then dipped in ash to simulate disuse. And one other thing: the hatchet's cutting edge matched the impressions in the victims' skulls.

There is no definitive proof of Lizzie Borden's guilt, but the mass of circumstantial evidence is very persuasive. Many alternate suspects have been suggested, including Bridget Sullivan; Lizzie's sister, Emma; and in 1991, Lizzie's alleged illegitimate brother, whose very existence had somehow escaped detection for a hundred years. None of them seem to have had the combination of opportunity, motive, and peculiar mental state that still, after all these years, points to Lizzie Borden.

H. H. HOLMES
1860–1896
"The Torture Doctor"

One thing can be said for H. H. Holmes—he was versatile. His criminal repertoire included wide-ranging pursuits. Despite a degree in medicine that could have led to a comfortable, legitimate living, his principal profession—if one could call it that—was swindling. His confidence game of choice was insurance fraud, but he was willing to try any other scam that presented itself as well. He also dabbled in bigamy and, throughout his life, maintained a steady sideline in murder—murder for profit, for convenience, to cover his tracks, and at times, apparently simply for pleasure.

Holmes's murders were often mundane, grubby acts reminiscent of

episodes in a hard-boiled crime novel. But other times they seemed to be plucked out of a gothic horror story, the kind that is inevitably set in a mysterious castle filled with secret passageways and torture chambers. In all, Holmes's crimes earned him the notoriety that was matched in his day only by the exploits of Jack the Ripper.

Predictably, H. H. Holmes, the constant practitioner of deception, did not use his real name. He was born Herman Webster Mudgett, coming into this world a year before the outbreak of the Civil War, in the small New Hampshire town of Gilmanton. Known as a strange boy, he was often victimized by both his father, a deeply religious man who believed in beating righteousness into his son, and by other boys in town, who bullied him mercilessly. He was not popular. In fact, he had only one friend. And that friendship didn't last too long. One day, Mudgett's friend died after falling from a second-floor landing in an abandoned house. The boy might have been pushed; standing directly behind him at the time that he made his fatal plunge was young Herman Mudgett.

New Hampshire could not have been a happy place for Mudgett, and when he was of college age, he went all the way to Michigan to earn his medical degree. While there, he saw opportunities in his access to hospital wards and dissection rooms that were not likely to occur to most people. He saw that he could get ahold of corpses. These in turn could be passed off as the remains of someone, either a fictitious individual or a living accomplice, who had a life insurance policy. When the insurance company paid off, at least part of the cash could end up in Mudgett's pocket. Before long, Mudgett had his start in the business of insurance scams.

In 1886 the twenty-six-year-old Mudgett was in Chicago, now using the name of Dr. Henry Howard Holmes. He was a bigamist by this time, and his activities in the Windy City would continue to involve a succession of women. First, there was a Mrs. Holton, the owner of a pharmacy who hired Holmes as an assistant. Setting a pattern for so many people who would come into contact with Holmes over the years, Mrs. Holton mysteriously disappeared. And she did so at a conspicuously convenient time for Holmes. He had recently become her partner in the store, and now, with her gone, he was the sole owner of the establishment.

Among the other females who passed in and out of Holmes's life was a married woman named Julia Connor. Charmed and seduced by Holmes, she became pregnant, and Dr. Holmes volunteered to abort the fetus. Julia Connor died when Holmes botched the operation—perhaps Holmes decided that she had become a burden. With her out of the way, he then had to consider Connor's teenage daughter, who might talk about her mother's death. Holmes got rid of her with a dose of poison.

The sale of bogus medicines and other ventures brought in enough money after a while for Holmes to build himself an enormous house across the street from his pharmacy. Holmes called it "The Castle." It became the scene of his most bizarre murders, a purpose for which it was perfectly suited. As extravagant as it may seem, accounts of the case maintain that secret passageways connected over a hundred rooms, each outfitted with a peephole so that Holmes could monitor what was going on inside, and a gas vent allowing piped-in poison gas.

One of the people to be gassed in this way was Emeline Cigrand, a beautiful employee of Holmes's and his lover, who made the mistake of declaring that she would not stay with a man who had no plans for marriage.

Men didn't necessarily fare any better with Holmes. A janitor got on Holmes's wrong side and ended up sealed in a room. Through the peephole, Holmes relished the sight of the man's agonies as he slowly starved to death. As gruesome as this was, however, Holmes was capable of worse. Diabolically ingenious, he engineered a device for igniting gas as it escaped its vent so that a fireball would shoot out and incinerate the person inside the room.

During the Chicago World's Fair of 1893, the Castle was especially busy as Holmes rented rooms to tourists staying in town for the exhibition. While the income from lodgers might have seemed sufficient to most people, Holmes saw other, additional possibilities. He killed some of his guests and sold their corpses and skeletons to local medical schools engaged in anatomical research.

Chicago went sour for Holmes when insurance investigators became suspicious of the origins of a fire that damaged part of the Castle. To avoid trouble, Holmes moved on to other states and other scams, working with a partner named Ben Pitezel. In 1894 the two men came up with a scheme that involved splitting the payment on Pitezel's life insurance policy once they had found a corpse that could double for Pitezel's body. But Holmes decided to cut corners: he saved himself the trouble of finding a suitable corpse by killing Pitezel, thus avoiding the necessity of splitting the money. He also decided not to pay off another of his living partners. This was the mistake that eventually led to his arrest, because the ripped-off partner got even by telling the police about the scam. More than a month later, detectives finally tracked down the elusive Holmes, but not before more murders were committed. Pitezel's wife and children had been included in the insurance scam plan. Holmes murdered three of the children to prevent them from ever talking, and would have gone on to kill Mrs. Pitezel and the remaining two children if he hadn't been apprehended in November 1895.

Labeled the American criminal of the century, H. H. Holmes confessed to twenty-seven murders. Some wild-eyed accounts have claimed that he killed as many as two hundred, but between these two figures may be the true number, probably around fifty. Holmes was hanged on May 7, 1896.

Theo Durrant

1871–1898

"The Demon in the Belfry"

Eighteen-year-old Blanche Lamont came to San Francisco from her home state of Montana. While in the Bay Area, she stayed with her aunt and uncle and took classes in preparation for a future teaching career. A respectable young woman, she was also a member of the Emanuel

Baptist Church. On April 3, 1895, at around three o'clock, she found a young man waiting for her as she came out of the Powell Street Normal School. His name was Theo Durrant, and he was a friend of Lamont's from Emanuel Baptist's social society. He had been waiting for her outside the school for nearly an hour.

When it came to late-Victorian righteousness, Theo Durrant had compiled quite an imposing re-sume. At the age of twenty-three, he was already shouldering administrative duties at Emanuel Baptist and was pursuing high-minded secular pursuits as well. He studied at Cooper Medical College to prepare himself for a life devoted to healing, and civic minded as he was, he was also a member of the California militia signal corps. But ultimately it was within the confines of his church that Theo Durrant achieved notoriety. In particular, it was his commission of two acts within the walls of the church—the first of which would take place on this afternoon of April 3—that garnered the rapt attention of the entire nation and made people ponder what seemed to be the imponderable: how could such a fine young man be so hideously monstrous?

Lamont and Durrant walked away from the school, and she accompanied him to the Emanuel Baptist Church library. Now they were alone. According to a later police reconstruction of the crime, Durrant strangled Lamont in the library, then dragged her up the stairs, perhaps by the hair, and lugged her into the belfry. After stripping off her clothes, he sexually assaulted her corpse.

A few days later, when the police began to investigate Blanche Lamont's disappearance, several witnesses could have come forward to testify that they had seen Durrant with Lamont shortly before she vanished. But no one did. Theo Durrant was just not a plausible suspect. Exploiting his effective immunity from investigation, Durrant had the unspeakable gall to volunteer information to Lamont's aunt. He said he had reason to believe that Lamont had not been killed but was instead in a house of prostitution, the victim of white slavers. He promised to do what he could to retrieve the hapless, fallen young woman.

On Good Friday, nine days after Lamont's disappearance, when no one else was about, Durrant escorted another young woman into the church library. She was twenty-one-year-old Minnie Williams. Since no bloodstains would ever be found on Durrant's clothes, police later surmised that he left Williams alone in the library for a few moments, then returned completely naked. A young woman would later testify that Durrant had once done the same thing with her; in that instance, however, the woman had been able to run away. Minnie Williams was not able to run. To stifle her screams, Durrant ripped off a patch of her clothing and rammed it down her throat. Then he stabbed her over and over again. When he was done, he once more engaged in necrophilia.

The next day, the body was discovered by three women who were decorating the church for Easter. Minnie Williams's flesh was slashed in many places; the knife blade, broken free of its handle, was still lodged in her breast.

Once again, witnesses had seen Durrant enter the church with a young woman, but this time they felt compelled to tell their story to the police. When they searched Durrant's rooms, police discovered that he had Williams's purse in his overcoat pocket. A more thorough search of the Baptist church broadened the ghastly scope of the case: in the belfry the police found Blanche Lamont's body. Subsequent testimony from people who had seen Durrant with Lamont on the day of the murder made it clear who had put the body in the bell tower. Durrant was arrested while out on maneuvers with his militia detachment.

At the trial the jury arrived at a verdict with remarkable efficiency: they needed just five minutes to find Durrant guilty and deserving of execution.

Since Durrant, like other criminals of his day, was not subjected to the sort of extensive psychiatric examination that has become common today, we have little information on the upbringing of this homicidal degenerate. But the behavior of his parents after Durrant's hanging at San Quentin provides us with a strange glimpse into the people who raised him. His parents received his body in a prison waiting room. At that time they chose to avail themselves of the warden's hospitality and were served some food. They ate a full meal while Theo Durrant's body—the face horribly disfigured from his violent asphyxiation—lay in an open coffin a few feet away.

The public was so outraged by Durrant's crimes that the murderer's parents had to go as far as Los Angeles, more than three hundred miles away, to find a crematorium that was willing to dispose of Durrant's body.

JOSEPH VACHER
1869–1898
"The French Ripper"

Serial killers come in all physical types. They don't necessarily appear to be thoroughgoing ogres, a fact demonstrated in recent years by Ted Bundy, whose monstrously murderous mind was camouflaged by an affable, attractive exterior. Appearances, as we all know, can be misleading.

But not in the case of Joseph Vacher.

Vacher, the dreaded "French Ripper" of the 1890s, was a thoroughly seedy tramp who suffered from paralysis on the right side of his face and had a right eye that frequently discharged pus. Sometimes he had difficulty forming words with his twisted, scarred lips. His demeanor was equally unappealing, guaranteeing that anyone who might have been inclined to feel pity for his physical afflictions would feel distinct aversion instead: as he traveled the country roads of southeastern France, he would knock on farmhouse doors and insist, in the most offensive tones, on being fed. In this he might have been quite shrewd: people would often gladly give him food just to get rid of him.

Vacher's obvious physical problems stemmed from a wound he inflicted upon himself at the age of twenty-four. In 1893, while on leave from the army, he shot a young woman three times after she had spurned him—she survived the attack—then turned the gun on himself and fired at his head. The damage caused by the bullet resulted in his partial paralysis.

Vacher would later maintain that people's abhorrence for his physical condition played some part in driving him to his hideous crimes. But the fact is that he was already headed in that direction by the time of his self-inflicted head injury. At the age of nineteen he had attempted to rape a boy, and during his army stint he had frequently alternated between botched suicide attempts and paranoid threats against his fellow soldiers. After his 1893 arrest for the shooting of the woman who would not be his lover, he was committed to an insane asylum where he was treated for "persecution mania."

Incredibly, after repeated escape attempts, Vacher was declared cured and was set free on April 1, 1894, less than a year after he entered the asylum. Beginning a month later, Vacher roamed the countryside—with an assortment of knives, a pair of scissors, and a cleaver—searching for women as well as teenagers of both sexes to butcher.

When he had his victim overpowered in some isolated spot, Vacher would attack with a demonic frenzy. He stabbed and strangled and disemboweled and mutilated sex organs. Often he sexually assaulted the ravaged corpses. People living in the vicinity of the murders told police about an ugly, ill-mannered tramp passing through their regions, but Vacher was always on the move, and besides, there were hundreds of other vagabonds to be suspected as well. For three years and three months Vacher stalked and slaughtered.

He was finally arrested in August 1897, for the monumentally understated charge of offending public decency. His capture resulted from his attempt to kill a woman at a time when her family was nearby. Vacher pounced on Marie-Eugenie Plantier outside Tournon, where the woman was combing the woods for pine cones. She managed to give him a stiff fight and also made enough noise for her husband and sons to hear what was going on. Soon Vacher was in the grips of the entire

Plantier family. His indecency infraction landed him in jail for three months. In the meantime, however, the authorities began to suspect that this tramp, who fit the descriptions of the French Ripper so well, might be guilty of much more serious crimes.

A great deal of investigative legwork produced a number of witnesses who swore that Vacher was the suspicious character they had noticed near various murder scenes. As he became increasingly implicated in the French Ripper crimes, Vacher came to the conclusion that the time had come to confess, and in his written account he freely divulged all the sickening details of his murders. Perhaps he confessed out of demented pride.

Vacher was tried for only one murder, the savage killing of a shepherd boy committed in the same district where he had been arrested for the abortive attack on the Plantier woman. But according to his confession he was guilty of eleven such murders, and may have, in fact, killed as many as fourteen in all. He tried to argue that his crimes were the result of a madness caused by rabies, which he claimed to have contracted from a dog bite at the age of eight. Not convinced, the court judged him responsible for his actions. He was guillotined on December 31, 1898.

JANE TOPPAN
1854–1938

Death swept through the Davis family in the summer of 1901. On July 4 Mattie Davis, a chronic diabetic, died of heart failure while staying with a friend in Cambridge, Massachusetts. Two weeks later, one of Mrs. Davis's married daughters, Annie Gordon, died during a visit to the Davis home in Cataumet, on the west coast of Cape Cod. The official cause of death, again, was heart failure, although in the manner of the times, the woman's demise was also ascribed to grief at the loss of her mother.

On August 9 the father of the family, Capt. Alden Davis, died of a massive stroke. Just four days later, death came to the Cataumet house

yet again. This time it was the Davis's second married daughter, Mary Gibbs. The cause of her death was not immediately apparent to the family's doctor.

Four members of the Davis family had now departed—within less than six weeks. There was an obvious common denominator in these deaths—a forty-six-year-old nurse named Jane Toppan. She had been the friend Mattie Davis was visiting in Cambridge, and Toppan had cared for Davis when she became ill. Following the funeral, Toppan had been invited to stay in the Davis's Cataumet home. During her stay she had given tonics or injections to the three people who died there. Relatives of the Davises became especially suspicious of Toppan when they learned that the nurse had prevented Dr. Latter, the family physician, from performing an autopsy on the body of Mary Gibbs; claiming to speak for the family, Toppan told the doctor that the Davises would have been opposed to any such procedure.

What made it difficult to believe Toppan's possible involvement in the Davis deaths was the sterling reputation she had earned over the previous twenty years. Some of the best Boston families had hired her and were willing to vouch for her professionalism and compassion. Just the same, the Massachusetts state police were brought in, and the autopsy of Mary Gibbs was finally done. Examiners found evidence of morphine poisoning. A warrant was made out for Jane Toppan's arrest, but by this time she had moved on.

Detective J. H. Whitney tracked her to her hometown of Lowell, above Boston, where she had gone to stay with the family of her foster sister—her late foster sister, that is. It seemed the woman had died of a sudden illness the year before. Toppan had nursed her.

Whitney was not able to catch up to his suspect in Lowell, as Toppan had already gone on to her next destination. But before leaving

Lowell, Detective Whitney learned, Toppan had spent some time in the local hospital. It seemed she had tried to kill herself. The hospital believed she might have tried to overdose on morphine.

On October 29, 1901, Whitney found Toppan at the home of friends in Amherst, New Hampshire. When the state policeman informed her she was under arrest for the murder of Mary Gibbs and under suspicion in the deaths of others, Toppan was willing to return to Massachusetts and face the charges without going through extradition procedures. She acted like a woman anxious to prove her innocence. On the way back to Massachusetts, according to a contemporary newspaper account, she mentioned to police that she was "frequently troubled with her head."

The investigation, meanwhile, continued, and autopsies of other patients treated by Toppan over the years revealed the combined presence of morphine and atropine. Atropine counteracted the morphine's tendency to constrict the pupils, thus leaving the pupil size normal and making it difficult to detect morphine poisoning without an autopsy.

As for Toppan's claims of innocence, they began to unravel once psychiatrists attempted to determine her mental condition. During her third session with the doctors, she admitted poisoning Mary Gibbs with a combination of morphine and atropine. She then went on to talk about other murders. In all, she confessed to killing eleven of her patients.

At her trial on June 23, 1902, with the jury influenced by the testimony of the examining psychiatrists, Jane Toppan was found not guilty by reason of insanity and was sentenced for life to the Taunton Insane Hospital. In the words of one doctor, Toppan had been "born with a weak and nervous mental condition," and she suffered from a "lack of moral sense and defective self-control." There was reason to believe her condition was hereditary: both her father and sister had ended up in insane asylums.

The public was shocked by this angel of mercy who had fatally poisoned eleven of her patients. They became even more shocked when additional confessions were made known. To her jailor and her chief counsel, Toppan admitted that, in fact, she had murdered as many as thirty-one people. Questioned about her motive for mass murder, she replied, "That is something I won't tell. . . . But it was not for money." She also seemed to take great pride in the way she had bamboozled the psychiatrists into certifying her insanity. "I know all about insane people," she said, "and I was fully aware that their opening remark to doctors when they are to be examined is that they are not insane, so I used my knowledge to advantage. I said to the doctors, 'I am not insane, and I don't want you to make me out insane,' but you see they have."

During her first years at the Taunton Insane Hospital, Toppan was prone to violent outbursts and was often straitjacketed. She then became a more cooperative inmate. She died at the hospital on August 17, 1938, after thirty-six years of confinement.

JOHANN HOCH
1862–1906
"The Stockyard Bluebeard"

Jacob Huff had his own way of dealing with his wife's untimely death. His first order of business was to look after her possessions. Over the years, his wife Caroline had managed to put nine hundred dollars in the

bank, a considerable sum in 1895. Soon after she died, the account was empty. Caroline also had owned a house. Jacob Huff sold it. And then, of course, there was his wife's life insurance policy. After Huff received the twenty-five-hundred-dollar payment on the policy, he took care of his final bit of business. He left town in the middle of the night and faked his death by leaving his clothes and a suicide note along the Ohio River. He did just one more thing before rowing downriver away from his recent home of Wheeling, West Virginia: he tossed a package into the water, a package that contained his ex-wife's entrails.

This was the end of Jacob Huff. The man who set out on the Ohio River that night would never use that name again.

Three years later, a middle-aged German immigrant was arrested in Chicago for swindling one of the merchants in town. The charge was minor, and the suspect, a former stockyard worker, was, as far as the local police were concerned, just one of a long procession of petty crooks passing through the Chicago jails. No further thought would have been expended on him, and the prisoner would have remained merely a face in a vast criminal crowd, if it weren't for happenstance.

The prisoner's photograph happened to appear in a Chicago newspaper after his arrest. Then, in West Virginia a clergyman named Haas happened to get ahold of that paper. The face in the picture brought the Reverend Mr. Haas up short. He wasted no time writing a letter to the Chicago police.

The letter had to do with a man named Jacob Huff.

Three years ago, the Reverend Mr. Haas of Wheeling, West Virginia, had paid a call to an ailing member of his congregation, a woman who had suddenly been taken ill by what appeared to be kidney disease. During the visit the woman, wrecked by a relentless, torturous pain, was given medicine by Jacob Huff, her husband. The reverend thought he saw that the medication took the form of white powder.

A few days later the woman died.

The dead woman's maiden name had been Caroline Hoch—an intriguing coincidence. The swindling stockyard worker currently in custody in Chicago was named Johann Hoch, or at least that was what he was calling himself. Could Johann Hoch the swindler, as the Reverend Mr. Haas contended, have taken on the woman's name after poisoning her and looting her estate? The photo of the dead woman's husband, enclosed with the clergyman's letter, indicated that Hoch was indeed the same man as Jacob Huff. And if the German immigrant in the Chicago jail was a wife-killer, what had he been up to in the three years since his cold-blooded West Virginia escapade?

The authorities launched an extensive investigation. What they uncovered was a series of suspicious marriages, from one end of the country to the other, that might have involved Johann Hoch, under one name or another. Many of the wives had been left fleeced and abandoned. Others had been left fleeced and dead, victims of sudden illness that might have been caused by arsenic poisoning. As for the Caroline Hoch case, the woman's body was exhumed so that the stomach could be studied for traces of arsenic. It was a short study. The corpse's entrails were missing.

They were now somewhere along the bottom of the Ohio River.

The picture that emerged of murder and greed was extraordinary, but there was little in the way of hard evidence. Johann Hoch served a year in jail for his swindling of the Chicago merchant and was set free. A few years later, though, when Hoch began to operate too quickly, the Chicago police got another crack at the man who would be dubbed "the Stockyard Bluebeard."

Hoch married Marie Walcker of Chicago in December 1904. He poisoned her a month after the wedding. As if that weren't fast enough, he then went to work on Walcker's sister, Amelia. Not only didn't he wait for his wife's body to go cold, he didn't even wait for his wife to become a corpse before he proposed to the sister. He must have been persuasive; Amelia married him a few days after her sister was put underground.

Amelia ensured a premature end to her marriage when she handed over $750 from her savings. This generosity may have also saved her life, because now Hoch would not have to resort to life insurance fraud to get his prize. The next thing Amelia knew, both her husband and her money were gone. She filed a complaint against Hoch with the Chicago police, who, in turn, ordered an autopsy of the body of Amelia's sister. Arsenic was found in the stomach.

Now there was finally a case against Hoch. When he was spotted in New York City, thanks to a photo of him circulated to newspapers across the country, local police picked him up and put him on a Chicago-bound train.

Despite the overwhelming evidence against him in the Marie Walcker murder, Johann Hoch was not about to give up on a lifetime of deceit. Even as the hangman's noose was tightened around his neck in February 1906, he made unconvincing claims of innocence. We will never know exactly how many women he victimized, but one of the more conservative estimates puts the figure at twenty-four wives swindled, twelve of them killed.

BELLE GUNNESS
1859–?

When she came to the United States in her early twenties, Belle Paulson (later Gunness) started her new life in humble circumstances. Locating in Chicago, she moved in with relatives who had preceded her from her native Norway, and like so many immigrants of her day, she took on whatever menial work she could find. But washing and sewing other people's clothes were not things that Belle Paulson intended to do for the rest of her life, and she took an important step to correct this condition by marrying fellow Norwegian Mads Sorenson in 1884.

The acquisition of a working husband, however, was not enough by itself. The watchman's salary that Mads Sorenson brought home did

nothing to elevate their economic position, and the subsequent addition of children to the family put an additional strain on their limited resources. The opening of a family-run confectioner's shop provided new opportunities for Belle. Now she had a mate, a family, and property. In years to come, she would realize her version of the immigrant American's dream by parlaying all three into monetary gain.

In 1896 fire destroyed the Sorensons' shop, and the insurance company paid Belle and her husband for their loss. Now they could afford to buy a house. Other lucrative fires would follow, but Belle didn't confine herself to the monetary potential of property. To her mind other forms of equity surrounded her. She proceeded to insure the lives of two of her infant children. They both died suddenly. And before long, husband Mads was also converted into ready cash. Like the children, Mads officially died of natural causes, suffering from symptoms that, we know now, could have been triggered by poison. Mads's natural death was especially opportune. He happened to die on the one day that he was covered by both his old life insurance policy and the new policy that was just going into effect.

Thanks to a succession of insurance awards, Belle began to make a prosperous life for herself in her adopted country. In fact, she had accumulated enough money to purchase a farm for herself and her remaining children. Fortuitously, the new property was outside La Porte, Indiana, just over the state line from Chicago, where her string of profitable hardships must have started to seem suspicious to insurance investigators. Belle married one more time, to a man named Peter Gunness, who soon died when a sausage grinder somehow slipped off a shelf and just happened to land on his skull, causing a mortal fracture. After collecting on his net insurance worth of twenty-five hundred dollars, Belle Gunness moved on to the next phase of her climb up the financial ladder.

Hired hands, who also doubled as lovers, came and went at the Gunness farm. So did prospective husbands. Over the next few years, men who answered Gunness's matrimonial ads and came to live on her farm had been known to make large withdrawals from the local bank just prior to dropping out of sight. The gruesome story behind these disappearances was revealed after the Gunness house was razed by fire, the last and most spectacular blaze associated with Belle Gunness.

The fire on April 28, 1908, apparently killed four people, who were identified as the three Gunness children and Belle Gunness herself. This last scorched body was distinguished by the peculiar absence of a head. A little over a week later, police discovered that more corpses were nearby; the farmyard turned out to be a secret murderer's cemetery. Buried there were at least twelve people, ten men and two women; the number of additional bodies was only hinted at by the unearthing of various, assorted bones. Identifying the victims was difficult; most of them had been carved up into six pieces. The murderer's application of quicklime had accelerated the process of decomposition. Three of the male remains were identified as men who had responded to Gunness's ad, while two others were believed to have been hired hands. One of the females was Jennie Olsen, Gunness's adopted daughter, who had disappeared two years earlier at the age of sixteen. She may have been an inconvenient witness to Peter Gunness's supposedly accidental death.

A disgruntled former Gunness farmhand named Ray Lamphere was implicated in the deaths of the four people found in the basement, but he was never convicted of murder. The case remained substantially unsolved. No one doubted that Belle Gunness was responsible for the more than twelve bodies buried in the farmyard; the principal issue instead was the identity of the decapitated woman in the farmhouse basement. Lamphere claimed that Gunness had killed a woman to serve as a substitute in her faked death. She then supposedly made her getaway with the $100,000 she had secured through mass murder. Over the years Gunness was allegedly sighted in the Midwest, the Northeast, and as far away as Los Angeles, but none of these sightings was ever substantiated.

BELA KISS

1872–?

"The Monster of Czinkota"

In 1916 the Austro-Hungarian army needed gasoline to fuel its military efforts in World War I. Every possible source in the empire's cities and towns was tapped, and by June the army's search reached the lazy resort town of Czinkota. The village constable, although eager to help the soldiers, didn't think there was anything he could offer, at first. Then he remembered something.

Back before the war there had been that business about the large metal drums being kept in the house of Bela Kiss, the retired tinsmith. Town gossips had circulated the rumor that he was using the drums to store illicit liquor, but then Bela Kiss had revealed to the constable what he was really up to. War was coming soon, Kiss had predicted, and these drums of gasoline would come in handy when fuel became scarce.

As he now brought the soldiers to Kiss's vacant house, the constable must have been impressed with Bela Kiss's shrewdness. Unfortunately, Kiss didn't have the luck to go with it. He never had the chance to profit from his foresight; he had been drafted and killed in the agonizing attempts to conquer Serbia in the early phases of the war.

Inside Kiss's house the constable and the soldiers found that the drums were still there, seven of them in all. They pried one of them

open to check its contents, then stopped and stared. The fluid inside the drum—not gasoline, it turned out, but wood alcohol—made it difficult to discern at first what lay below the surface. But soon the soldiers and the constable realized what they were looking at: the naked, discolored body of a woman, tied with rope in a doubled-up position so it could fit inside the container.

That wasn't the only corpse they found.

Each of the six other drums also held a female body. All of the women had been strangled. And an inspection of the grounds near the house revealed shallow graves and even more female bodies.

Residents of Czinkota were about to learn something about the middle-aged man named Bela Kiss who had once lived so quietly in their midst.

The first important clue to the nature of Kiss's murderous secret life was found in the collection of papers uncovered in his house soon after the discovery of the corpses. They clearly showed that Bela Kiss had been finding women—and victims—through personal ads he had placed in newspapers. Subsequent investigations, coordinated with the efforts of the nearby Budapest police, sketched in the rest of the picture.

At its best the portrait of Bela Kiss is quite hazy. At the height of World War I's mass slaughter, Austro-Hungarian officials had more pressing things to worry about than the crimes committed by a man who had already been killed himself; inquiries into the Kiss case weren't as thorough as they might have been. Consequently, accounts of his life give different versions of the facts, making Bela Kiss seem more like some ominous figure of folklore—a sort of a twentieth-century Grimm's fairy-tale villain—than a real-life criminal.

One of the facts that is agreed upon is that Bela Kiss moved to the town of Czinkota in 1912. He was forty years old and married to a woman named Marie who was fifteen years younger. Marie had an affair with an artist by the name of Paul Bihari. They ran off together—

or so the story went. In 1916 Marie would turn up as one of the bodies buried near the house.

When he killed his adulterous wife, Kiss discovered murderous impulses that had previously lain dormant inside him for many years. Either that, or he became a sex maniac who was driven to partake of, and permanently dispose of, one woman after another. Both explanations have been offered by chroniclers of his exploits. In either case, he sought women by advertising in newspapers for female correspondents. Some women were lured by the prospect of marriage, others were interested in Kiss's alleged fortune-telling talents. Once Kiss had them in the apartment he kept in Budapest, he would strangle them, take their valuables and drive their bodies out to Czinkota. He would fold the bodies into drums and leave them hidden and preserved in alcohol until the opportunity arose to bury them outside. In total, Kiss murdered between twenty and thirty women.

Perhaps the most intriguing aspect of this case is the ultimate fate of Bela Kiss. As Mark Twain might have put it, rumors of Kiss's death might have been greatly exaggerated. In early 1916 the residents of Czinkota were notified that Kiss died in a Belgrade military hospital, but the nurse who tended to him later swore that he was a mere boy, even though Kiss was over forty at the time. For this reason it is believed that he did not die in combat, but rather switched his identification papers with a dying young soldier. Alleged sightings from both sides of the Atlantic kept Bela Kiss's legend alive: perhaps he returned to Budapest; maybe he joined the French Foreign Legion; maybe he settled in New York City. Despite all this alleged globetrotting by Kiss, no other murders were ever attributed to him.

HENRI LANDRU

1869–1922

"The Bluebeard of Paris"

When he was discharged from the French army in 1894, twenty-five-year-old Henri Landru was a bright young man who seemed to be en route to a life of legitimate success. The product of a solid working-class family, he had compiled a good record as a soldier. He went on from there to become a white-collar office employee, apparently on the verge of a comfortable, middle-class existence. He was even appointed subdeacon in his church. True, he had strayed from the straight and narrow when he had impregnated one of his female cousins in 1891, but Landru eventually got around to doing the honorable thing by marrying the young woman two years later. Despite this rocky beginning, the

marriage went smoothly at first. Several years later, however, Landru began to find it difficult to spend much time with his wife. That was because he kept getting sent to prison.

As it turned out, Landru was simply not interested in leading a respectable life; the life of a con man was far more appealing, even if he kept getting caught at it. From 1900 to 1914, he was in prison as often as he was at home with his wife and growing family. Still, his wife learned to live with the problems created by her husband's criminal career. We know from Landru's subsequent ventures that he was a consummate deceiver of women, and he got considerable practice at this craft with his wife. Over the years, he would make her believe that he was a good husband, in his way. He was certainly a conscientious provider; he kept the cash coming in, and he supplied furniture for the home and jewelry for adornment. If his wife wondered where the money came from, or why the furniture and jewelry were invariably secondhand, she never pressed her questions. For this reason she had no way of knowing that her bald, bearded husband was turning into France's most infamous woman-killer.

For Landru the transition from ordinary fraud to murderous swindling occurred sometime in 1914 when he was in his midforties. He was such a devious man, and so effective in his secrecy, that little is known about the reasons for this transition. Perhaps it was simply a matter of a psychopathic mind perceiving an irresistible opportunity. World War I was just beginning to engulf Europe, and perhaps Landru judged that the conflict's mass slaughter would be the ideal cover for some discreet homicide.

Landru approached the business of murder for profit with great efficiency. He first contacted his female victims through ads he placed in newspapers. Sometimes he claimed to be a widower in search of a new bride, other times he presented himself as a used furniture dealer looking for secondhand merchandise. He would cultivate several women at the same time, just as a salesman pursues many prospective customers in the hope of landing one sale. When he was satisfied that he had hooked a woman who was both prosperous and sufficiently lonely, Landru would proceed with a whirlwind romance that would culminate in the woman's accompanying him to the villa he kept outside Paris, in the town of Gambais.

Landru was so good at covering his tracks that his exact method of murder was never revealed. We do know, however, that once the deed was done, he would dismember the corpse and burn the pieces in his stove. The victim's possessions would then be his. If he had not been able to wangle arrangements to his liking while the woman was alive, he would, through forgery, gain access to the woman's savings and securities after her death. Scavenged furniture and jewelry would add to his profit.

Landru's use of many aliases, as well as eleven different residences in Paris, made it difficult for the police to detect any pattern in the increasing number of missing-women cases. In the end it was incriminating information supplied by sisters of two of the victims that put the Paris authorities on Landru's trail. They placed him in custody in April 1919, pending further investigation.

The police were never able to produce any *corpus delicti*—Landru's disposal of his victims was so thorough—but they uncovered a great deal of other evidence: human bone fragments in the stove at Landru's villa; extensive correspondence between Landru and his prospective victims; testimony that Landru was the last person to be seen with many of the victims; and a little notebook containing the names of the missing women. In all, Landru was charged with the murder of ten women, along with the sixteen-year-old son of one victim.

In court the great mass of circumstantial evidence made for a powerful case against the man who became known as "the Bluebeard of Paris." But Landru never admitted to anything. Instead, he continued to exercise the kind of slipperiness that had evidently fooled so many gullible women. At one point, when doctors testified that he was legally sane and not entitled to any special consideration, Landru found a way to twist things around to his benefit: since he was sane, he claimed, he could not have committed the eleven alleged murders, because they were clearly the acts of a madman. The judge and jury, however, were not impressed by this feat of backward logic. The jury convicted him of all murder charges, and the judge sentenced him to death.

Maintaining his facade of innocence to the end, Landru was beheaded by the guillotine in February 1922.

THE AXEMAN OF NEW ORLEANS
1918–1920
Unidentified Serial Murderer

Two weapons were used in the New Orleans murder of Joseph Maggio and his wife on May 23, 1918. An ax smashed their heads while they slept, and a razor was used to slash their throats. Although the final, killing strokes were delivered with the razor—used so savagely on Mrs. Maggio that she was nearly decapitated—it was the bloody ax found on the rear steps of the house that would become the gruesome trademark for the night's horror. The specter of an ax blade plunging through the darkness toward a sleeper's head would haunt the people of New Orleans for the next two years.

Immediately following the Maggio murders, speculation arose throughout the city that a crazed multiple murderer was on the loose. According to a story in the *New Orleans States*, the Maggio killings were connected to three earlier ax murders, committed seven years before and still unsolved. Recently this theory has been disputed by Michael Newton in his book *Hunting Humans*; he asserts that there is absolutely no record that these earlier killings even occurred. But for the citizens of New Orleans in 1918, this debate over criminal history

would have been moot, as their fears about a relentless homicidal maniac soon proved to be justified. On June 28, a little over a month after the Maggio murders, the Axeman struck again.

Beginning in June, there were three attacks in as many months, leaving two wounded and two dead. All were perpetrated by an unknown, ax-wielding assailant who struck in the middle of the night, usually gaining entrance to his victims' homes by cutting a panel out of the back door. Two witnesses caught a glimpse of the killer during the last of these raids and described him as "dark, tall, heavy-set, wearing a dark suit and a black slouch hat." This would be the police's only lead.

Panic swept through the city. Jittery citizens went to the police with one story after another about suspicious characters, panels cut out of back doors, strange sounds heard in the middle of the night. Eventually the hysteria would reach such a point that sardonic humor became a desperate way of defying the oppressive fear. New Orleans residents threw "axeman parties" in honor of the fiend who was terrorizing the city, and a popular tune of the day was "The Mysterious Axeman's Jazz."

As often happens in serial murder cases like this, the attacks ceased for a while, creating a false sense of security. Then on March 10, 1919, the city's peace of mind was shattered once again. On that night, in the town of Gretna on the other side of the Mississippi River, Charles Cortimiglia and his wife, Rose, were discovered, both with fractured skulls; they would survive the savage assault, but their two-year-old daughter Mary had been axed to death. Another wave of attacks was about to begin. The Axeman struck four homes between March and October, wounding four and killing two.

Wild accusations and capricious arrests became part of the Axeman hysteria. A man named Louis Besumer, for example, was accused not only of being the killer, but of being a German spy as well (World War I was at its height at the time). Eventually, Besumer was acquitted, but Iorlando and Frank Jordano, falsely named by neighbor Rose Cortimiglia as the killers of her daughter, didn't fare as well. Acting out of personal animosity, Cortimiglia gave testimony against them in court that directly led to their convictions; the father, Iorlando, was sentenced to life imprisonment and the son, Frank, sentenced to hang. The incarceration of these men, however, did nothing to stop the Axeman's forays. In December 1920 Rose Cortimiglia confessed to lying about the Jordanos, and the two men were set free.

By then, the Axeman case came to a sudden, if indefinite, conclusion. The reason may have been a shooting death more than fifteen hundred miles away in Los Angeles. The victim was a man named Joseph Mumfre, and the shooter was the widow of Mike Pepitone, the Axeman's last victim. The woman claimed that Mumfre was the Axeman and that her killing of him was an act of vengeance.

Was Joseph Mumfre really the Axeman of New Orleans? There is some reason to believe so. A habitual criminal, Mumfre had been in and out of jail for the last ten years, and all the periods he had been at large coincided with the times of Axeman attacks. Also substantiating the Mumfre-as-Axeman theory is the fact that the epidemic of New Orleans ax murders came to a halt after his death. Unfortunately, beyond this circumstantial evidence, there is nothing to link Mumfre *directly* to all the attacks.

Some writers have speculated that the Axeman murders may have been part of a Mafia extortion scheme. The problem with this theory is that the Mafia at that time confined itself to extorting fellow Italians, and several of the Axeman victims were not Italian. Another theory is that there may have been more than one culprit responsible for the Axeman terror, the evidence being that the *modus operandi* was not exactly the same in all the attacks. As yet, no theory has attracted enough hard evidence to be completely convincing. The identity of the Axeman of New Orleans, one of America's first real-life bogeymen, may never be known.

GEORG GROSSMANN
1863–1921

During World War I, life in Berlin was transformed. The once-prosperous center of the kaiser's empire became a place where the everyday business of life was a harsh struggle. The Allies' naval blockade prevented all sorts of needed goods from reaching German hands, including quite a bit of that most elemental of supplies—food. Exacerbating the situation was the military's drain on healthy workers, which left fewer farmers to raise homegrown crops and livestock. The government issued food rationing cards just five months after the outbreak of war, and restrictions became increasingly severe as the fighting dragged on. As early as 1915, meat and other staples started to become a scarcity.

Berliners, desperate for food, were often to be found on food lines during World War I and its aftermath. Exploiting their hunger, Georg Grossmann turned many of them into unwitting cannibals.

In this time of privation and disruption, unscrupulous men could flourish. The same could be said for depraved men. Georg Grossmann was a horrendous example.

Early in the war, Grossmann, a man in his fifties, was living in an apartment house in one of Berlin's slum districts. He started to make strange demands upon his landlord, insisting that he have his own entrance to the house's kitchen and that he enjoy special privileges there: no one was to disturb him while he made use of the room, not even the landlord himself. In hard times, and in an impoverished neighborhood, a landlord might tend to overlook eccentricities in a tenant as long as he paid his rent on time. Grossmann met that requirement, no matter how mysterious his means of support might have been. It's likely that he also could be very persuasive. He was a big man, and known to be ill-tempered. Perhaps one reason the landlord gave in to Grossmann's arrogant demands was that he knew his tenant had a violent, criminal past.

Grossmann had been arrested twenty-five times. Three of those arrests were for assaulting children, each resulting in a sentence of hard labor; in one of these instances the attack resulted in the child's death. Over the years he often supported himself by begging and street peddling, but at one point he pursued a more legitimate vocation, that of a butcher. This particular career path would prove to be useful training for his wartime activities.

During the war Grossmann made a habit of bringing prostitutes back to his rooms. His neighbors concluded that he was sexually insatiable and didn't give it any more thought than that. The fact that he brought the women to the kitchen was not of any significance to them, which is only reasonable. There was no way for them to guess the twisted truth: Grossmann viewed the prostitutes as a way to capitalize on the city's meat shortage.

After having sex with one of these women, Grossmann would kill her, then butcher her body and carve the flesh into cuts of meat, as he had once done with the carcasses of cows and pigs. On the streets of Berlin, where meat was hard to come by, Grossmann the peddler would pass off human flesh as beef or pork.

He carried on this hideous enterprise throughout the war, then continued to make unwitting cannibals out of his fellow Berliners in the chaotic postwar years as well. As long as he paid his rent, and as along as he murdered his victims quietly, Grossmann went undetected. Then, in August 1921 he brought home a prostitute who gave him a loud, if futile, struggle.

The landlord followed the noises to their source in the kitchen, Grossmann's domain. He called in the police, who burst into the kitchen to find a woman, already dead, lying on a cot. Nearby, Grossmann had his butcher knives ready.

Despite further investigation, the police were not able to fix a definite total of victims, and Grossmann was not willing to supply any information. But the police knew their prisoner had been peddling his curious meat since the beginning of the war, which meant he had been at it for seven years, and they estimated that Grossman had killed and butchered over fifty women in that time. A more complete account of these grisly crimes might have come from Grossmann himself, after he was convicted and sentenced to death, once he had nothing to gain from further silence. But soon after his trial, he sidestepped both the executioner and the investigators by hanging himself in his cell.

VASILI KOMAROFF
1871–1923
"The Wolf of Moscow"

During the turmoil of the early 1920s, Soviet Russian authorities were obsessed with enemies. They had just left their military opposition vanquished on the battlefields of a horrific civil war, but their work was far from over. As Premier Lenin suffered his first of a series of strokes in 1921, the fate of the new revolutionary regime was still in question, and the Cheka, the Soviet secret police, carried out its brutal campaign against enemies of the people, both real and imagined. In this intensely politicized atmosphere, ordinary, nonpolitical crime was not of the foremost concern in the nation's capital, Moscow, but the corpses that mysteriously appeared at regular intervals on the city's empty lots forced authorities to make an exception to this rule. The discovery of twenty-one murder victims in just two years' time was clearly no ordinary matter, and proof that not all enemies of the people were political.

The first body was found in 1921. Like all the others that

would follow, the corpse was male and was bound by rope in a doubled-up position so that it could be stuffed inside a sack. Most of the victims were found on the south side of the Moskva River, and the majority of those in the Shabolovki District. The cause of death was either strangulation or bludgeoning of the skull.

At first the Moscow police had absolutely no clues, then a clear pattern began to emerge. The bodies were discovered either on a Thursday or a Saturday. This pattern took on significance when the police realized that the Shabolovki horse-trading market was open for business on Wednesdays and Fridays, the days before the grisly discoveries. The horse market became the focus of investigation.

The police learned of a horse trader named Vasili Komaroff, who not only showed up at the market on Wednesdays and Fridays but, more significant, had some peculiar habits. As often as he came to market, it seems he rarely brought any horses to sell. He was known, however, to walk away with a prospective customer at his side.

When the police checked up on Komaroff, they put together a report that described this husband and father of three as "a genial, smiling man." According to *The New York Times'* account of the case, the only characteristic they could discern about him out of the ordinary was, of all things, the pupils of his eyes, which were observed to be "unusually small in comparison with the white." In light of the man's solid reputation, the police decided to move with caution: they searched Komaroff's property, but not, ostensibly, for the purpose of investigating mass murder; they explained to Komaroff they were merely looking for an illicit liquor still.

Their caution turned out to be unwarranted.

Beneath a pile of hay in Komaroff's stable they found a sack containing a trussed-up male body, a corpse that was being hidden until Komaroff could dispose of it in his usual manner on one of the city's vacant lots. When the corpse was found, Komaroff jumped out a window and managed to elude the police for a few days, but he was finally apprehended and placed in prison. Soon he confessed.

The body found in the stable brought the total number of known victims to twenty-two, but the police now learned that there were eleven others that had never been uncovered. Komaroff directed the authorities to five more corpses scattered among the city's southern districts and explained that the remaining six had been dumped into the river, from which they were never recovered. His confession also revealed that his wife, Sophia, was an accomplice in his crimes. As the police suspected, Komaroff found his victims at the horse market. From there he brought them to his stable, supposedly for the purpose of showing them a horse that could be had for a pittance.

The reason for his murdering thirty-three men? To this question Komaroff offered the incredible comment "I needed money for food and drink." Ironically, the murder and robbery of thirty-three people had brought in a grand total of $26.40, or 80¢ per victim; it seems reasonable to assume that some other, psychological motive drove Komaroff to commit these crimes. The police learned, for example, that Komaroff's homicidal streak had cropped up at other times in his life. Once, when his eight-year-old son had done something to displease him, Komaroff fashioned a hangman's noose, tightened it around the boy's throat, and strung him up. If his wife hadn't come in time to cut the rope, the boy would have been hanged.

While this incident demonstrates that Komaroff didn't need the incentive of profit—and picayune profit at that—to resort to violence, the Moscow authorities were not terribly interested in exploring the fine points of motivation. Komaroff and his wife were convicted and sentenced at a trial that lasted just one day. To the highly vocal approval of the spectators who crowded the courtroom, "the Wolf of Moscow" and his wife were condemned to death.

Just before the trial Komaroff had shown considerable bravado, saying he hoped the conviction and execution would come quickly. Once sentenced, though, he tried to appeal the decision, an effort that failed. Komaroff and his wife faced the firing squad on June 18, 1923. Indicative of the outrage Komaroff's crimes inspired, some Moscow citizens were not especially impressed with the sentence. One woman said at the time, "If they cut Komaroff slowly in bits, others might be frightened, but shooting—bah! That's nothing."

FRITZ HAARMANN
1879–1925

"The Vampire of Hanover"

For Germany the years following World War I were a time of economic collapse, growing decadence, and political chaos. In this time of social disintegration, Germany's cities also seemed to be the breeding ground for some of the most vile killers that modern Europe has known. One of the worst was Fritz Haarmann, a man who preyed on boys for their meager possessions, for the thrill of killing—and for the flesh on their bones.

During the early 1920s the northern German city of Hanover was not aware of the scope of the horror being carried out in its midst. Boys were vanishing, but mostly they were refugees, dislocated by the war, whose disappearances simply might have meant that they had moved on. Some curious discoveries along the banks of the Leine Canal, however, provided ominous hints about what might have been the truth behind the reports of missing boys. In the spring of 1924, several human skulls and a sack containing human bones were found there. Another indication of the true, horrifying nature of the case—which was not correctly evaluated by the police—was a suspicious incident involving some meat sold by one of the city's many sidewalk peddlers. A woman complained to the police that there was something peculiar about one of the "steaks" she had purchased, but a police analyst came back with the conclusion that the meat in question was merely pork. The peddler whose wares had aroused the woman's suspicions was Fritz Haarmann, known to the police as a confirmed petty crook and

sexual deviant. The police might not have made any connection between Haarmann and the missing boys if they hadn't arrested him around this time on charges of indecency.

As a result of this arrest, police searched Haarmann's rooms and uncovered incriminating evidence: boys' clothing. They also discovered something incriminating about the coat being worn by the son of Haarmann's landlady: it was traced to one of the missing boys. Suddenly, and apparently by happenstance, Haarmann became the prime suspect in what was beginning to look like a case of mass murder. Once he was linked to the disappearances, Haarmann confessed. He told his tale readily and in ghastly detail.

Haarmann began committing hideous murder around 1919, at the age of forty, following one of his many stints in prison. His most recent jail term had been for sexual assault against a seventeen-year-old boy; other offenses over the course of his seedy life had included pickpocketing, fraud, smuggling, and burglary. At the age of seventeen, at the start of his criminal career, he had been described by a doctor as "incurably feebleminded." Between 1919 and 1924, however, he proved to be cunning enough to avoid detection while slaughtering perhaps more than fifty boys.

To Haarmann the young male refugees who thronged to Hanover at the end of World War I were irresistible targets. His accomplice in hunting down these victims was Hans Grans, a male prostitute, a younger, handsome man who also happened to be Haarmann's lover. Haarmann would entice a hungry boy to his rooms with the promise of a meal. When the boy was finished eating and was lulled by a full stomach, Haarmann would attack. Grans would often help pin the boy down, but it was Haarmann alone who proceeded from there. He would lunge at the boy's throat, and then the man who later became known as "the Vampire of Hanover" would chew through the boy's flesh. When Haarmann was done, the boy's head would be practically severed from his body. The experience would often make Haarmann achieve orgasm.

Haarmann committed these grotesque crimes for five years. Along with sating a demented sexual appetite, the murders also had a sickening larcenous motive. Haarmann and Grans would sell cuts of the young men's flesh at a market across from the Hanover railway station. Like the woman who had complained that one of these pieces of meat was peculiar, customers thought they were buying steak. The killers also made a little extra money by selling the victims' clothes.

But not every part of the victim and his possessions was put up for sale. Much of the boys' flesh was eaten by Haarmann himself. Those parts of the bodies that he couldn't digest or sell would be dumped in the Leine Canal, where some of the victims' bones would eventually be found.

Aided by the killer's confession, the police were able to find enough evidence to charge Haarmann with twenty-seven of his fifty-odd murders. He went on trial in December 1924, an experience he seemed to enjoy as he voiced a running commentary throughout the proceedings and offered a series of what he considered humorous asides. Found guilty, the forty-six-year-old Haarmann was condemned to death by decapitation. His accomplice, Grans, received a prison term of twelve years.

Haarmann's execution took place on April 15, 1924. Just moments before being beheaded, he announced that he considered his execution to be his wedding.

THE TOLEDO CLUBBER
1925–1926
Unidentified Serial Killer

Although largely forgotten now, the maniac who stalked the women of Toledo, Ohio, in the mid-1920s was regarded as one of the most frightening criminals of his day. On and off for a year and a half, the mad killer carried out a reign of terror, creeping along darkened streets and clubbing his victims in a demonic frenzy. Even out-of-state newspapers chronicled the case, while in Toledo itself the most extraordinary measures were taken to protect the city's women and bring the deranged slugger to justice. Despite all this, the Toledo Clubber was never found.

A measure of the fear that the Clubber inspired can be gleaned from the description of the mystery culprit, compiled from statements of several Clubber-attack survivors. The authorities made it known they were on the lookout for "a beastlike man, more than six feet tall, of dark hue, with long woolly hair, protruding front teeth, fiery eyes, and almost superhuman strength." It would seem safe to assume that this profile, which could pass for a description of a folk-tale ogre, was probably colored by the victims' trauma, but it's also obvious that the fears of Toledo's women were justified.

The onslaught began one night in May 1925. A forty-eight-year-old woman named Emma Hatfield was bludgeoned with some sort of heavy club until her skull was crushed. She was still alive when she was found, sprawled in an alley, but died several weeks later. For three months the Clubber wasn't heard from; then in August he beat a second woman to death. The attacks accelerated in the fall; seven women were bludgeoned in October and November. No deaths resulted, but several victims were put in critical condition, and the frightening rapidity of the assaults plunged the city into panic.

The pattern was now clear. The Clubber, prowling the city's west side, hunted for women as they walked alone down poorly lighted streets. The first blow came from behind, incapacitating the victim before she had a chance to scream.

With no substantial clues to follow, the police conducted a roundup of "mental defectives" and in the process reincarcerated some escapees from mental institutions. At the height of the panic, the American Legion put a thousand men in the street to aid in the search for the culprit, and the city's Medical Service Bureau provided escorts for any woman who was understandably afraid to walk the streets by herself. To a great extent streets were empty at night, and stores closed before nightfall.

The public's perception of the mystery fiend as some sort of unnatural creature was reflected in some of the alleged sightings of the Clubber. In one instance witnesses said they saw the culprit standing on the roof of a house one night, firing a

HUNT TOLEDO GIANT WHO FELLS WOMEN

Mysterious Man Has Clubbed Ten In Ten Days, Two Dying From His Blows.

APPEARS AT MANY PLACES

American Legion Joins Police in Determined Effort to Rid the Streets of Strange Terror.

Special to The New York Times.

TOLEDO, Ohio, Nov. 21.—This city began a determined search today for a crazed man who has struck down ten women in the last ten days, two of whom died from fractured skulls. Police, firemen, citizens and special officers have failed to find a single clue that would lead to the identification of the terrorist. He appears in widely separated parts of the city, carrying a huge club with which he crushes the heads of his victims.

Tonight 1,000 members of the American Legion are helping police comb the city for "a beastlike man, more than six feet tall, of dark hue, with long woolly hair, protruding front teeth, fiery eyes and almost superhuman strength." This identification was given the police by several of his victims who obtained glimpses of his face as he fled after making attacks.

While the city was engaged in the man hunt tonight, two more women were attacked. Miss Lorine Braun, 18, was hit over the head in the front yard of her home. She was unconscious when found and was rushed to the hospital in a serious condition.

Soon afterward the maniac clubbed another woman, who has not been identified. She also is in a serious condition.

The two victims tonight brought the maniac's list to ten.

Officials are endeavoring to suppress the reports of the fiend's activities to quiet the alarm that has spread through the city. Chief of Police Harry Jennings and Police Inspector William Delahanty this afternoon denied that two women had been attacked last night. They declared that one of the women had been a victim of a delusion while the other had since denied that she had been attacked. But two dead and six seriously injured women provide plenty of proof that a murderous maniac is at large.

It is a well-known fact that the man is a lunatic and women are his prey. On no occasion since his appearance on Toledo streets has he even threatened a man or child.

Mrs. Frank Hall was the first woman to encounter the clubber. She was attacked in front of her home and sustained a fractured skull, broken nose and other injuries. She has been confined to her bed since the meeting with the killer and her condition is serious. Mr. Hall said that attending physicians declared it would take years for his wife to recover, if she ever regained her health.

Mrs. Emma Hatfield and Mrs. Lydia Baumgartner were struck over the head with a club and died of their injuries. Both were attacked on the street and, in dying statements, gave identical descriptions of their assailant. Mrs. Cora Bachelor met the man as she was returning to her home and was struck down. She has a broken nose and serious facial lacerations. Miss

Continued on Page Twenty-seven.

pistol and emitting a "weird cry." In another case two women, who claimed they had a close call with the Clubber, described the attacker as a bizarre man with green circles painted around his eyes.

The citywide alert seemed to drive the maniac into hiding, but only temporarily. On the night of January 19, 1926, the Clubber smashed in the skull of Mary Handley. She was found dead in an alley the next morning. The Medical Service Bureau escorts were called out again, the American Legion patrols resumed, and the city's safety director called for the hiring of more police officers to pursue the case—he had already put his entire existing force on homicide duty. Once again, the police picked up suspicious characters, but no convincing suspect was found. For some reason the attacks stopped again, and the city was quiet for nine months. More fatalities, however, were to come.

The Clubber struck twice on October 26. A twenty-six-year-old schoolteacher named Lily Croy, returning home from night classes at the University of Toledo, was beaten to death; she was also raped, perhaps after the clubbing had rendered her unconscious. Later, forty-seven-year-old Mary Alden was found in her own kitchen, half-naked and battered to death. As an all-too-familiar fear swept through the city, the alert was on once more.

The day after this double killing, the police arrested two suspects. But the authorities didn't have much hope that they had finally solved the case. Even while the suspects were in custody, police vehicles carrying shotgun squads were sent out to patrol the city. Predictably, nothing came of the police interrogation of the latest detainees. But what the police didn't know at the time was that the attacks were over.

Perhaps the latest roundup of escaped asylum inmates, prompted by the October 26 murders, succeeded in incarcerating the man known as the Toledo Clubber. We will never know for sure. The madman who had killed five women and savagely wounded seven others had somehow dropped out of sight.

EARLE NELSON

1897–1928

"The Gorilla Murderer"

On February 20, 1926, a young man arrived at a San Francisco boardinghouse inquiring about a room to rent. Despite coarse features—a short, thick build, protruding lips, a heavy brow—he came across as a well-mannered, respectable individual, and the landlady, an elderly woman named Clara Newman, had no compunctions about letting a room to him.

The spinster Newman was sixty years old, not the sort of woman that would ordinarily be sexually enticing to a young man, but to this new boarder she held some attraction—a dark, twisted attraction. As soon as he was alone with Clara Newman, he clasped his big hands around her throat and strangled her, then sexually violated her dead body. He was gone well before the murder was discovered.

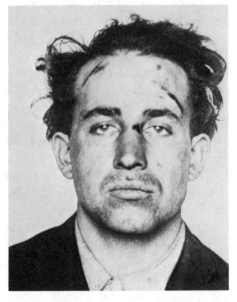

The man's name was Earle Nelson. This was his first murder. It would be far from his last. What exactly brought the twenty-eight-year-old Nelson to Clara Newman's boardinghouse on this particular day is entirely a matter of conjecture, as are his whereabouts and activities for the previous two years and three months. What we do know is that he had compiled a history of sexual violence in his early twenties and that his animallike appearance was a true physical reflection of the primitive, savage impulses that lay within.

Earle Nelson's career as a serial killer may have been more a matter of nature than nurture. A criminologist once even claimed that he could detect Nelson's inborn degeneracy in a photo of the killer as a three-year-old toddler. Whether an observation like this can be considered valid or not, from an early age Nelson had been known to be a peculiar, extraordinarily moody boy. The aunt who adopted him as an infant, after his mother died of syphilis, did everything she could to impart her righteous Christian beliefs to young Nelson. He absorbed these teachings, but they became jumbled in his mind with other, not-so-righteous notions. He would often lock himself in his room and mutter nonstop, as if intoning some sort of magical chant. Passages from the Bible were included in this litany. So was foul-mouthed obscenity.

Whatever congenital disorder may have plagued him, his condition got drastically worse at the age of ten, when he suffered a life-threatening head injury. After that he became increasingly violent toward girls. He crossed the line into outright criminality at the age of twenty-one. That was when he was arrested for the attempted rape of a preadolescent girl and was sentenced to a state penal farm.

Over the next few years the authorities tried to keep Nelson incarcerated for his sexual assaults—one of which was committed against a woman who had the misfortune of marrying him—but he soon became an escape artist *par excellence* and was never behind bars for very long. After his escape in November 1923, Nelson, for all intents and purposes, vanished. By the time he went to Clara Newman's boardinghouse in 1926, he was prepared to start a way of life that was devoted to nothing else but killing and necrophilia. Even when considered in terms of today's more murderous times, Earle Nelson's killing spree was appalling.

Always on the move, always a step ahead of the police, Nelson strangled and raped ten landladies in an area ranging from San Jose, California, to Portland, Oregon, within just nine months. With the West Coast in a panic, he then drifted to the Great Plains and preyed on more females there. He killed and violated one woman in Council Bluffs, Iowa, and two more in Kansas City. The last of these women had a baby daughter. Nelson strangled her too.

Through all this, the authorities were able to accomplish one thing: they developed a description of the monster they were trying to catch. Witnesses agreed that the killer had a simian appearance. Nelson became known as "the Gorilla Murderer."

Drifting again, Nelson hit Philadelphia, Buffalo, Detroit, and Chicago, and when he was done, five more women were dead. His next stop was Canada. Nelson was shrewd enough to get away from the U.S.

manhunt that was furiously trying to track him down, but his caution ended there. He wouldn't stop killing long enough for public alarm to fade. Because of that he was caught.

After murdering two women in Winnipeg, he was spotted on his way out of town, and his features were matched up with the picture on a wanted poster. Canadian police were then able to arrest the man who had successfully eluded authorities across the width of the United States. As was his custom, Nelson escaped from jail but was recaptured for good just hours later.

Nelson was convicted in November 1927 and was hanged in Winnipeg two months after that. Reverting to old habits learned in childhood, he mounted the scaffold with Bible in hand. The man who had killed twenty-two people in sixteen months then informed the spectators, "I forgive those who have wronged me."

CARL PANZRAM
1891–1930

Anyone searching for an argument for the bad-seed theory should take a long look at the life of Carl Panzram. True, he suffered hardship growing up on a meager Minnesota farm and also, at an early age, underwent the trauma of his father's desertion of the family. But it is difficult to see how these experiences led directly to a life of crime that began at the age of eight and eventually climaxed in some ten years of unrelenting plunder, sadism, and murder.

Panzram's first arrest at the age of eight was a drunk-and-disorderly charge, a sort of infraction one might expect from a boy twice his age, but still relatively innocuous. Panzram would grow out of that innocuousness quickly. Just three years later, he was burglarizing neighbors' houses, got caught, and was sent to reform school. Taking a dim view of the institution, he burned down one of its buildings. The first chance he had, after his release at the age of fourteen, he ran away from home and took to the road where he could better acquire new and more offensive ways of breaking the law. Except for those times when he was forcibly detained, he would drift for the rest of his life.

Panzram's apprenticeship as an incorrigible criminal included

incarceration in and escapes from a string of brutal reformatories, as well as diligent practice in the burglar's craft. To amuse himself when not robbing anyone, he would find the nearest church and burn it down. His final master classes in criminality were taken during three harsh years in the military prison at Fort Leavenworth. He landed there after enlisting in the army and discovering that there were things in army camps that could be stolen.

When released in 1910, at the age of nineteen, he regarded the entire country, and ultimately the wide world, as the theater for his depredations. He wandered west to California and up the Pacific Coast, then eastward across the northern Great Plains and eventually drifted to the Eastern Seaboard. Everywhere he went there were homes and businesses to rob, people to assault and kill. Among his murder victims were young men and boys, whom he also sodomized. To Panzram's mind he had some sort of license to do this because of the time, while a teenager, that he had been gang-raped by hoboes. According to his later confession Panzram killed twenty-one people in all and committed over one thousand acts of sodomy.

In the 1920s, when roaring self-indulgence became the signature life-style of the day, Panzram too went on a binge, taking his criminality to far-flung places and even more atrocious heights. In 1920 he used stolen money to buy a yacht, hired ten sailors to get the craft shipshape, then showed his appreciation for their work by inviting them on board to get drunk on a stash of bootleg liquor. The liquor turned out to be drugged. When the sailors were out of commission, Panzram raped them. Then he shot them all and pitched them overboard. Later, after hiring on as a merchant seaman to West Africa, he gunned down six Africans whom he had supposedly hired for a crocodile-hunting expedition. Panzram did, in fact, find some crocodiles. He fed the six corpses to them.

By the late 1920s Panzram was back in America, working his way down from Massachusetts to Washington, D.C. There, on August 16, 1928, he was arrested for burglary and received a stiff sentence of twenty-five years, to be served at one of Panzram's least favorite places, Fort Leavenworth, this time at the federal, rather than military, prison there. Making it clear that he had no intention of slowing down, he announced, "I'll kill the first man who bothers me." It seems his definition of "bothers" was rather loose. Soon after arriving at Leavenworth, Panzram smashed in the head of a laundry foreman, someone who had clearly done nothing to provoke him.

This would be the murder that would send Panzram to his execution. After he received his death sentence, his cause was taken up by the Society for the Abolition of Capital Punishment. No one else was interested in commuting Panzram's sentence, including Panzram. He went so far as to write President Hoover demanding that he was entitled to what he considered to be his constitutional right to be hanged, which he was on September 5, 1930. Panzram spent his last moments on earth complaining that the hangman wasn't working quickly enough.

PETER KURTEN

1883–1931

"The Monster of Dusseldorf"

In fictional form the unspeakable crimes of Peter Kurten acquired a lasting, international fame in the classic German film M. Made in 1931, the movie broached the appalling subject of child-killing, as carried out by a relentless psychopathic strangler portrayed by a young Peter Lorre. As disturbing as the film was at the time of its release—and still is, for that matter—it paled in comparison to Kurten's actual deeds. Not that the filmmakers pulled their punches—they simply must have realized that a single movie could not have possibly embraced the full murderous scope of the man known as the Monster of Dusseldorf.

Child-killing was the most reprehensible of Kurten's crimes, but it constituted just one part of his activities. He also killed men and women. His methods of murder constantly changed, and his killings were often accompanied by rape, and on occasion by necrophilia and vampirism. Throughout Kurten's life he equated sexual excitement with bloodletting and death.

Peter Kurten grew up in an impoverished home in western Germany that was a veritable hothouse for the cultivation of demented criminality. From his father he learned brutality and out-of-control sexuality; one of the father's more conspicuous offenses was the at-

tempted rape of one of Kurten's sisters, for which Herr Kurten earned a prison sentence. And when Kurten felt he had to get away from his hated father, he turned to his chosen role model, a dogcatcher neighbor who tutored him in the torture and masturbation of animals. When Kurten was nine, he went out rafting with two of his friends, an excursion that ended with both friends drowning. This might have been Kurten's first act of murder.

By the time he was in his teens, Kurten was a habitual thief and a frequent jailbird. In total he would spend twenty-seven of his forty-seven years in prison. Between 1899 and 1928, during those periods when he managed to remain at large, he may have committed as many as three murders, none of which were pinned on him. He was also responsible for many other attacks, often nonfatal strangulations of women. For Kurten, it seems that choking someone was not necessarily a means of murder; he apparently regarded it as a form of sex play. Another source of sexual stimulation for him was the torching of barns, something he did frequently.

The woman he married in 1921, however, was not of any great erotic interest to him. He looked upon her as merely a companion, but a companion that for some reason he felt he absolutely had to have. When he first courted her, the woman resisted his marriage proposals.

She gave in when Kurten modified his proposal somewhat: either she married him or he would kill her.

Kurten's infamy as "the Monster of Dusseldorf" was clinched in 1929, when he was in his forties. The torrent of violence he unleashed in that year has rarely been equaled. In a year's time he attacked twenty-three people, many of whom died. He began in February 1929 by pulling a woman off the street and stabbing her twenty-four times—somehow, she survived—then went on to stab a man to death just ten days later. The worst of the attacks came to an end in November with the strangling and frenzied stabbing of a five-year-old girl, Gertrude Alberman.

The city of Dusseldorf was terrorized for more than a year, and the police did everything they could think of to bring the attacks to a stop. They questioned nine thousand people, investigated three thousand clues, even consulted psychics. Unfortunately, the authorities were unwilling to assume that the horrific violence was all the work of one man. The mistake was understandable. The attacks did not have a consistent pattern: the victims didn't fit one particular type, and the methods of murder ranged from stabbings and stranglings to bludgeonings with a hammer. And one other thing made police think that more than one killer was responsible: the attacks were so frequent, sometimes more than one a day, that it seemed unreasonable that one man would even attempt such a thing.

But then, Peter Kurten was hardly reasonable.

He was so unreasonable, in fact, that he once anonymously helped the police with their investigation. In November 1929 he sent a letter to a newspaper that directed the police to the remains of the five-year-old girl Gertrude Alberman, as well as the body of a housemaid named Maria Hahn. The latter had been stabbed twenty times and had been sexually violated after death. Kurten's letter made it obvious he was proud of himself. But he was also starting to act like someone who didn't care if he was caught.

In May 1930 he convinced a woman to take a walk in the woods with him, and then, after his inevitable attempt to choke and rape her, he backed off when she put up a fight. He even let her go with the promise that she wouldn't turn him in. He couldn't have been too surprised when the woman's story, eventually relayed to the police, led to his arrest.

He quickly agreed to confess all his crimes to the police, as if he had been waiting to tell someone the story of his life. According to Kurten's account, he had been responsible for seventy-nine crimes all told, and in particular, at least thirteen murders. He revealed that in some instances he drank the blood of his victims. In April 1931 Kurten's confession aided in his conviction on nine counts of murder.

In the memorable conclusion to the film M, Peter Lorre, as the killer, makes an impassioned, anguished plea for mercy, asking that his accusers try in some way to understand the deadly compulsions that he cannot control. In the real crime story that inspired the film, Kurten also made a plea, requesting that the court take his insanity into consideration. But after considering evidence of crime upon hideous crime committed by the defendant, the panel of three judges had little mercy to spare; they sentenced him to be decapitated.

Once the judges handed down the death sentence, Kurten accepted his fate philosophically. He spent much time wondering what pleasure he might derive from his own execution. He was convinced that if he could hear his own blood gush from his neck stump in the instant after the blade dropped, he would leave this world a happy man. He got his chance to find out on July 2, 1931, when he stepped up to the guillotine at Klingelputz Prison.

SYLVESTRE MATUSCHKA
1891–?

Like many men besieged by bizarre, homicidal obsessions, Sylvestre Matuschka could convey the impression of normalcy, and highly proficient normalcy at that. After the outbreak of World War I, when he was in his early twenties, he enlisted in the Austro-Hungarian army and went on to serve with distinction as an officer of the Sixth Honved Regiment. Following the armistice, he went into business for himself in Budapest and was a success again. From there he moved on to Vienna, where he pursued several ventures at once, becoming involved in the construction business, a lumber company, and the running of a delicatessen. He had a wife and daughter, lived in a comfortable house on the outskirts of the city, and went to church regularly.

The one chink in his armor of respectability was his arrest for fraud in Budapest after the war, but even then he was acquitted. And the hint of business impropriety was hardly an indication of the strange thoughts that increasingly crowded his mind. Those thoughts stayed with him through the 1920s and gathered momentum until they took hold of him completely in 1930. That was when he came to the conclusion that he had to wreck trains—trains that carried coaches filled with people.

Matuschka's first two attempts to put his compulsion into action were not particularly successful. On the night of December 31, 1930, he sabotaged some tracks east of Vienna, but the train was halted just shy of the dismantled track. On his second attempt Matuschka tied lengths of steel to the tracks at the same spot. This time the train derailed, but it had already started to slow down and damage was minimal. Matuschka now devoted himself to trying another tack—he would use explosives next time.

Matuschka approached the problem with the professionalism and thoroughness that had characterized his legitimate enterprises. He knew he would be leaving a distinct trail for the police to follow if he purchased the explosives under his own name. To give himself a solid alternate identity, he went as far afield as a Berlin cafe and, introducing himself as a baron, got into a conversation with a stranger, an Irishman working as a translator in Germany; the conversation revealed both the man's name and his background. Matuschka assumed the Irishman's identity when he bought the dynamite and detonators. He then purchased a rock quarry, where he could learn how to use the dynamite through a series of test explosions, and he devised a means of detonating the explosives with a system of battery-run electric cables. By August 1931 he was ready to move ahead.

Setting off the dynamite from a hiding place along the right-of-way, Matuschka blew up tracks outside Juterbog, Germany, and sent a train barreling out of control. Seventy-five passengers were injured. Matuschka was getting closer to his deranged goal.

A connection was made between this train wreck in Germany and the two previous attempts in Austria, prompting German and Austrian authorities to work together. As Matuschka had hoped, the police traced the remnants of the Juterbog explosives setup to the place where they had been sold—which in turn put them onto the false name and information used for the purchase. The German police arrested the Irishman whose identity Matuschka had used, but soon discovered that the Irishman was not their man.

Matuschka struck again on September 12, 1931, detonating sixteen sticks of dynamite at the Biatorbagy Viaduct in Hungary. The first five passenger cars of a Hungarian Railways train veered off the track and plunged eighty feet to the gorge below. The crash killed twenty-two people. As for Matuschka, who watched the fatal disaster from behind some bushes, the experience was profoundly exciting. He reportedly had an orgasm.

Not content with his enjoyment of this catastrophe, Matuschka went on to file a lawsuit against the Hungarian Railways, claiming he had been one of the injured passengers on the train he had wrecked. This act of arrogance eventually brought about his arrest. Investigators learned that Matuschka had bought a ticket for the doomed train, but no one remembered his being on board. The police then went back to the Irishman in Berlin who had been falsely arrested. The Irishman was shown a photograph of Matuschka, and he identified him as the man who had presented himself as a baron in the Berlin cafe. The net began to close around Matuschka. When the police arrested him in October, they found a map in his house that indicated plans to wreck trains in such places as Paris, Marseilles, and northern Italy.

Although uncooperative at first, Matuschka eventually confessed to his crimes and explained his motivation: "I wrecked trains because I like to see people die. I like to hear people scream."

He was tried in Vienna for his first two wrecking attempts and was then sent to Budapest to stand trial for the twenty-two deaths he caused at Biatorbagy. While passing through the judicial systems of two nations, Matuschka offered a bewildering series of explanations for his murderous actions: he was the slave of an evil hypnotist who had entrapped him while he was a boy; he wrecked trains to stop the spread of atheism; he blew up tracks to draw attention to his knack for inventions; he was compelled to commit his crimes by a conspiracy of five demons, all of whom were named Leo. If all of this was an attempt to secure leniency by appearing insane, the judges he faced were not open to the idea. In his first trial in Vienna, Matuschka received a prison sentence of six years, and at his mass-murder trial in Hungary he was sentenced to hang. The death sentence was later commuted to life imprisonment, due to a legal technicality.

The ultimate fate of Sylvestre Matuschka is not clear. It is believed he escaped from prison during the chaos of the final stages of World War II; after that nothing more is known. Another, more extravagant theory is that, while sweeping through Hungary in 1944, the conquering Soviets took him out of prison. It seems, the story goes, that the Red Army needed a man who knew his way around explosives.

ALBERT FISH

1870–1936

"The Cannibal"

Albert Fish belonged to one of New York's most prominent families. In the mid-nineteenth century, Hamilton Fish rose through the political ranks to become Secretary of State during President Grant's administration. A son and a grandson of his followed in his footsteps with careers in Congress, while another son went on to become president of the hugely successful Illinois Central Railroad.

Not all branches of the Fish clan, however, were able to emulate these accomplishments. Albert Fish's branch was poor and undistinguished. It was also, quite prophetically, riddled with insanity. But even this streak of madness, as pronounced as it may have been in this part

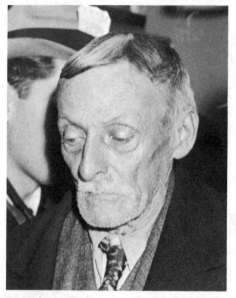

of the family, was not adequate foreshadowing of the dementia that possessed Albert Fish for so many years. Dr. Fredric Wertham, a psychiatrist who came into contact with many twisted criminals in his long career, would state unequivocally that Fish was the most wildly depraved person he ever examined.

Fish's particular form of depravity was a mixture of religious fanaticism and sadomasochism. His experience at a parochial orphanage as a child seemed to crystallize this unnerving fusion. He was sent to St. John's Refuge at the age of five after his father died and his mother found herself unable to support her children anymore. There he received intensive religious instruction, often interrupted by disciplinary measures that involved beating a child while he or she stood naked in front of the other children. In his own way Fish took the religious indoctrination to heart and also found pleasure in the punishments: he would often have an erection while being thrashed by his teacher.

For years his bizarre obsessions simmered. He made a scant living as a housepainter and handyman, he got married, he became the father of six children. Then his wife left him for another man. Around this time, his madness began to overwhelm him. He subjected himself to excruciating punishments: beating himself with a spiked paddle, eating his own feces, inserting needles into his crotch. Much later, after his arrest, an X ray would confirm that there were twenty-nine needles left inside his body from this practice. His religious experiences took the form of hallucinatory visions and voices that instructed him how to live his life. The commandments he received ultimately involved what he should do to children. He became convinced that he was an incarnation of the biblical Abraham who had been willing to sacrifice his own child for God. Fish would serve God and wash away his own sins, he believed, by killing children.

Fish began to travel across the country, taking odd jobs where he could find them. His nomadic life gave him a vast selection of children to prey upon. He may have molested as many as several hundred boys and girls. As for the number he mutilated and killed, it has conservatively been estimated at five, while some information indicates the total is as high as fifteen. Although he was arrested on occasion for the relatively minor crimes of theft and embezzlement, he escaped detection when it came to more serious offenses. His appearance helped him to avoid suspicion; he was so innocent looking, especially in later years, when he seemed to be nothing more than a gentle old man. The best-documented of his murders was his killing of ten-year-old Grace Budd. It was this sickening crime that eventually led to Albert Fish's arrest and conviction.

Back in New York City in 1928, the fifty-eight-year-old Fish came into contact with Grace Budd while setting his sights on her older brother. The eighteen-year-old Edward Budd had placed a classified ad announcing his desire to find farm work outside the city. Fish, using an alias, came to the apartment of the boy's family and presented himself as a Long Island farmer. Liking the looks of the boy, Fish intended to make him his next sacrifice, but on a subsequent visit he met pretty little Grace and decided she would be preferable. Under the pretext of taking her to his niece's birthday party, he led her away. She never came back.

Detective William King of New York's Missing Persons Bureau made the Grace Budd case his personal crusade and spent six years tracking down the girl's abductor. The case broke after Fish sent an anonymous letter to Grace Budd's mother in November 1934. The letter made it very plain what he had done to Grace: after taking her out of the city and up to Westchester County, he strangled her and chopped up her body; then he cooked pieces of her flesh and ate them.

On the stationery used for this note was the letterhead for a chauffeurs' association. The dogged Detective King learned the identity of a man who had pilfered some stationery from this association, then discovered that the petty thief had left the stationery behind in a rented room. The room's current resident was Albert Fish. Detective King finally found his man.

After his arrest Fish gave a detailed account of his horrible crimes, leaving no doubt as to his guilt. Predictably, he was convicted of Grace Budd's murder, the strongest of the cases against him. The only real issue to be settled at his trial was whether an insanity plea would prevent his execution. The jurors didn't question his complete insanity, but they weren't about to let that consideration stand in the way of what they considered to be proper punishment for an unspeakable crime. They recommended the death sentence.

On January 16, 1936, sixty-five-year-old Albert Fish was taken to the electric chair at Sing Sing, for what he had earlier predicted would be "the supreme thrill of my life."

DR. MORRIS BOLBER
1890–1954

Dr. Morris Bolber rarely did any actual killing himself, but through accomplices acting under his supervision, he is believed to have been responsible for more than thirty deaths. During the Great Depression he displayed an enormous talent for exploiting hard times and personal greed, as well as a remarkable ability for finding and enlisting others who regarded cold-blooded homicide as nothing more than a means to a desired end. For five years Bolber's South Philadelphia medical practice was the hub of one of the most ruthless insurance-fraud operations ever devised.

Even before 1932 Dr. Bolber was obviously a man who would travel some shady routes to make an extra dollar, but he didn't show any clear inclination toward murder. He had various ways of enhancing his practice in Philadelphia's immigrant Italian community: he would offer faith healing to those who were unwilling to accept modern medical techniques, would sometimes use his doctor's degree as a cover for the illicit sale of drugs, and was reputed to be available to local gangsters in need of emergency mending after a gangland battle. Then in February 1932, when he was in his early forties, Bolber came upon a set of circumstances that, to his mind, presented a great financial opportunity—if only he were willing to overlook certain moral precepts about killing fellow human beings.

A female patient complained to him about her drunken, unfaithful husband, a grocer by the name of Anthony Giscobbe. While talking to this woman, Dr. Bolber happened to notice that a friend of his was outside, a local tailor named Paul Petrillo. A tireless ladies' man, Petrillo had an arrangement with Bolber for acquiring new mistresses: Petrillo would supply the doctor with free suits as long as Bolber kept introducing the tailor to his lonely female patients. Bolber now considered both Mrs. Giscobbe's predicament and his friend's Casanova talents. Suddenly, murder didn't seem to be a very great obstacle.

At Bolber's direction Petrillo seduced the unhappy wife and persuaded her that she deserved to collect on her no-good husband's life insurance. All that was required was Anthony Giscobbe's sudden demise, which, Petrillo pointed out, could be arranged quite skillfully with the help of a clever doctor like Bolber, who would only ask for half of the insurance payment for his services.

Bolber's devious mind was more than equal to the task. One chilly night, when Anthony Giscobbe came home stinking drunk, his wife waited till he passed out, then took off the man's clothes and opened the window next to his bed. By morning the frigid air blowing in had brought on a severe illness. Thinking of everything, Bolber instructed Mrs. Giscobbe to bring in an honest doctor, who, as Bolber expected, came to the conclusion that the woman's husband was in danger of contracting pneumonia. Bolber then got hold of the medicine that had been prescribed and treated it with hemlock. When Giscobbe died, he was apparently just another pneumonia victim.

Bolber split the $10,000 insurance payment with Mrs. Giscobbe and handed a share of it to Petrillo, who promptly brushed off the widow so that he could move on to another equally unhappy, and unscrupulous, wife.

Over the next five years Bolber came up with a series of ingenious variations on his vicious scheme. When many Depression-era immigrants in his community proved unable to afford life insurance, Bolber called in the services of Petrillo's cousin, Herman Petrillo. A spaghetti salesman and professional counterfeiter who also fancied himself an actor, Herman would acquire an insurance policy while pretending to be a target husband. After Bolber took care of the first insurance premium payments, the husband would then be ready for a premature death.

Bolber also sought to increase his murder ring's profits by cashing in on double-indemnity clauses, which required that the victim die of an apparent accident. During this phase of Bolber's operations, insured husbands had a habit of dropping off the tops of buildings or tumbling over the sides of boats—with a push in the right direction from Herman Petrillo. At this point Bolber took a more direct role in the proceedings as he ran over one victim with his car. But he came close to being discovered in the act and subsequently decided that "accidents" involved too much risk. The next method he devised was brutally simple and effective. He instructed his henchmen to pound victims over the head with a sandbag. A few blows would produce a cerebral hemorrhage but would leave no obvious wounds the way a blunt object would have.

As time passed, Bolber broadened his enterprise to other Philadelphia neighborhoods by making a deal with Carino Favato, a self-styled witch and faith healer from another part of town. The woman supplied names of potential disgruntled wives in exchange for a cut of the money. Ultimately, Herman Petrillo betrayed Bolber's schemes by taking it on himself to bring in yet another victim finder. While getting drunk with a recently released prisoner one night in 1937, Herman told the man how he could make extra cash by finding well-insured men to be murdered. The ex-convict told the police about this proposition, and Herman Petrillo was arrested on suspicion of murder.

Once in custody, Petrillo tried to save himself by informing on his partners. Then, like rats jumping off a sinking ship, the rest of the Bolber gang supplied more and more information as they were picked up by the police, each trying to heap the majority of the guilt on someone else.

In the end the ones who got the worst of this back-stabbing orgy were the Petrillo cousins. More directly involved in the actual killings than others in the ring, they both received death sentences. Dr. Bolber, the leader of the murderous pack who so often distanced himself from the dirty deeds, managed to turn over enough evidence to escape the electric chair. While serving a life sentence, he wrote five unpublished books on religious history. In 1954, he died of a heart attack in Pennsylvania's Eastern Penitentiary.

ANNA MARIE HAHN
1906–1938

Anna Marie Hahn never studied or trained to be a nurse, but among her fellow German immigrants in Cincinnati, her qualifications to care for the sick were not questioned. What, after all, is really required in nursing other than attentiveness, diligence, and a willingness to help? And the fact that Hahn was a young, attractive blonde certainly didn't make her presence unwelcome in the sickrooms of older, ailing men. Between 1932 and 1937 she cared for quite a few of these men, and as far as Cincinnati's German community could tell, the final days before death must have been made easier for these patients by Hahn's dutiful ministrations.

The good deeds Hahn performed did not go unrewarded, either. After the death of her first patient, Ernest Kohler, she took possession of the man's house. But only the mean-spirited would find something suspicious about that: the house had been bequeathed to Hahn in Kohler's will, just his way of repaying her for her kindness in his time of need.

For five years Hahn continued her self-styled nursing career. Then, in the summer of 1937, when Hahn was in Colorado, miles away from her usual Cincinnati haunts, police noticed some peculiarities about the young woman. First, while investigating a robbery, the police discovered that she had in her possession some diamond rings that had recently been stolen from the owner of a hotel in Colorado Springs. Hahn, it turned out, had been observed in the hotel with an elderly Cincinnati man named George Obendoerfer. Soon after checking into the hotel, Obendoerfer had died suddenly. This death raised further suspicions when it came to the local police's attention that Obendoerfer's entire savings were now in Hahn's name.

Cincinnati authorities got word of these developments, and they did some snooping of their own. While an autopsy was conducted on the body of Obendoerfer in Colorado Springs, three corpses were exhumed and examined in Cincinnati—the bodies of three men who had been nursed by Hahn. Pathologists found poisons in all three Cincinnati corpses, as well as in the body of Obendoerfer. The investigation accelerated.

Police were soon speculating that Hahn had poisoned as many as eleven men in order to take control of their money or possessions. In the case of Ernest Kohler, she got hold of the ailing man's house by maneuvering herself into his will; in other cases she simply stole outright whatever valuables were left in the house upon the man's premature death. Testimony from her estranged husband made it clear that her murderously greedy ways had begun at home. Years before, she had tried to convince him to take out a life insurance policy, one that, naturally, would have profited her had he died. When her husband didn't go along with this idea, he suddenly became sick. He left Hahn before she had a chance to make him any sicker. Another indication of how Hahn operated came from the testimony of a man named George Heis, who had been nursed by the woman but managed to live to tell the tale. He had become suspicious enough to dismiss her when he couldn't help but notice that flies were dying on the surface of the beer Hahn insisted on serving him.

Turned over to Cincinnati authorities, Hahn was eventually indicted for two murders. By the time her trial began in the fall of 1937, the prosecution concentrated on the death of a man named Jacob Wagner and presented an overwhelmingly convincing case. Through it all Anna Hahn remained unflappable. She maintained that her only goal in life was to make enough money "to take care of the poor unfortunates, the old people and the children."

The jury, on the other hand, failed to detect much charity in Hahn's actions. They found her guilty of first-degree murder. For its first 135 years, the state of Ohio had a policy of not executing any female criminals. The judge and jury in Hahn's case decided to make an exception to the rule. Hahn, the murderous nurse who preyed on the old and ailing, was electrocuted on December 7, 1938.

JOE BALL
1894–1938

In 1976 movie director Tobe Hooper, the man who had previously been responsible for the notorious *The Texas Chainsaw Massacre*, made a little-known horror film entitled *Eaten Alive*. Set in the Lone Star State—like Hooper's previous film—*Eaten Alive* concerned the owner of a wayside inn who fed his guests to the pet crocodile he kept in a pool beside the hotel. The story may sound like just another overheated attempt by horror filmmakers to top themselves in terms of sheer bizarre gruesomeness. In actuality, though, not much imagination was required in formulating the film's basic premise, which was very similar to a real Texas murder case, the story of Joe Ball, a tavernkeeper who devised a peculiar diet for his pet alligators.

Little has been recorded about Joe Ball's early life other than his enlistment in the army during World War I and his occupation as a bootlegger during Prohibition. Variously described as a "stocky, ugly man" and a "towering, square-jawed, leathery-skinned man," Ball started to sell liquor legally once America's experiment in sobriety came to an end. He opened a bar in Elmendorf, Texas, just southeast of San Antonio. Called the Sociable Inn, Ball's establishment had a distinctive feature that set it apart from other taverns in the area, or in any other area, for that matter: a cement pool behind the inn that was home to five alligators. Feeding time was one of the entertainments offered at the Sociable Inn. Ball would toss chunks of horsemeat into the alligator maws, or sometimes, as a more exotic touch, he would serve up live dogs or cats.

There was also something else unusual about the Sociable Inn. Male patrons were pleased to find themselves served by pretty waitresses, who also roomed at the inn, but the customers also couldn't help but notice that Joe Ball's waitresses came and went awful quickly. Ball, reputed to be romantically involved with the women who worked for him, was noncommittal about these comings and goings, saying only that waitresses were a footloose lot. Those prone to be suspicious might have wondered about this constant changeover of female employees. But whatever vague suspicions people might have had, nothing ever crystallized into a definite allegation—not, that is, until 1937, when relatives of three former waitresses began to ask questions. It seemed that the young women had not only left the Sociable Inn suddenly but had also disappeared.

In all three cases the police got a simple explanation from Ball: the young woman had left town. In the case of the second and third missing waitresses, though, the police became skeptical. One waitress had supposedly left the region without taking any of her clothes, and the other had neglected to close out her savings account at the local bank. The circumstantial evidence might have convinced the police that there had been foul play at the Sociable Inn, but they knew they would have to find some physical evidence before they made an arrest.

A local grim joke maintained that Ball's waitresses ended up in the alligators' digestive tracts. Perhaps, the police wondered, this wasn't a joke after all. The contents of the meat barrel that Ball kept by his alligator pit, they figured, might provide the evidence they were looking for. Arriving at the Sociable Inn on September 24, 1938, the police made it clear what they wanted.

Ball must have decided that pat explanations and evasions would no longer do any good, but he must have also decided not to tell the truth about his motives and methods. That would explain why he took a handgun from the cash register till and shot himself in the head. He was dead by the time he hit the floor. As they suspected they would, the lawmen found human flesh in the barrel out back.

Since there was no chance to put Ball on trial, many of the details of this case were never firmly established. But police learned enough to establish that Joe Ball had been a mass murderer. After attempting to track down all the waitresses who had worked at the Sociable Inn, the police found that fourteen women could not be traced. Willie Sneed, the Sociable Inn handyman, then came forward to make it clear that the sardonic regional jokes were true. Sneed said that Ball had forced him to help feed the murdered waitresses, piece by piece, to the five alligators in the rear pit.

With the chief culprit permanently out of the picture, the authorities went ahead with tying up loose ends. Convicted as an accessory after the fact, handyman Willie Sneed, who had helped get rid of the bodies, was sent to prison for four years. On the other hand, the five alligators, who had consumed so much incriminating evidence, got off easy. They were put on display at the San Antonio zoo.

THE CLEVELAND TORSO KILLER
1934–1938

For the people of Cleveland during the mid-1930s, the dire hardship of the Great Depression was compounded by citywide terror. Over a four-year span, the periodic discovery of ravaged human parts was unnerving evidence of a monstrous killer at large. As for evidence of who the killer might possibly be, there was precious little. The county sheriff's office, the city police, even legendary crimebuster Eliot Ness each carried out intensive investigations. But for all their efforts nothing conclusive was ever learned about the perpetrator of the Cleveland

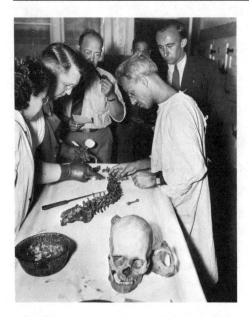

*The scant remains of one of the
Cleveland Torso Killer's victims.*

Torso Murders, the killer who was known as "the Mad Butcher of Kingsbury Run."

The trail of senseless murder began on September 5, 1934, in the sands of Euclid Beach, bordering on Lake Erie. All that was found of the first victim was a section that included the lower torso and part of the legs, from the waist down to the knees. The discarded remains belonged to a woman, but no identification was ever established. A year later, it became clear that the killer was not singling out a particular sex when the bodies of two men were found. Both corpses were incomplete, without heads or genitals. The missing parts were subsequently discovered a short distance away.

The scene of this discovery was Kingsbury Run, a long gully used as a railroad right-of-way through the city. Many of the Torso Murder remains would be uncovered along or near this desolate cut, thus providing the authorities with the geographical component of the killer's *modus operandi*. As the carved-up bodies continued to crop up, another recurring trait that manifested itself was the difficulty in identifying victims. From this the police speculated that the Torso Killer's targets tended to be transients, prostitutes, and other social cast-offs. And one other pattern came into focus in the harrowing months of 1936 and early 1937: many of the remains were being found without a head. The grisly possibility arose that the Mad Butcher of Kingsbury Run might be keeping the heads as souvenirs.

Sections of torsos, cut off at the waist, along with dismembered arms and legs, were discovered with relentless regularity. By the summer of 1937, the Torso Killer's tally of victims had reached ten. With the escalation of fear throughout the city came increasing pressure on the authorities to find the killer. Two exceptionally tenacious detectives by the names of Peter Merylo and Martin Zalewski spearheaded the city police's investigation and explored every possible lead that came their way. More in the public spotlight were the efforts of Eliot Ness. Ness had come to Ohio after making a name for himself as the leader of the Treasury Department's Untouchables, the special strike force that had played a part in the battle against Al Capone in Chicago. In his new capacity as Cleveland's director of public safety, Ness had already distinguished himself in campaigns against mobsters and police corruption, but his hunt for the Mad Butcher of Kingsbury Run turned out to be an exercise in frustration.

The only headway Ness succeeded in making was the interrogation of a mentally unstable premed student in 1938. Given the pseudonym Gaylord Sundheim by Ness's biographer, Oscar Fraley, in order to protect the true name of a man who was never officially charged with anything, this student was touted by Ness as a prime suspect, but the famed Untouchable never had a chance to prove his case. Sundheim had himself committed to the sanctuary of a mental hospital before he could be prosecuted.

The county sheriff's department, meanwhile, had their own ideas about the identity of the Torso Killer. In the summer of 1939, the sheriff's office extracted a confession from a Bohemian immigrant by the name of Frank Dolezal. But once more, law enforcement officials ran into a brick wall. The confession given by the sheriff's suspect was compromised by discrepancies, and whatever might have been of value in this confession was then recanted by Dolezal. The man would later hang himself in his cell. Some have asserted that this suicide was suspicious, alleging that it was a cover-up for police brutality.

The four-year Torso Murder onslaught claimed twelve victims. No one was ever prosecuted. Detective Merylo, who continued to investigate the case after his retirement from the police force, believed that the killer continued his atrocities in other regions for ten more years. But like all other theories about the Cleveland Torso Killer, no conclusive proof was found to back up the claim.

GORDON CUMMINS
1914–1942
"The Blackout Ripper"

In 1942 terror was an accepted fact of life for the people of London. The worst of the Blitz may have passed—the German Luftwaffe no longer dropped bombs on the city every night—but the air raids were far from over. On any given night German bombers might still invade the city's skies. Sudden death could come at any time.

But terror did not originate only from above.

For a few days in February 1942, there was another horror, one that emanated from the London streets, carried out not by a wartime enemy but by someone sworn to defend his fellow British citizens. Over the course of four nights, while Londoners were on their guard for the

next blackout and the next blast of German bombs, Aircraftman Gordon Cummins of the Royal Air Force stalked and slashed unescorted women like a modern-day Jack the Ripper.

Before February 9, 1942, the worst that could be said about Gordon Cummins was that he was irresponsible and prone to fanciful boasting. Before enlisting in the RAF in 1935, he had been unable to hold a job for any length of time, and while in the air corps, he had been fond of making apocryphal claims that he was actually the illegitimate son of a member of the House of Lords. His fellow members of the RAF may have jeered at him by referring to him as "the Count," but they certainly didn't consider him to be any sort of mortal threat. But, on the night of February 9, the twenty-eight-year-old Cummins, then in training as a fighter pilot, struck up a conversation with a female pharmacist named Evelyn Hamilton as she walked from a restaurant to her boardinghouse. She was later found sprawled in the entrance to a brick air-raid shelter. She had been strangled.

We don't know how long the compulsion to murder had been incubating inside Cummins, but we do know that, once unleashed, it propelled him to kill again soon—and more savagely.

The next night, in Piccadilly Circus, the affable Cummins met another woman, an ex-showgirl named Evelyn Oatley who now earned a living as a prostitute. She trusted Cummins enough to take a cab with him to her Soho apartment. There he slit her throat, then indulged in a hideous orgy of mutilation. Using a can opener, he slashed away at the flesh around her genitals.

During his four-day murder spree, Cummins displayed a puzzling attitude about getting caught. At some point he went to the trouble of forging a leave pass that fraudulently established that he was out of London at the time of the killings. But in other ways he was exceptionally careless. When he abandoned the bloody scene of the Oatley murder, for example, he left behind the can opener, covered with his fingerprints, and left other prints on a small mirror from Oatley's pocketbook.

This discovery did not enable the police to get any closer to Oatley's murderer; Cummins had no police record and thus the authorities did not have his prints on file. But the discovery did tell the police something else. The fingerprints belonged to somebody's left hand, and the bruises on the neck of Evelyn Hamilton, the first victim, indicated that her killer was also left-handed. The link between the two killings tipped the police off to the fact that they were on the trail of a multiple murderer, a Jack the Ripper–type killer who was likely to strike again.

Once more, Cummins didn't wait long. He killed Margaret Lowe in her apartment the next night, February 11, and killed Doris Jouannet in her home the night after that. Both were strangled, and then mutilated in the same ghastly manner as Oatley had been. The police were able to lift more fingerprints, which conformed to the previous prints, but still they had no lead that would take them to the killer. In desperation they started to check fingerprints found at all recent violent crimes in the hope that something would match up. That search ended, though, on the night of February 13. Cummins attempted two strangulations that night and showed little concern about leaving behind incriminating evidence.

In one case he tried to strangle a woman named Greta Heywood in the doorway of an air-raid shelter, but when the woman dropped her flashlight, the clatter against the sidewalk caught the attention of a delivery boy passing nearby. Cummins ran away to escape discovery. In the other attempt Cummins talked Catherine Mulcahy into inviting him home. This time it was his victim's screams and violent struggling that rattled him and made him run off. Now the police had two would-be victims who could provide descriptions of the so-called "Blackout Ripper." More important, though, was the gas mask he left behind in the Greta Heywood incident. Not much detective work was required to deduce the significance of this piece of evidence: printed inside the gas mask were Cummins's name, rank, and serial number. He was arrested at his quarters in St. John's Wood.

The combination of fingerprints, eyewitnesses, and the telltale gas mask were overwhelming proof of Cummins's guilt. Still, he refused to admit anything, even after such bogus alibis as his forged leave pass were exposed by police investigators. The jury at his trial saw nothing ambiguous in the evidence that was presented; they convicted him after a scant thirty-five minutes of deliberation. Aircraftman Cummins was hanged on June 25, 1942.

BRUNO LUDKE
1909–1944

A murderer during a time of institutionalized, wholesale murder, Bruno Ludke was a shadowy serial killer who drifted along the fringes of Nazi German society for years. While preoccupied with isolating and exterminating Jews, gypsies, cripples, and all other officially designated undesirables, Nazi authorities failed to track down the man who was waging his own personal campaign of terror outside the nation's capital.

After more than ten years of murder, the truth about these gruesome crimes came to light only after the discovery of a woman's body in early 1943 in the town of Kupenick, just east of Berlin.

Death and devastation were hardly unheard of in Hitler's Third Reich, even if the German people were shielded from the harshest of the facts. German soldiers were being decimated on the Eastern Front and were on the run in North Africa in the face of an Allied counteroffensive, and all the while, civilians were being herded on trains for mass deportations to the Nazi death camps. But here in Kupenick was a murder of someone racially acceptable, right in the heart of the Fatherland.

The victim was Frieda Rosner, a hardworking, middle-aged *hausfrau* who had last been seen setting off for the woods on the outskirts of Kupenick, where she had gone to gather firewood. She never got out of the woods alive. An examination of her body revealed that death by strangulation was only part of the horror that had been directed at Rosner; the woman's corpse had also been sexually violated.

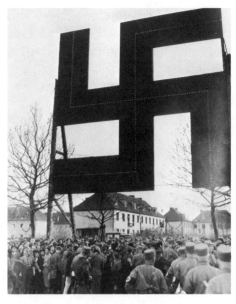

While proving so brutally efficient at weeding out non-Aryans, the Nazi police state allowed mass murderer Bruno Ludke to slip through its fingers for more than ten years.

Supervising the investigation was Kriminal Kommissar Franz. As Claude Rains would have put it in the film *Casablanca*, the kommissar rounded up all the usual suspects. In the process of pulling in a collection of local riffraff with established criminal records, the police picked up a thirty-three-year-old laundry deliveryman named Bruno Ludke. Franz had no reason to suspect him any more than the others. Ludke may have been a known thief, but he had never been considered homicidal. His most significant brush with the law had occurred earlier in the war, when he was arrested for molesting a woman. While in custody for this crime, he was labeled a mental defective. In accordance with the Nazi eugenics policy of purifying the German genetic pool, Ludke was sterilized. Then he was set free.

Kommissar Franz put Ludke through some routine questioning

about the Frieda Rosner murder and drew out an admission from Ludke that he had known the victim. Franz went on to ask point-blank if he had killed the woman. Something snapped inside Ludke. He lunged at the interrogating officers and put up a fierce struggle before he was finally beaten into submission. Once under control again, he confessed to the murder.

But this mental defective wasn't completely mentally deficient. He was familiar with Nazi law and pointed out that, according to a provision known as Paragraph 51, mental defectives were not subject to normal criminal prosecution.

Ludke sensed he had scored a legal point. Confident that he had placed himself beyond the reach of the law, he now kept talking— compulsively. He told the police officers about another murder he had committed. And another. And yet another.

The confession dragged on.

When Ludke was finally done, he admitted to an astounding total of eighty-five homicides. The first had been committed when he was only nineteen, back in 1928, five years before Hitler took control of the government. The killings then continued through the period of the Nazis' consolidation of power in the thirties and into the war years. His victims were all female, both girls and women, either strangled or stabbed. Often he raped his victims; sometimes he engaged in necrophilia.

Franz and his men investigated Ludke's claims to see if they could be corroborated and concluded that most, if not all, of Ludke's confessed murders were genuine. The question now before the authorities was what to do about this vile, remorseless killer. Ludke had been right in thinking that he would be exempt from usual criminal procedures, but not for legalistic reasons. The authorities were not about to bring this case into a court of law where their inability to apprehend Ludke for so many years would be publicized (innocent men had even been executed for some of Ludke's murders). The peculiar problem required an unorthodox solution.

Not only had Ludke failed to gauge the Nazis' willingness to circumvent their own laws; he had failed to appreciate that serial killers had no monopoly on cruelty in Germany at that time. The murderer was shipped off to a Vienna hospital as a medical specimen, a human guinea pig to be used in Nazi experiments. In April 1944, when the doctors were done with him, Ludke was given a lethal injection.

LOUISE PEETE

1883–1947

"The Duchess of Death"

One of the most notorious murderesses of her day, the incorrigible Louise Peete didn't always have to rely on overt violence in her destruction of people. Over the years, she committed two murders for which she was convicted—and killed at least one and perhaps as many as two others—but she could also do her dirty work in other ways: she had the uncanny ability to drive men to suicide. In classic black-widow fashion, she could make husbands drop like flies, a talent in which she was known to take great pride.

The first man to die for her was her first husband, R. Henry Bosley, a hotel manager in her native Louisiana. Her extramarital affairs made

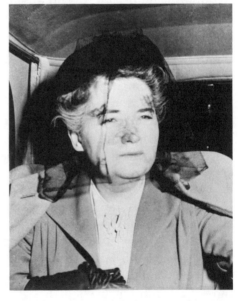

him sick with jealousy, especially on one occasion when, in 1906, the twenty-three-year-old Louise allowed herself to be discovered in bed with one of her lovers. Unable to take it anymore, Bosley killed himself. Her second husband, Harry Faurote of Dallas, had a similar reaction to her sex life. But he didn't go down to the basement to hang himself just because she was taking on an extra lover or two; what pushed him over the edge was the fact that she was brazenly carrying on a career of prostitution. In between husbands number one and two, Louise also had a fling with a Texas oilman who didn't fare any better, even though he had no intention of snuffing himself. In this case Louise shot her man in the head and took his collection of diamonds. She got away with this murder by putting on a dazzling performance before a grand jury, which believed her story that she had simply been defending herself against an attempted rape.

Louise Peete is unique among murderers in that she went through two separate, highly publicized homicide trials. In 1921, at the age of thirty-eight, she was brought up on the charge of murdering Los Angeles millionaire Jacob Denton. The year before, while living with Denton in his three-story mansion, she had broached the subject of marriage, even though her third husband, a man in Denver named Richard Peete, was still alive and legally bound to her. Denton was not interested in her proposal. Shortly after that, she shot Denton in the back of the neck, an act that allowed her to take possession of the man's house and to forge checks in his name. Denton's body was later found in the mansion's basement vault.

At the 1921 trial for this crime, Louise Peete was found guilty of first-degree murder and was given a life sentence. Incidental to this case—and absolutely typical of this woman's life—her husband, Richard Peete, grew despondent when she suddenly stopped corresponding with him from prison. Eventually, Richard Peete reached his wit's end and put a bullet in his head. According to those who observed her in prison at the time, Louise Peete was quite vain about this suicide, viewing it as a tribute to her feminine wiles.

Peete's prison sentence ended with a parole in 1939. Her next headline-grabbing murder would take place five years later.

In the intervening years, Peete had been relatively well behaved. She might have been responsible for the death of a female friend, who dropped out of sight in 1942, but no case was ever made against her. The disappearance of Margaret Logan two years later, however, was something else again.

Margaret Logan and her husband, Arthur, were Peete's parole sponsors and, as far as they knew, her good friends. But in 1944 the sixty-one-year-old Peete saw them as a means to a financial end. At the end of May, Peete ended her relationship with Margaret Logan the same way she had with Jacob Denton: she shot the woman in the back of the neck. For good measure she then turned the pistol around and used the butt to bash in Logan's skull.

Peete still had the ailing Arthur Logan to deal with, and while fending off questions about Margaret Logan's disappearance, she put him out of the way by getting him committed to the Patton State Hospital for the Insane. He conveniently died there of natural causes near the end of the year. Now came the payoff. Peete forged the Logans' checks, wangled possession of their house, and got herself listed as Margaret Logan's life-insurance beneficiary.

Peete eventually tripped herself up by going one forgery too far. As part of her parole responsibilities, Margaret Logan had been sending regular reports about Peete to an officer of the parole board. After May 1944 this officer noticed that Logan's signature at the bottom of these documents did not look genuine, and for good reason: Peete was forging the reports. Police were sent to the Logan home to investigate. When they saw neighborhood dogs poking at a peculiar mound of dirt in the backyard, they decided to take a closer look. Beneath the mound was Margaret Logan's corpse, already in an advanced state of decomposition due to an application of lime that Peete had administered.

Peete's second, sensational homicide trial began in April 1945. Once more, she was convicted of first-degree murder, but there would be no leniency such as she had received in her 1921 trial. She was sentenced to die in the gas chamber. On April 11, 1947, the sixty-four-year-old Louise Peete became the second woman in California history to be executed.

One sidelight to Peete's final murder conviction: Shortly before murdering Margaret Logan, Peete had gone to the altar for the fourth time, marrying a sixty-seven-year-old bank manager named Lee Borden Judson. He was living in the Logan house with Peete when the body was discovered in the backyard, and for this reason he came under suspicion as a possible accessory. The case against him never amounted to anything—he was exonerated at a preliminary hearing—but once more Louise Peete had left her mark on a man. Profoundly mortified by his association with a reprehensible cold-blooded murder, Judson jumped out a ninth-story window on January 12, 1945.

DR. MARCEL PETIOT
1897–1946

On a late winter day in 1944, black smoke billowed from the chimney of 21 rue Le Sueur, spreading an overpowering stench through the neighborhood. For Jacques Marcais, who lived next door, the odor was especially hard to take. He telephoned the Parisian authorities and demanded that they do something about the nuisance.

Firemen broke into the empty building, proceeding on the assumption that the chimney itself might be catching fire, and went down to the basement to check the furnace. There they discovered something infinitely more disturbing than a blaze about to go out of control. Burning inside the furnace were human limbs. And stacked on the basement

floor, like so much firewood, were mutilated corpses.

The police took stock of the remains found in the basement charnel house and determined that twenty-seven bodies were stashed there. Many were dismembered. Some were slit down the entire length of the torso, as if readied for scientific dissection. As the investigation of the scene continued, Dr. Marcel Petiot arrived and was identified as the building's owner.

Only the extraordinary set of circumstances that existed in Paris at that time could have led to what happened next. The Allied D-Day landing on the north coast of France was three months away, and Paris was still under the thumb of Nazi occupation. The spirit of resistance, however, simmered under the surface, and it was this kind of sentiment that Petiot must have sensed in the police sergeant who took him aside at 21 rue Le Sueur. He explained to the policeman that the bodies in the basement were those of Nazis and their collaborators; they had been assassinated by the French Resistance, and Petiot had merely been disposing of the corpses, all for the good of France, of course. It turned out that the police sergeant really was a Resistance sympathizer. He let Petiot go free.

Petiot dropped out of sight.

That June, the Allies invaded France, and by August Paris was a free city again. The grisly discovery made in the basement on rue Le Sueur, which had become public knowledge, was still on Parisians' minds, but now it was being given a new interpretation. A newspaper article suggested that Petiot had been a Nazi collaborator, murdering patriots for the Gestapo. From hiding, Petiot sent a letter to the newspaper in defense of himself. Once more, he claimed to have been an agent of the Resistance. The manhunt for Petiot began. On October 31, 1944, he was found and arrested on his way into a subway station. This time the authorities did not let him slip away. The matter was going to be settled one way or another.

The investigation revealed that the bodies in the basement had nothing directly to do with either the Gestapo or the Resistance. The killings had been done out of insane cruelty and greed.

When Dr. Marcel Petiot first settled in Paris in 1933, he already had a record of petty theft, drug peddling, and mental illness, and had been suspected in the deaths of two of his patients. His shady ventures continued in Paris, while at the same time his legitimate medical practice began to prosper. But he was not content with his success. After the Nazis overran France, he saw new opportunities for illicit gain, far more lucrative and far more ghastly than anything he had attempted before. He purchased the house at 21 rue Le Sueur, ostensibly for his medical practice, but he had it remodeled for a different enterprise altogether.

Petiot let it be known that he was a member of the Resistance and that he was willing and able to smuggle Jews and other fugitives out of the country. When these desperate people showed up at 21 rue Le Sueur—with all their money and valuables—Dr. Petiot would give them a shot, to immunize them, Petiot said, against diseases found in other countries. Then he would take them to a specially built room in the back of the house. Supposedly, the refugee would meet a Resistance escort in the backyard, but when the fugitive tried the rear exit, he or she would find it was a false door. By then the shot—a lethal injection— would begin taking effect. The soundproofed walls would muffle the victim's screams, while a peephole allowed Petiot to watch the fugitive's final, agonizing moments. In the early phases of this deadly venture, Petiot would hasten decomposition of the bodies in a lime pit in his backyard, shielded from view by the rebuilt, and especially tall, garden walls. Later, he decided to speed up the process by incinerating the bodies in the furnace.

The proceeds Petiot looted from his victims between 1941 and 1944 were estimated to be the equivalent of a million English pounds. And as it turned out, there were more victims involved in the case than the twenty-seven found in the basement.

At his trial Petiot stuck to his defense that he had been a loyal operative of the Resistance, and in an attempt to demonstrate his ardor for the Free France cause, he stated that he had killed and/or disposed of as many as sixty-three enemies of the French people. His claim that he had been active in the Resistance was undermined by his complete inability to name any of his fellow anti-Nazi operatives. His claim of sixty-three victims, though, was much more plausible. Police believed that many murdered refugees not found in the rue Le Sueur basement had been dumped in the Seine River.

In the end the jury determined there was sufficiently conclusive evidence to link Petiot to twenty-four murders. Playing the part of the wronged man to the end, Petiot left the courtroom shouting, "I must be avenged!" Ultimately, the people who were avenged were the dozens of trusting, helpless victims of Petiot's cruel scam: on May 26, 1946, Dr. Marcel Petiot was beheaded on the guillotine.

ALFRED CLINE
1889–1948
"The Buttermilk Bluebeard"

No one heard much from Eva Delora Krebs after she got remarried and left her native Chicago in May 1944. Her relatives back home were concerned. True, Eva Delora might have been just too busy in her new life to correspond, but on the other hand, she was a seventy-three-year-old woman, and it was natural for her family to become somewhat anxious when months went by without any word from her.

An inquiry about her annuity payments revealed that Eva Delora's monthly five-hundred-dollar checks from the life insurance company were being cashed on schedule, so it would appear there was no reason to become alarmed. But still, each time relatives placed a call to her in Portland, Oregon, the nice churchgoing man she had married always gave some excuse for Eva Delora's not coming to the phone: she was out shopping, she wasn't feeling well enough to talk—it was always one thing or another. All this behavior then took on a sinister cast in November 1945 when relatives received a telegram informing them of Eva Delora's death. The cause given was cerebral hemorrhage.

The relatives of Eva Delora Krebs, last known by her married name of Cline, were not convinced.

When Portland authorities got word of the Krebs family's suspicions, a trace was put on Eva Delora's recent widower, a

fifty-six-year-old man known as Alfred Leonard Cline. On December 3 police in San Francisco spotted him and put him into custody on suspicion of forgery in connection with his cashing of Eva Delora's annuity checks. Gray-haired and bespectacled, Cline looked like he could have been a Presbyterian minister, and indeed he had been a singer in a church choir, but the investigation initiated by the San Francisco district attorney's office produced an altogether different picture.

Picking through the sparse facts about the man's early life, detectives were able to establish that Alfred Cline had been born in the American heartland of Kansas and had been employed as an insurance broker for a while. There was more precise information about the two prison terms in his past. In 1929, at the age of forty, he had served a year in Colorado State Prison for grand theft, and in 1934 he began a nine-year stretch for drugging a Los Angeles businessman in order to separate the man from his money. An especially interesting fact the district attorney's office picked up was that Cline was currently wanted in Dallas, Texas, for suspicion of murder.

It seemed that a woman named Alice Carpenter had checked into a hotel there in the company of Cline—while Cline was still legally married to Krebs. Carpenter soon died of what was officially designated as heart failure. Dallas police suspected this was a case of poisoning. Nothing would ever come of these suspicions, however, because there was no possibility of an autopsy: Cline had made sure the woman's body was cremated immediately after death. Intriguingly enough, Eva Delora Krebs had also been cremated right after she died.

The story of Cline's life began to come into focus as reports came in from other police departments—in Florida, Georgia, Indiana, Ohio, and Oregon. In each of these places, a woman had married Cline, had taken a room in a hotel with him, and had then drunk a glass of buttermilk given to her by Cline. Before long, the woman was dead. In most cases the apparent cause was heart trouble, and in all cases death was followed by cremation. Four women died this way in the two years between 1943 and 1945. Then investigators discovered four other similar deaths in southern California during the 1930s, between Cline's two prison terms. Three of the victims were women, and one was a wealthy male evangelist. In each case Cline inherited money. His total inheritance over the years was estimated at $82,000.

Edmund Gerald Brown, San Francisco's district attorney, had no doubts about it: the man he had in custody was an extremely skillful and utterly amoral Bluebeard. The problem was how to prove it.

In the end there was no way to make a case for murder; without any bodies to examine for traces of poison, there was no way to establish what Cline had put in the glasses of buttermilk. Taking the next best route, the district attorney's office won convictions against Cline on nine counts of forgery. During the trial the prosecution succeeded in putting Cline's larceny in an especially ominous light by presenting the testimony of two women who had survived poisoning attempts by Cline. Cline's sentencing proved to be an example of how the flexibility of the legal system can sometimes serve the interests of justice. The judge ordered that the nine forgery sentences be served consecutively, amounting to a prison term of 126 years.

Cline ended up serving only two years of his sentence; he died of a heart attack in Folsom Prison on August 5, 1948. Although never prosecuted for murder, there was never any significant dispute as to what sort of criminal he really was. Even the sedate *New York Times* headlined its obituary for Cline with the words "KILLER OF 8 WOMEN DIES."

NEVILLE HEATH
1917–1946

Military titles were very important to Neville Heath. They were so important, in fact, that he acquired three officer commissions in just a few years' time, each with a different military service. He might not have held all these commissions under the same name, and he never left a military outfit without the benefit of a court-martial, but he always looked the part. Tall, handsome, and rugged, he seemed to be the Hollywood ideal of the British soldier-hero.

Heath's military career began in 1936 when he became an officer in the Royal Air Force. Unauthorized use of other people's cars, along with abandoning his post without leave, earned him a dismissal just a year

later. His second go-round came when Britain entered World War II. Fresh from a stint in prison for jewelry theft and check forgery, he decided to try the army. While serving as an officer in the Middle East in 1941, he was drummed out for various petty offenses and was put on a ship to be sent back to England.

Tiring of the boat ride as he approached the Cape of Good Hope, Heath took it upon himself to reroute his itinerary and jumped ship at the South African harbor of Durban. Before long he was in Johannesburg passing himself off as a war-hero captain by the name of Selway. He swiftly changed names again—to Bill Armstrong—in order to join the South African air force. Carrying his third officer's commission, he was transferred back to the RAF, his original military employer, and even saw some legitimate action as a bomber pilot in Europe. Predictably, when he returned to the South African air force at the end of the war, he was dishonorably discharged again, partly because of his habit of wearing medals he had never earned. He was still wearing bogus ribbons when he returned to his native England in February 1946.

Up to this point in his life, Heath might have been characterized as a comically incorrigible imposter. But there was little humor to be gleaned from his subsequent escapades. While staying in a London hotel, he brutalized a woman—an initially willing sex partner who went to his room and discovered Heath had tying-up and beating in mind. Since no one filed charges, Health was free to indulge new savage urges.

He took the next step on June 20, 1946. Heath's soldierly bearing— he was presenting himself as Colonel Bill Armstrong these days—his good looks, and his suave manner often made a favorable impression on women, and on this summer night Margery Gardner, a thirty-two-year-old dilettante who dabbled in film acting and fine arts, was taken in. She accompanied Heath to his room at the Pembridge Court Hotel. Their sexual fling turned into a night of monstrous murder.

Margery Gardner's body was found the next afternoon, sprawled beneath bloody sheets on one of the room's beds. Heath had killed her by suffocating her in some way, most likely by forcing a gag down her throat. The blood came from massive mutilations; Gardner's flesh was lashed with a sort of whip that might have been a riding crop, and her vagina was lacerated. Her nipples were partially removed, the evidence indicating that they had been bitten.

The identity of the culprit was obvious. Although he had introduced himself to his victim as Bill Armstrong, Heath had registered at the Pembridge Court Hotel under his real name. Authorities circulated his photograph among police departments throughout England, and the manhunt began.

Neville Heath was not especially concerned.

He drifted south from London to the coast of the English Channel, moving from one hotel to another and living on credit. Taking on the name of England's doomed poet-hero of World War I, he now called himself Captain Rupert Brooke. The only thing he did to keep the police at bay was to send a letter to Scotland Yard in which he claimed that the murder had taken place while he was not in the hotel. After sending the letter, Heath continued along England's southern coast. He stopped in the town of Bournemouth just long enough to commit his second murder.

As the charming Captain Rupert Brooke, Heath went to dinner with a young woman named Doreen Marshall and attacked her while walking her back to her hotel. Marshall put up a struggle as he gagged her, but Heath was too strong for her. He slit her throat, then mutilated her as he had Margery Gardner. It would take five days for the police to find the missing woman's ravaged body along a shrub-covered rise known as Branksome Chine. By that time Heath had already delivered himself to the authorities.

Heath's behavior since the Gardner murder in London had not been especially elusive, as if he half wanted to be caught. But his actions on July 6, two days after he killed Doreen Marshall, were particularly self-destructive. He went to the Bournemouth police station to volunteer his help in the search for Marshall. With a picture of Heath on hand, the police had no trouble identifying the fugitive murderer. They placed him under arrest.

Among the pieces of evidence collected by the police were the mutilation instrument (a metal-tipped riding crop found in Heath's suitcase) and a handkerchief fashioned into a gag that was covered with blood and that contained some of Doreen Marshall's hair in its knot. The trial against Heath proceeded quickly, and the jury needed only fifty-nine minutes to convict him of murder. He was hanged on October 16, 1946. Throughout his three months in custody, he maintained his stoic regimental demeanor. No one ever learned what turned this imposter into a sadistic killer.

WILLIAM HEIRENS
1929–

With the skill of a practiced, if extremely young, thief, sixteen-year-old William Heirens slipped into an apartment on Chicago's North Side on December 10, 1945. He searched the darkened rooms for money or valuables for the taking, but stealing was not necessarily his only reason for being here. As always, just sneaking into someone's apartment made him excited. He could find sexual stimulation in this act, without any contact with a woman. But then the bathroom door opened and a woman appeared.

Standing in the doorway was thirty-three-year-old Frances Brown. Heirens turned to her. The two people facing each other reacted according to their first impulses: Brown screamed, and Heirens pulled out a pistol and fired. In another moment the woman was motionless on the floor. Next, Heirens found a knife and thrust the blade into her throat, stabbing with such force that the knife's tip protruded out the other side.

A strange sort of panic seized the young man. In an attempt to somehow erase his deed, he took the dead woman into the bathroom, stripped off her now crimson clothes and washed the blood off her. But still there was a gruesome reminder: the knife still lodged in her neck. He found a housecoat at hand and draped it over her neck and shoulders to hide the blade. None of this washing and covering up, though, could put his mind at ease. Before he left, as a last, desperate measure against his own impulses, he wrote a message on the bedroom wall with Brown's lipstick: "For Heaven's sake catch me before I kill more. I cannot control myself."

William Heirens had good reason to believe he would murder again. A highly intelligent young man, he knew that the strange obsessions that had started plaguing him at an early age were still driving him on.

Three things seemed to be inextricably entwined in Heirens's mind: sex, which he had been taught was filthy; violence, which he found fascinating (he had stockpiled firearms in his early teens); and burglary, which he had already started to commit regularly by the time he had gained early entrance to the University of Chicago. This trio of obsessions had now become a deadly combination.

After the Frances Brown murder, and the discovery of the chilling message scrawled on the victim's wall, the Chicago police were on the alert, but Heirens's warning/plea did not really prepare them for the next hideous crime that he felt compelled to commit.

This time, when he broke into an apartment on January 7, 1946, he was surprised by the awakening of six-year-old Suzanne Degnan. Later that night, the police found the dismembered pieces of the girl in various nearby sewer drains. They were not, however, able to pick up any trace of the killer. For five months Heirens continued to elude them. He then helped the police find him by entering an apartment without any serious attempt at covering his tracks.

He walked through an open apartment door just before dinnertime in June 1946. After they chased him through the building, two police officers trapped and subdued Heirens. In accordance with his professed wish, he had finally been stopped.

Fingerprints lifted at the crime scenes provided persuasive physical evidence; Heirens's confession provided the details. Among other things, he now made it clear that he had killed before the Frances Brown murder. The victim had been forty-three-year-old Josephine Ross, killed, like Brown, when she had discovered Heirens burglarizing her apartment. Heirens now revealed that he had experienced one orgasm after another immediately following this murder. He also said his crimes were actually committed by his alternate personality, a personality that was so real to Heirens that he had even given him a name, George Murman.

In exchange for his full confession, the court refrained from condemning him to the electric chair. Instead, he received three life sentences to be served consecutively, for the three murder counts lodged against him. Now in his sixties, Heirens continues in prison, despite a judge's abortive attempt to declare him fit to reenter society in 1983.

Rudolf Pleil

1924–1958

"The Death-Maker"

There was some element of doubt as to whether Rudolf Pleil really intended to kill when he clubbed the hapless salesman with an ax. Perhaps, the West German court considered, the death was merely the result of a momentary, uncontrollable rage, with no premeditation on the part of the chubby, twenty-three-year-old defendant. This interpretation became the official ruling, and in 1947 Pleil was convicted of manslaughter and given a prison sentence of twelve years. West German authorities had no reason to give the man any further thought. They would have come to a different view of the matter, however, if they had been aware of the memoirs Pleil was writing to while away

his time in jail. The title he chose for this work was *Mein Kampf*, a disturbing allusion, obviously, for anyone concerned about the possible resurgence of Naziism in postwar Germany, but not nearly as disturbing as the by-line Pleil assigned to his efforts. It read, "by Rudolf Pleil, death dealer (retired)."

Soon the full meaning of Pleil's self-description would become clear. A refugee from East Germany named Lydia Schmidt went to the police with a story about the young man recently imprisoned for manslaughter. She had come upon Pleil along the border between East and West as she was fleeing the Soviet-controlled zone. Pleil was posing as a policeman. He said that he would help her, that he could make it easier for her to get beyond the reach of East German guards. And, in fact, he did get her safely to the West, but only so far. As soon as they were in an isolated spot, he attacked her.

He started beating her until, he thought, she was senseless. Actually, she pretended to be unconscious in order to save herself and had to continue to do so while Pleil sexually assaulted her, then left her for dead.

Following up on this story, the police began to dig for more information about Pleil's past. They soon unearthed a portrait of a mass murderer who had emerged as a sexual psychopath during the atrocities of the Hitler era, then exploited the turmoil of the subsequent Cold War to his own homicidal advantage.

Pleil discovered his overwhelming appetite for human suffering as a German soldier during World War II. One day, a train that was deporting prisoners to a concentration camp stopped near Pleil's military post, and Pleil had the chance to see the Gestapo at work. The officers of the secret police ordered the bodies of those prisoners who had died of starvation to be dumped off the freight cars, then they tore off the corpses' clothes and flung the lifeless human forms into a wagon. As Pleil later put it, watching this was his "finest sexual experience."

After the war he put his sadistic tastes into action. Relying on the technique used with Lydia Schmidt, he prowled the no-man's-land that separated East Germany and his West German state of Saxony, and preyed upon women making desperate flight to the West. Typically, he raped his victims, then killed them and mutilated the bodies. His weapons varied. Sometimes he slashed with hatchets or knives, other times he bludgeoned with a hammer or heavy stone. At one point he enlisted the aid of two accomplices, young men by the names of Karl Hoffman and Konrad Schuessler, who helped trap his victims. The actual act of murder, however, Pleil insisted on doing himself.

During his string of murders in 1946 and 1947, Pleil tended to draw moral lines in some peculiar places. He had a falling-out once with Hoffman because the accomplice demanded that they decapitate a victim. Pleil was outraged with what he considered to be his underling's disgusting behavior.

Pleil's ax murder of the salesman in 1947 was out of character for him. The victim was male, and Pleil acted on the spur of the moment, without sufficiently covering his tracks. Because of that, he was finally placed in custody and his other crimes detected.

The police eventually charged Pleil with nine rapes and murders. As he had been during the falling-out with his partner, Pleil was once again outraged for twisted reasons all his own. At his trial in 1950, he demanded that his number of victims be corrected to its true total of twenty-five. He was exceedingly vain about his appalling career of murder. "You underrate me," he announced in court. "I am Germany's greatest killer. I put others, both here and abroad, to shame." He also insisted that, for posterity's sake, the trial transcript should duly note that he was "the best death-maker of Germany."

The court might have minimized the murder total due to lack of evidence, but it certainly was impressed by the defendant's viciousness. Following Pleil's conviction, the judge voiced his disappointment that West German law did not allow the death penalty, forcing him instead to sentence Pleil merely to life in prison.

That prison term was cut short in February 1958 when Pleil hanged himself in his cell.

THE BLACK DAHLIA AVENGER
1947

The Los Angeles police found the naked body on a vacant lot on the morning of January 15, 1947. Once the body had been that of a beautiful young woman. Now it was reduced to hideously mangled flesh and bone. It was carved in half at the waist, the flesh slashed in sadistic fashion. Pathologists later determined that the victim had been mutilated with a knife while she was hung by the ankles; the mutilations had been inflicted while she was still alive. At first the police had no way to identify the woman; the one immediate clue was a pair of cryptic initials, "BD," sliced into one of the thighs, a grotesque parody of the sort of inscription a lovestruck boy might carve into the bark of a tree. Only after the victim's fingerprints were forwarded to the FBI was there a name to attach to the ghastly, severed carcass.

The FBI would not have been able to help if the victim had had no police record or period of employment in a defense plant. As it turned out, the fingerprints were matched with those of a twenty-two-year-old woman named Elizabeth Short, who had been picked up by police five years before while drinking, underage, in a Miami, Florida, bar. The

The Black Dahlia's blood-stained clothes are discovered near the horribly ravaged body.

connection between Short and the BD initials became clear when police spoke to the owner of a Long Beach drugstore that Short used to frequent; the pharmacist said that the murder victim's nickname was the Black Dahlia. She was known as a striking woman with gray-green eyes who had a habit of dressing in black clothes, to match her lustrous black hair. She skirted the edges of the Hollywood life, working sometimes as a film extra, and led a promiscuous existence. If the killer was one of her ex-lovers, then the police faced a difficult task indeed in narrowing down the list of suspects.

The brutality of the murder made the Black Dahlia case one of the most notorious of its day. The attractiveness of the victim, and her evocative nickname, also seemed to inspire writers to speculate on the life of Elizabeth Short, a woman who has been romanticized as a tragic beauty whose murder was the inevitable conclusion to an ill-fated existence. The few known facts of her brief life certainly seem to lend themselves to this interpretation. In 1942, while working as a waitress in Miami, the seventeen-year-old Short fell in love with a young serviceman. Soon after that the young man was sent off to do his bit against the Axis enemy and was killed in action. Short's hard-drinking, sexually active life was supposed to have begun after this emotional shock.

It was around this time that she had her brush with the police. Believing the teenager just needed a fresh start, the police released her without pressing charges. Still restless, Short traveled cross-country and ended up in Santa Barbara, California. Once more she fell in love, and again she was struck by tragedy. Her fiance, an air corps major, was sent to the Pacific theater and succeeded in getting through the war alive, only to die in a plane crash a year after Japan's surrender. In an apparent attempt to put the grief behind her, she settled in Hollywood and started over again.

Short now cultivated the Black Dahlia persona. As one of many attractive young women seeking to break into the movie business, she hit upon the scheme of all-black attire to attract attention. As the so-called Black Dahlia, she may have made a name for herself on the scruffy fringes of Hollywood, but film stardom did not beckon, and even extra work started to peter out. Before long she moved on to San Diego. She was a waitress again.

In trying to reconstruct the last few days of Short's life, the police could only come up with a sketchy picture. The picture indicated she had become a melancholy drifter, but it offered no solutions to the mystery of her death. After leaving San Diego six days before the murder, she was seen in several Los Angeles bars and hotels, some-times with men who may have been lovers, sometimes with women of ill repute. She was also spotted back in San Diego the day before the killing, but was showing no signs of settling down: her luggage was still in a bus station locker.

The police came their closest to the killer when they received an anonymous mailing, the words of which were assembled from letters snipped out of a newspaper. The message: "Here is Dahlia's belongings. Letter to follow." In the package were Short's address book, her birth certificate, and the bus station claim check for her luggage. Another letter, presumably from the same person, promised that the sender would turn himself in. The note was signed "Black Dahlia Avenger." But there was no such surrender. A final letter simply stated, "Have changed my mind." Further frustrating the police was a steady stream of confessions from people who were clearly cranks.

The so-called "Black Dahlia Avenger" was never identified, and the person who ended Elizabeth Short's life with such mind-boggling cruelty was never found.

JOHN GEORGE HAIGH
1909–1949
"The Acid-Bath Killer"

In one respect the jury is still out on convicted British killer John George Haigh: was he a fantastically depraved maniac who literally thirsted for the blood of his victims, or was he merely a monstrously cold murderer for profit? Granted, the moral distinctions are blurry, to say the least, but for students of bizarre crime this is a question of great interest. It is also a question that does not have an easy, clear-cut answer.

To begin with what we know for fact, John George Haigh devoted his early adult years to practicing his craft as a swindler. He was in and out of jail throughout his twenties and early thirties, getting arrested for such scams as selling bogus company stocks. A convincing argument could be made that all these years of fraud led directly to his first homicide in 1944, which, in many ways, was a classic case of money-mad murder.

At this point in his life, Haigh was passing himself off as a mechanic/engineer. His principal client was an amusement arcade owner named Donald McSwann, who had his pinball machines repaired in Haigh's shop. One day Haigh invited McSwann to his basement workshop in South Kensington and smashed in his skull with a hammer. Putting all his defrauding skills to use, Haigh then wangled possession of the deceased McSwann's arcade. This greed-motivated killing, however, had some bizarre features that set it apart from the mundane homicidal fraud.

During one of his stretches in prison, Haigh had managed to scrounge up the means to conduct weird experiments: he had made a study of how well sulfuric acid could dissolve the flesh and bones of dead mice. The ghastly knowledge gained from these experiments came into use in Haigh's basement workshop, where he kept a forty-gallon vat. After killing McSwann, he disposed of the *corpus delicti* by carving it into pieces, putting the pieces in the vat, and pouring in sulfuric acid.

This grisly method of murder was successfully employed against four other victims in as many years: McSwann's mother and father (who asked too many questions about their son's disappearance), and Dr. Archibald Henderson and his wife, Rosalie. Haigh, the veteran bilker, got control of the estates of all of these people and parlayed their deaths into a great deal of money. His hideous career came to an end in 1949 when he shot and acid-bathed an aging widow named Olive Durrand-Deacon.

A friend of Durrand-Deacon told the police that the victim had been on her way to meet Haigh the day she disappeared. The policewoman who interviewed Haigh detected something dishonest about his manner and requested a check for past convictions. When the police got a look at Haigh's extensive criminal record, they searched his workshop.

By the end of the search, the police had found a .38-caliber revolver that had been recently fired, twenty-eight pounds of human fat that had not been dissolved, and a set of dentures that was identified as Durrand-Deacon's. Haigh understandably saw no advantage in denying any charges in the face of such evidence; he soon began his confession. As far as the police were concerned, they had an open-and-shut case of calculated, cold-blooded murder, perpetrated for material gain. The methods may have been especially nasty, but still it was simple murder for money nonetheless.

Then Haigh started confessing to vampirism.

He said he had obsessive nightmares about forests dripping with blood, and these dreams, he explained, drove him to commit murder. After killing his victims, and before destroying the bodies in acid, he would slit their throats and drink their blood by the glassful. Haigh told the police that his bleeding-forest visions had started while he was a child; he had been mad for years, it seemed.

Or was he just inventing this vampire motive in order to support an insanity plea?

Since the only witness to these alleged blood-drinking rituals was Haigh himself, there was no way to corroborate his claims—or to conclusively disprove them. A psychiatrist hired by the defense examined Haigh and testified in court that the validity of Haigh's vampirism claims was "pretty certain." The prosecution, on the other hand, pointed out that Haigh was a lifelong liar and con man. This characterization, obviously, could not be denied, but while in prison, Haigh made it patently clear that he was willing to imbibe grotesque fluids: he drank his own urine. Was he so much of a con man that he would go to that length for the purpose of deceit?

In the end the jury declared Haigh legally sane and convicted him of murder.

The question of whether Haigh really was a vampire on top of all his other crimes remains unanswered. John George Haigh, the only witness to this alleged perversity, was hanged on August 6, 1949. For many people in Britain, seeing Haigh face the ultimate penalty was more important than discovering the true psychological nature of his sickening murders.

RAYMOND FERNANDEZ
1916–1951

MARTHA BECK
1920–1951

"The Lonely Hearts Killers"

Forty years ago, the Michigan town of Byron Center was small enough that people would have been likely to notice the comings and goings of their neighbors. Of course, a conspicuous *absence* of comings and goings would also be noticed.

In February of 1949, the neighbors of Delphine Dowling became suspicious when they saw neither the twenty-eight-year-old widow nor her twenty-month-old daughter for some time. The only people the neighbors did notice around the Dowling place were those two curious

The "Lonely Hearts Killers" exchange a loving glance over their guard.

visitors, a slim Hispanic man and an obese woman, who had arrived a few weeks earlier and settled in as if they intended to stay. The police were called, and officers showed up at the Dowling house to ask some questions.

The Hispanic man and his overweight companion presented themselves as brother and sister, and acted like people who had nothing to hide. They raised no objections to the police request to search the premises.

The mystery of Delphine Dowling's disappearance was solved when the police took a close look at the basement. There they discovered that a pit had been dug out of the basement floor and covered by a layer of cement that was obviously still fresh. In the pit were the corpses of Delphine Dowling and her baby daughter.

Under questioning, the alleged brother and sister, who in reality were unmarried lovers by the name of Raymond Fernandez and Martha Beck, confessed to the double Dowling murder. Soon it became clear why the culprits had agreed so readily to a search of the house even though there had been no warrant: their devil-may-care response had been the last-ditch, cocky bluff of experienced con artists. Swindling, it turned out, had been their game for the last two years, in particular the ruthless bilking of lonely women. Once in a while difficulties had arisen in the execution of this game. That was when murder had entered into the scheme.

Fernandez and Beck had met in Pensacola, Florida, in 1947. By this time Fernandez was already a bigamist and money-grubbing gigolo. He would win his way into the hearts of lonely women with his smooth, if somewhat oily, charm and his Latin looks, which included a mound of thick, dark hair that looked almost too good to be true (in fact, it was— Fernandez worked his romantic trade with a wig covering his bald scalp). He met Martha Beck the way he usually met women—through a lonely hearts correspondence club.

By the time of her meeting with Fernandez, the two-hundred-pound Beck was a three-time divorcee, a registered nurse, and the superintendent of a home for crippled children. As for her own children, a court had declared her unfit to care for them.

For whatever reason, the first date for the seemingly mismatched Fernandez and Beck was sexually charged. Instead of victimizing Beck, Fernandez quickly became her passionate lover. For her part Beck was so smitten with her Latin Romeo that she wanted to become a partner in his cruel lonely-hearts swindles. She came up with the idea of posing as his sister to help put over the scams, and before long she was no longer just an accomplice; she was the driving force behind their criminal enterprise.

After finding a suitable spinster or widow through a lonely-hearts service, Fernandez would trap the pigeon with his gigolo ways, then together he and Beck would persuade the woman to sign over her savings. Working their scam from one state to another, they often succeeded in ripping off their victims without resorting to extreme measures. But sometimes the lonely women weren't sufficiently cooperative.

Ultimately, only three murders would be definitively established, but there may have been as many as twelve. The helplessness of the victims and the brutality of the known murders would prove enough to thoroughly outrage the public.

In mid-January 1949 sixty-six-year-old Janet Fay of Albany, New York, accompanied Fernandez and Beck to a Valley Stream apartment on Long Island and allowed herself to be fleeced by Fernandez and Beck, but she made the mistake of being too desperate. After she couldn't buy Fernandez's permanent devotion with four thousand dollars from her savings, she resorted to pleading with him to stay on as her lover. Beck didn't care for this. She cracked the old woman's skull with a heavy ballpeen hammer. Not to be outdone, Fernandez then moved in and strangled Fay. A few days later, the ever-mobile Fernandez and Beck were in Byron Center, Michigan, winning the confidence of Delphine Dowling.

Dowling turned out to be especially vexing, even after she let the bogus brother and sister live in her house. Suspicious of their intentions, she failed to turn over any money. Prodded by Beck, Fernandez gave Dowling an overdose of sleeping pills. When she didn't succumb fast enough, he got his pistol and fired a coup de grace into the widow's head. Later, Dowling's twenty-month-old daughter complained about missing her mother. Beck, the former nurse, drowned the little girl in the bathtub.

Eventually, Fernandez and Beck were put on trial in New York for the Janet Fay murder, rather than in Michigan, where the Dowling murders had occurred. The reason was simple: New York still made use of the electric chair, the only fate that many people believed the "Lonely Hearts Killers" deserved. Fernandez and Beck were both convicted and sentenced to die. On March 8, 1951, Fernandez and Beck took turns sitting in Sing Sing's electric chair.

HOWARD UNRUH
1921–

Rita Unruh became deathly afraid of her son on the morning of September 6, 1949. Right after breakfast, twenty-eight-year-old Howard Unruh stepped out of the second-story apartment he shared with his mother and went down to the building's basement. He came back to their flat carrying a wrench. Rita Unruh found him in the living room, his back to her. Suddenly, he spun around on her, the wrench raised as if ready to attack. Perhaps even more unsettling were his eyes; as Rita Unruh would later tell reporters, he stared at her as though he had no idea who she was.

Rita Unruh ran away from her son and fled to a friend's home nearby. She would be one of the few people that morning to get away from him alive.

After his mother was gone, Howard Unruh selected a 9mm German Luger from his collection of firearms, some extra ammunition and a

small knife, and left the apartment a little before nine-thirty. Out on his section of River Road in East Camden, New Jersey, people were going about their everyday business after the long Labor Day weekend. Unruh's personal business that morning took him a short distance down the block to the shoe repair shop. He walked up to the shop owner, John Pilarchik, already busy at his workbench. Unruh leveled his pistol and shot the man once in the chest and once in the head. Wasting no time, but showing no sign of hurry, he returned to the street and moved on.

His next destination was the adjacent barbershop. Inside, a mother was watching her six-year-old son get a haircut. Unruh shot and killed both the boy and the barber. He let the mother live. By the time he stepped back onto the sidewalk, the gunshots had gotten the attention of the people on the street, and the first wave of panic was sweeping down the block. Like a deadly automaton, Unruh walked through the chaos, bypassing a group of children that raced past him in search of cover, then shooting a boy who appeared at a window overhead. The owner of a bar fired at him from the apartment above his tavern and managed to send a .38 bullet through Unruh's left thigh, but the wound had no noticeable effect. Unruh marched toward the corner drugstore owned by Maurice Cohen. At the doorway Unruh said, "Excuse me, sir," and shot a man who didn't get out of his way fast enough, then tracked down the Cohens in the upstairs apartment and gunned down Maurice Cohen, as well as Cohen's wife and mother.

Unruh wasn't through yet. Only minutes had passed since he had killed John Pilarchik, the cobbler, and the police had not yet had the chance to respond. With his way still clear, Unruh continued along the block, firing with deadly accuracy at shopkeepers, residents, and motorists. As police sirens drew near, he returned to his apartment.

In the preceding twelve minutes, he had killed or mortally wounded thirteen people.

Police surrounded the two-story building where Unruh lived. As the killer prepared for a siege, a local newspaper editor placed a call to Unruh's phone. In the course of a startlingly calm conversation, he asked Unruh why he was shooting people. "I don't know," Unruh replied. "I can't answer yet—I'm too busy. I'll have to talk to you later."

The standoff with the police ended quickly after a tear gas bomb was heaved through Unruh's bedroom window. Unable to withstand the fumes, the killer gave himself up.

At the police station Unruh gave police the explanation that he had been too harried to supply to the newspaper editor earlier. Of the neighbors he attacked, he said, "They have been making derogatory remarks about my character."

An in-depth psychiatric examination was clearly in order. Between the month-long evaluation by four psychiatrists, the investigation by police, and the snooping done by newspaper reporters, a picture was pieced together of the events that had preceded the horrifying slaughter of September 6.

Howard Unruh, it was learned, was a decorated World War II veteran who had distinguished himself as a tank gunner in the campaign up through Italy to Austria, France, and Germany. Among the engagements in which he took part was the dramatic relief of Bastogne in the Battle of the Bulge. Unruh's heroism on the field, however, did not translate into popularity among his fellow soldiers. He was known as an unusually tightlipped young man who preferred to devote his free time to cleaning his rifle and reading his Bible.

After his discharge in 1945, he moved in with his mother, now separated from her husband, and began preparing for civilian life by taking pharmacy courses at Temple University in Philadelphia, across the Delaware River from East Camden. His interest in religion continued; he took Monday-night Bible classes and escorted his mother to St. Paul's Evangelical Lutheran Church every Sunday. But soon Unruh's orderly life began to fall apart. He dropped out of his pharmacy classes and, by the spring of 1949, had even stopped going to church with his mother. Since he had no job, he had a lot of time to brood.

A great many of his thoughts focused on his neighbors and the way they treated him. He kept a journal of all the insults he felt had been directed at him. After some of these entries was the notation "retal," his abbreviation for *retaliate*. Concurrent with this cataloging of offenses was his continuing, and growing, interest in guns. His collection of weapons expanded, and he honed his aim by taking target practice in his basement.

On September 5, 1949, Unruh spent the night repeatedly watching a movie double-feature in Philadelphia and didn't get home until three in the morning. When he discovered the gate had been stolen from the wooden fence he had recently erected around his backyard, he felt this was one insult too many. He spent the rest of the night thinking.

Eventually, he decided that nine-thirty would be the best time to start shooting. When he threatened his mother with the wrench the next morning, he was considering killing her so that she wouldn't have to withstand the ordeal that his subsequent actions would cause.

Psychiatrists diagnosed Unruh as suffering from dementia praecox with "paranoid coloring." As an insane person, he was immune from criminal prosecution and was instead committed to a mental institution. He has been there ever since.

REG CHRISTIE

1898–1953

"The Monster of Rillington Place"

Reg Christie had the appearance of a respectable, if colorless, man. Bald, bespectacled, with a narrow build, he looked like a steady, lifelong clerk. But by 1938, when he and his wife moved into an apartment at 10 Rillington Place, in a shabby section of London's Notting Hill, this forty-year-old man had already lost three jobs due to his compulsive thievery. He had also suffered from hypochondria and was a known liar, often misrepresenting himself as a man of uncommon skills and elevated status.

His move to Rillington Place coincided with the last abortive attempts to avoid war in Europe. During World War II Christie's life would change.

Soon after Hitler's invasion of Poland, he became a constable in the War Reserve Police. Finally, he had acquired some semblance of the status that he had previously only pretended to possess. His newfound authority may have been petty, but he was quick to abuse it nonetheless, as he hounded fellow Londoners for the most insignificant violations of blackout rules. A year later, as Britain braced itself for the onslaught of Nazi bombing, another change occurred in his life. He started killing women.

One day while his wife was out of the city visiting her sister, Christie brought a woman named Ruth Fuerst to his Rillington Place flat. No doubt the apparent respectability that came with being a constable helped him persuade her to accompany him. At the apartment he was going to treat a respiratory complaint of Fuerst's with a therapeutic vapor that he had concocted. (A flair for medical remedies was one of those rare abilities he claimed to have.) While administering this treatment, Christie managed to slip a tube into his steaming mixture; he'd hooked up the other end of the tube to the flat's coal-gas fixture. The intake of gas made Fuerst pass out. Now that she was unconscious, Christie considered her a suitable object of sexual desire—a very deadly sexual desire. Simultaneously, he raped and strangled Fuerst. She ended up beneath the garden in back of Christie's house.

Three years later, Christie used the same method to rape and kill Muriel Eady, one of his wife's friends, then murdered no one else until 1949. At that time he learned that Beryl Evans, the wife of his upstairs neighbor, needed an abortion. The Evanses already had one child, a fourteen-month-old girl, and they didn't want another. Christie claimed that performing abortions was another of his skills, and when Beryl Evans was alone with him in his apartment to submit to this procedure, he beat her senseless and strangled her. Then he sexually violated her corpse. Still he wasn't through. Reaching a new depth of horror and depravity, he strangled Evans's baby daughter.

Beryl's husband, Timothy, was a dim-witted man. Perhaps this fact explains what happened next. When Timothy Evans came home to find his wife and child killed, Christie somehow convinced him to confess to the murders. Later, when he got hold of himself, Evans would retract the confession, but it would be too late. He was convicted of his daughter's murder and was hanged in 1950.

Christie's murderous sexual impulses remained in check until December 1952. Then, as if to eliminate any possible restraint on himself, he killed his wife. Dispensing with any careful concealment of the body, he simply placed the corpse beneath the dining-room floorboards. Within a two-month period in early 1953, he then gassed, strangled, and raped three women. The bodies were stuffed into the kitchen closet. Christie was now acting like a man who wanted to get caught.

True-crime writer Colin Wilson has speculated that the obsessions that had driven Christie to murder were now his master at this point, banishing all sense of caution from his actions. This interpretation would certainly account for what Christie did during his last weeks at large. In March 1953 he sublet his apartment, leaving four corpses in the flat when he left. The closest he came to concealing his crimes was applying a sheet of wallpaper over the kitchen closet that contained the three most recent bodies. The new resident uncovered these remains three days after Christie moved out and called the police. Before long, Mrs. Christie was discovered under the floorboards, and two bodies were unearthed in the garden. Christie was wandering aimlessly around the city when he was arrested at the end of the month.

Expedited by a detailed confession, the prosecution of Christie proceeded quickly. On July 15, 1953, only three-and-a-half months after his arrest, he was hanged at the Pentonville gallows.

WILLIAM COOK

1929–1952

Beneath the surface of American life in the 1950s was a dark undercurrent that coursed against the flow of an otherwise contented, orderly society. While most Americans seemed devoted to family, prosperity, and national purpose, there were others who drifted into lawlessness, often alienated young people who were regarded as an affront to everything decent. Motorcycle gangs, juvenile delinquency, street rumbles, the commission of crimes for kicks—these manifestations of a darker side of the national psyche deeply troubled and frightened middle-class parents of the day. Perhaps no one did more to propagate fears about surly, unpredictable young men in leather jackets than a misfit named

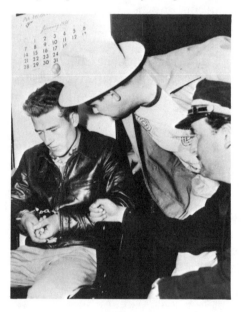

William Cook, who inaugurated the fifties with a harrowing spree of murders across the Southwest.

In 1950 William Cook emerged from the Missouri State Penitentiary. He was twenty-one years old, with a record of petty arrests and reform schools in his past, and a plan for the future that would make a perfect outline for a crime novel of random, existential violence. His first stop was his hometown of Joplin, where he looked up his father. Why he felt compelled to see the man at this point is not clear. There certainly couldn't have been much love between them. Cook and his seven siblings had been abandoned at an early age by their widower father. Even when the senior Cook had been around, he didn't exactly fit the post–World War II ideal of an able family provider: the home he had found for his children was the bowels of a deserted mine shaft.

Perhaps Cook's reason for seeing his father in December 1950 was simply to announce his plans. With his black leather jacket and brushed-back hair, Billy Cook was intent upon becoming a self-styled desperado, a sort of modern-day Billy the Kid. As he succinctly put it to his father, "I'm gonna live by the gun and roam."

Chances are that Cook didn't work out his plans in any great detail, but his subsequent actions suggest that the most important thing to him was the possession of people, the taking of hostages, as if he craved having people completely under his control. A few days after leaving his father, he hijacked a car at gunpoint outside Lubbock, Texas. In this case he wasn't vigilant enough to keep his hostage for more than a few hours before the man escaped. Cook didn't let that happen again.

On New Year's Eve, 1950, he commandeered the car of a family named Mosser on their way to visit relatives in New Mexico. This time, Cook held on to the father, mother, and three children for three days.

Except for the time he beat back an attempt by the father to get hold of his pistol, Cook did not physically brutalize the Mossers until the very end of those seventy-two hours. Keeping the family in the car and making the father drive him around seemed enough for him—at least for a while. All of which must have been enough to terrify the five Mossers. And not just because of the .32-caliber pistol that was trained on them. Cook himself was unnerving.

For one thing there was his deformed right eyelid, never fully open and never fully closed. When Cook was a child, this disquieting feature had spooked potential foster parents from taking him on after Cook's father had skipped; now it gave the young adult a weird, brutal appearance. And there were also the tattoos on his fingers. A trailblazer of sorts when it came to bizarre adornment, Cook was five years ahead of the psychopathic Robert Mitchum character in the 1955 film *Night of the Hunter*, who had the words *love* and *hate* inscribed on the fingers of his right and left hands respectively. Cook tattooed the words *hard luck* on his fingers.

After three days of forcing the Mossers to drift with him through four states, Cook decided the time had come to share some hard luck with his captives. He shot and killed both parents and all three children.

Driving on with his carful of corpses, Cook made another trip back to his hometown of Joplin. It may have been a visit of symbolic importance for him. He threw the five corpses into an abandoned mine shaft, one that was probably not much different, and not too far, from the shaft that had once been his childhood home.

Cook roamed some more.

The police now started to pick up Cook's trail. In Oklahoma they found the Mossers's abandoned car, the seats covered with blood, as well as the discarded vehicle belonging to Cook's first abductee. In the latter car they found a receipt in Cook's name, acquired in the purchase of a .32 pistol. Soon a manhunt was launched, involving police departments throughout the Southwest as well as the FBI.

Cook's wanderings, meanwhile, had taken him west to California. There he took another driver hostage, a traveling salesman by the name of Robert Dewey. Cook tired of him after a while and killed him. His next destination, in the manner of old western outlaws eluding dogged posses, was the sanctuary of Mexico. But Mexican authorities had been notified about Cook and were willing to cooperate.

Mexican police closed in on Cook as he sat in a restaurant with two American prospectors he had taken hostage—he still wasn't willing to stop pulling people into his net. But perhaps he knew he had reached the end of the trail, because for all his desperado defiance, he offered no resistance when Mexican police took away his gun and made the arrest.

Of the two states that wanted him, California got first chance at Cook for the murder of the salesman Robert Dewey. It turned out to be the only chance that was needed. Convicted of first-degree murder, Cook died in the gas chamber on December 12, 1952.

ED GEIN
1906–1984

Ed Gein came by madness rightly. It was a legacy from his mother, Augusta. Dementia was something she passed down from her generation to his, nurturing it in her son for nearly forty years before it fully blossomed and overtook Gein completely.

Augusta Gein's whole being was consumed by an insane hatred for what she considered the world's greatest evil—sex. She detected signs of smut and fornication on all sides of her in the Middle American city of La Crosse, Wisconsin, where Ed Gein was born, so she spared Ed and his brother the licentiousness of city life by moving the family some ninety miles away to the small town of Plainfield. But the ways of Sodom were to be found in this rural village too—or at least, Augusta Gein found them—and they moved again, to an isolated farm. As remote as their new home was, Augusta maintained her crazed vigilance, drumming any hint of carnality out of her sons.

By 1944 both Ed Gein's father and brother had died, leaving Ed to bear the full brunt of Augusta's suffocating mania. It was a burden he was more than willing to bear, for at the age of thirty-eight, he was totally dependent on the woman. When Augusta had a stroke the next year, Ed was her full-time nurse, taking care of her every need, alternately putting up with her verbal abuse and cuddling in bed with her like a little boy. A second stroke came only a few months after the first, and it would ultimately prove fatal.

Augusta Gein died at the end of 1945, but she lived on in Ed's horribly disordered psyche. Madness that had been cultivated for thirty-nine years would now bear grotesque fruit.

All alone in the Gein farmhouse, Ed subsided on occasional handyman jobs and spent much of his time poring over magazine articles on the gruesome details of the Nazi holocaust and the headhunting practices of South Seas tribesmen. He was also fascinated by new advances being made in sex-change surgery. All these interests meshed together in a psychotic muddle when Ed Gein started to make nocturnal visits to local cemeteries.

Gein robbed graves and brought the corpses home to provide himself with the raw material for his insane hobbies. Like the headhunters he had read about, he cut off heads and shrunk them. Like the Nazis, he turned human skin into lampshades. He also came up with his own ideas. The tops of skulls became soup bowls. The dried skin removed from female heads was stuffed and mounted on the walls. As for his sex-change obsession, he arrived at a nonsurgical way of flirting with the transformation that he desired. He would wear a female scalp and face and put on a vest made from the skin of a woman's torso—and then dance outside in the moonlight.

After a few years, Gein decided he didn't necessarily have to get all his corpses from the graveyard. In December 1954 he shot and killed the manager of a nearby tavern, Mary Hogan, a crude, profane woman whom Gein's mother would surely have considered worthy of damnation.

For three more years Gein went along in his demented way, a strange recluse viewed by his fellow Plainfield residents as nothing more than an odd little man. Then, on November 16, 1957, while most of the men in town were out hunting deer, Gein did some hunting of his own. He went into the Plainfield hardware store owned by Bernice Worden and shot the proprietor with a .22-caliber rifle, then drove the woman's body back to his farm.

Later, after finding a receipt in Worden's store that had been made out in Gein's name, local police went out to his house. If they were starting to suspect that there was more to Gein than garden-variety oddness, they still had no way to prepare themselves for what they would see when they looked inside the shed behind the Gein farmhouse. The fifty-eight-year-old Bernice Worden was there, naked, swinging by the ankles, her head and bowels removed. The unspeakable horror was then magnified when the police stepped inside the farmhouse. In addition to all the furnishings, costumes, and implements fashioned from human body parts, they discovered boxes filled with noses and vaginas. Bernice Worden's head was under a mattress; nails driven into her ears were connected by twine, as if the head were to be hung on the wall like a trophy.

Judged mentally unfit to stand trial for ten years, Gein's case was finally disposed of in 1968, when he was ruled not guilty by reason of insanity and was placed in a mental hospital. He died there in 1984.

Soon after the news of the case shocked the nation in 1957, author Robert Bloch wrote a novel inspired by the Gein horrors. This book in turn was the basis for Alfred Hitchcock's 1960 classic *Psycho*, which introduced a new bogeyman to the world of fright films. No longer did such fabled creatures as the vampire, werewolf, and Frankenstein monster seem so terrifying. Much more unnerving was the idea of an isolated man just down the road, harboring gruesome obsessions and willing to act them out. This Gein-inspired nightmare is still with us to this day.

PETER MANUEL
1927–1958

Peter Manuel was a bright child. Educated at Catholic schools in England and Scotland, he displayed both intelligence and creativity. He was especially well-read, capable of consuming such formidable books as the *Decline and Fall of the Roman Empire* while still in his early teens. This appetite for the written word eventually translated into a facility for expressing himself and a reputation as a precocious raconteur. His talent for language would one day prove valuable when he would address a jury and defend himself against eight charges of cold-blooded murder.

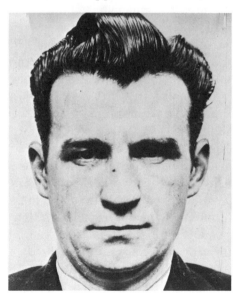

Like his appetite for books, Manuel's compulsion for crime began at an early age. His first burglary arrest came in 1939, when he was twelve. Soon he would begin a revolving-door existence, alternating between petty crimes on the outside and incarceration at increasingly severe penal facilities. Manuel would follow this pattern for the rest of his short life.

Although in the beginning he was primarily a burglar, Manuel occasionally showed an inclination toward violent crime as well. Sexual assault and rape were among the crimes he was convicted for in his late teens, and once, while burglarizing a home, he attacked the occupant with a hammer. In some cases he would ransack homes, then leave the premises without lifting the most obviously valuable items. Something was at work in Peter Manuel's mind other than the simple desire to steal.

As a young man in his twenties, when he was doing neither crime nor time, he lived with his parents in Glasgow and took on various menial jobs. His employers considered him to be a good worker. In the midfifties he also got engaged to a young woman who wasn't aware of his shady past. But the marriage never happened. His fiancee got cold feet when she received an unsigned letter outlining Manuel's almost nonstop record of arrests. The note was sent by Manuel.

His reasons for doing this will never be absolutely clear, but we do know that it was consistent with other things he did: he had a habit of snitching on himself—not always truthfully. Manuel was fond of confessing to celebrated robberies, crimes that were obviously much larger than anything he would have been able to handle. Between robbery confessions, Manuel also fancied himself a high-level espionage informant. At his most grandiose he let it be known that he could supply critical information about Guy Burgess and Donald Maclean, the notorious British diplomats who were exposed as Soviet spies after their defection in 1951.

After these various attempts at notoriety, Manuel started to become genuinely worthy of infamy in 1954 when he began his career in murder. In September of that year, he broke into a boardinghouse room in the Glasgow area and was surprised by the occupant, a prostitute named Helen Carlin. Acting on a sudden violent impulse, he strangled her with one of her stockings. Over the next two years he killed two more women, apparently out of pure homicidal compulsion, as neither crime involved a burglary.

Then, in September 1956 murder was coupled once more with robbery for an especially heinous act. Manuel broke into the house of the Watt family south of Glasgow, shot both the mother, Marion Watt, and her sister, Margaret, in the head while they slept, then went into the room of the Watts' sixteen-year-old daughter. The girl gave him a fight, but he shot her through the head as well. William Watt, the father of the family, was out of town that night. He was subsequently held on suspicion of murder for over two months before finally being set free.

As in the past, Manuel couldn't resist telling a tale. He contacted William Watt's lawyer and told him that he knew the identity of the man responsible for the triple murder. He wasn't willing, however, to come across with the man's name or to tell his story to the police. The lawyer reported Manuel's suspicious behavior to the authorities, who proceeded to investigate Manuel. But they couldn't uncover anything to link him to the murders.

Manuel went on a killing binge in December 1957. He murdered a man on the eighth, a woman on the twentieth, and committed yet another triple murder on New Year's Eve. Once more, the triple murder was committed after breaking into a house. He shot the entire Smart family: father, mother, and their eleven-year-old son. This time he also stole some money, specifically a wad of recently issued pound notes that could be traced to victim Peter Smart. If the police could find someone spending this money, they would be able to identify the killer. As it turned out, the murderer obliged them.

Manuel was known to be broke at the end of December, but right after the Smart murders he was suddenly flush, treating friends and family to drinks and presents wherever he went. After the police had a chance to identify some of the newly issued bills he had spent, they placed Manuel under arrest. Two days later he confessed to most, but not all, of his murders. He went to trial in Glasgow, facing eight homicide counts.

In court he asserted that his confession had been coerced out of him. Then, not trusting anyone else to put this argument across, he fired his attorney and represented himself. He received high marks from the trial judge on his handling of the defense, and he delivered a forceful, if apparently fraudulent, summation to the jury. His gift for expression, however, failed to save him. He was convicted of seven of eight murders and was sentenced to hang.

With nothing left to lose, Manuel now confessed again, this time to three murders with which he hadn't been charged: the prostitute Helen Carlin, killed in September 1954; Anne Steele, a fifty-five-year-old woman bludgeoned to death in her apartment in January 1956; and Ellen Petrie, beaten to death on the street in June 1956. He didn't mention taxi driver Sidney Dunn, shot and slashed in his cab on December 8, 1957. The omission might have been because the murder was committed in England, outside Scottish jurisdiction. But an inquest jury ruled that he had indeed been the culprit.

Manuel, the murderer of as many as twelve people, went to the gallows on July 11, 1958.

HARVEY MURRAY GLATMAN
1928–1959

Lorraine Vigil believed the mousy young man's story that he was a professional photographer. He might have been sort of creepy looking, but Vigil, a twenty-eight-year-old model in a city filled with young models, must have figured that she couldn't afford to be too choosy. She got into Harvey Murray Glatman's car on a September night in 1957 and let him drive her to his studio.

Glatman drove through the southern end of greater Los Angeles, then continued southward, soon leaving the city behind altogether. He passed Anaheim, Garden Grove, and Santa Ana, and still kept going. Something, obviously, was not right. On a remote stretch of road, he

finally pulled over. Then Glatman showed Vigil a handgun.

He said he was going to tie her up.

But Vigil surprised him by grabbing for the gun. They struggled for possession of the weapon in the front seat of the car, then their fight spilled out onto the road's shoulder. Vigil took a bullet in the thigh when the gun accidentally discharged, but she didn't stop fighting until she had the pistol in her hand, pointed at the alleged photographer. She didn't have to keep him there for long. A police car happened by and the attacker was taken into custody.

A subsequent search of Glatman's apartment revealed that the attack on Lorraine Vigil was not an isolated incident. The police found photographs of three young women who had recently disappeared. The pictures were a visual record of sadistic serial murder.

Harvey Murray Glatman was not, in the strict sense of the term, a snuff photographer, but he came all too horribly close. True, he didn't photograph the actual deaths of his female victims, but he took pictures of them bound and gagged, tormented and sick with fear, as they anticipated their terrible fates. He now told the police the story behind these photos, a confession he made willingly, in great detail, and with considerable relish.

The killings had started one month earlier, in August 1957.

Glatman, the owner of a TV repair shop at the time, began to pass off his amateur interest in photography as his bona fide profession. He sought to exploit the Los Angeles pool of underemployed actresses and models by offering them opportunities to pose for magazine covers, professional assignments that Glatman had never acquired. The type of magazines he pretended to work for were the sleazy true-detective publications that were popular at the time. Covers for these magazines inevitably required photos of attractive young women, their wrists and ankles tied. It was only natural that Glatman would be interested in photography that involved binding people with rope—while growing up, he had regarded choking himself with a noose as a sexual thrill.

The first victim Glatman selected for his particular brand of demented murder was a beautiful young model named Judy Dull. She agreed to pose for some bound-and-gagged shots in Glatman's apartment. When Glatman had her trussed up, he raped her twice, then drove her out to the desert, as if he intended to let her go. Instead, he took more photographs of her all tied up. When he had had enough of her, he strangled her with a rope. The second and third victims were Shirley Bridgeford, a young divorcee whom Glatman met through a lonely hearts service, and Ruth Mercado, a model and stripper. He followed the same murderous procedure of rape, bound-and-gagged photography, and strangulation in each case. The photographs of the three women, literally scared for their lives, are profoundly unsettling glimpses of Glatman's sadism.

Perhaps Lorraine Vigil, Glatman's would-be fourth victim, should have been more suspicious of the strange little man when he first proposed to photograph her—as all Glatman's victims should have. But once Glatman had her in his car and out on his desert killing ground, she had decided she was not about to let herself be intimidated into submission during those critical moments when the previous women's fates had been sealed. Vigil's fierce counterattack put an end to Glatman's two-month career of torture and death.

After he was convicted of first-degree murder, Glatman seemed to have no regrets that he had been caught. Perhaps, as has been stated in Colin Wilson's book *The Serial Killers*, Glatman truly did feel tormented by his compulsion to rape and kill. As a way of removing that compulsion forever, he wanted to forgo any appeal and get on with his execution. He got his wish on August 18, 1959, in the gas chamber of San Quentin.

CHARLES STARKWEATHER
1939–1959

On January 21, 1958, Charles Starkweather went to the Bartlett house in Lincoln, Nebraska, with the intention of waiting there for his girlfriend to come home from school. The exact nature of the argument that flared up between Starkweather and the elder Bartletts on that day is not known. Perhaps the exact cause is not important. There was enough deep-seated antipathy between Starkweather and his girlfriend's parents to make an explosive confrontation inevitable.

Nineteen-year-old Starkweather was not any parent's idea of an ideal boyfriend for a young daughter. For one thing he was five years older than Caril Ann Fugate, Velda Bartlett's child from a previous marriage. Something else to put a parent off was his appearance. A self-styled rebel, the short, bowlegged Starkweather went around in scruffy jeans, dungaree jacket, and cowboy boots, with his longish hair combed up and back in the manner of James Dean, his idol. In other words, he struck the pose of the sort of shiftless, rootless youth that most parents in the fifties dreaded.

Appearances, of course, can be deceiving. But Velda Bartlett and her husband, Marion, had no reason to believe that this was the case here. They knew Starkweather was a ninth-grade dropout whose greatest occupational achievement to date had been winning a job as a garbageman. And even that job had proved to be too much for the lazy teenager. Currently unemployed, he had been padlocked out of his boardinghouse room for failure to pay rent. And then, of course, there was also the business with the rifle.

As Starkweather sat in the Bartlett house that afternoon waiting for Caril Ann, he cradled a .22-caliber slide-action hunting rifle, his almost constant companion. He was also fond of his shotgun; it was then in his rundown '49 Ford, which was parked in front of the Bartlett home. The constant proximity of firearms, along with all of Starkweather's other qualities, was enough to make the Bartletts uneasy about this young man. What they didn't know—and what the local police didn't know—was that Starkweather had used the shotgun just seven weeks earlier; he had blown out the brains of a gas-station attendant during the course of a holdup. No doubt if they had been aware of this, the Bartletts would have been more cautious in their treatment of the young psychopathic loner on the afternoon of January 21.

Soon after Starkweather and Velda Bartlett began to exchange heated words, Velda got fed up with the teenager and slapped his face. Starkweather slapped her back. Then the husband, Marion, stepped in. In Starkweather's mind this sequence of actions constituted a threat. He fatally shot and stabbed the couple.

Caril Ann came home around this time. Whether or not the fourteen-year-old actually witnessed her parents' murders has been a point contested over the years. In any case, Starkweather's rampage wasn't yet done for the day. Still in the house was Caril Ann's two-year-old half-sister, Betty Jean. Starkweather beat the child with his rifle butt, then slashed her throat. After stashing the three bodies around the property, he decided he was hungry and went into the kitchen to make some sandwiches, then joined Caril Ann on the couch. She had been whiling away the time watching TV.

For six days Starkweather and Fugate fended off nosy relatives with the story that the entire Bartlett family was sick with the flu. They made the murder house their little teenage love nest. According to Starkweather's later confession, "We knowed that the world had give us to each other. We was goin' to make it leave us alone."

Starkweather was determined to maintain that resolution as he and his underage lover hit the road in his '49 Ford on January 27. Over the next three days he killed seven people. The first of them was seventy-year-old farmer August Meyer. Starkweather blasted him in the head with his shotgun, apparently because he was frustrated that his car had gotten stuck in the snow on Meyer's property. From there he and Fugate hitched a ride with a wholesome high-school couple. Starkweather took them to a nearby deserted storm cellar, shot the seventeen-year-old boy in the head six times, then raped and shot to death the sixteen-year-old girl. Taking his victims' car, Starkweather drove with Fugate to the well-to-do section of Lincoln. He and his girlfriend then broke into the house of C. Lauer Ward, a steel company president. He killed Ward, as well as the man's wife and housekeeper. Now Starkweather had Ward's luxury Packard to drive. He used it to escape a massive manhunt. While the police and National Guard staked out the southeastern portion of the state, Starkweather and Fugate headed west into Wyoming.

Starkweather's final killing led to his capture. He pulled the Packard over to the side of the road outside the town of Douglas, and thinking the time had come to get a new vehicle, he approached another car parked nearby. Inside was Merle Collison, a traveling salesman from Montana who was taking some time out for a nap. Starkweather shot him nine times. When he tried to start the car, however, he couldn't release the emergency brake. A driver came to his assistance, not seeing the body of Collison until he was right next to the killer. He and Starkweather started fighting for possession of the killer's rifle. The fight ended when a deputy sheriff drove onto the scene.

Fugate, who had been with Starkweather throughout his insane murder spree, now ran to the lawman, yelling that Starkweather was a killer and had to be arrested. Before the deputy sheriff could make a move, Starkweather jumped into the Packard and sped off. With the assistance of other officers, the deputy sheriff overtook him after a high-speed chase.

In custody Starkweather readily confessed to all eleven murders and was even willing to shield Fugate from any guilt. But her subsequent claims that she had been nothing more than a blameless hostage proved too much for him. He went on to maintain that she had been an eager accomplice in his crimes.

This discrepancy between their stories would not be legally resolved for many years. In 1958 the courts were not willing to believe Fugate's protests of innocence and convicted her of first-degree murder, the same charge of which Starkweather had been found guilty. Their sentences, however, were not the same. Starkweather was electrocuted on June 24, 1959. Fugate was sent to prison for life. But by the seventies a groundswell of sympathy had arisen for the woman who had been imprisoned since the age of fourteen, and the Nebraska Parole Board came to share that sentiment. Caril Ann Fugate was released in June 1976. She told reporters that all she wanted was unexceptional domesticity: "I just want to be an ordinary dumpy little housewife."

MELVIN DAVID REES

1933–1961

"The Sex Beast"

Glenn Moser of Norfolk, Virginia, didn't have any serious doubts about his friend Melvin David Rees until January 10, 1959. Until then, Rees had seemed to be a bright, talented young man, somewhat rootless, perhaps, but that was one of those things that went along with his friend's chosen profession as an itinerant jazz musician. But on January 10 Moser had a strange conversation with Rees.

Rees, speeding on Benzedrine at the time, started talking about murder. He had an opinion on the subject that was unusual, to say the least. "You can't say it's wrong to kill," he told Moser. "Only individual standards make it right or wrong."

Future events in the Middle Atlantic region made Moser wonder about the significance of his friend's curious comment. The next day, January 11, a family by the name of Jackson disappeared while driving home from a visit with relatives; the car they had been driving was found abandoned along the side of the road. Two months later, the bodies of Carroll Jackson, the father, and his one-and-a-half-year-old daughter, Janet, were found in a ditch outside Fredericksburg, Virginia. The father had been shot through the head and had been heaved into the ditch on top of the baby, who was subsequently smothered to death under her father's weight. Less than three weeks later, outside Annapolis, Maryland, the bodies of Mildred Jackson, the mother, and Susan Jackson, the five-year-old daughter, were also discovered. The mother had evidently been raped several times before being murdered, either by strangulation or savage bludgeoning—the physical evidence was ambiguous. The child had been beaten to death.

The timing of the Jacksons' abduction, coming as it did a day after Rees's amoral philosophizing about murder, disconcerted Glenn Moser. He confronted Rees, asked him outright if he was responsible for the Jackson killings. Rees's response could not have been more suspicious: he would not give a direct answer.

Moser considered the implications of all this. If Rees was involved in the Jackson murders, there was reason to believe he might have been involved in at least one other murder as well, because by this time the police were linking the Jackson murders to an earlier killing of a young woman named Margaret Harold. Harold had been found, shot in the head and sexually violated after death, near the spot where the bodies of Mildred and Susan Jackson had been uncovered. In May 1959 Moser decided to notify the police of his suspicions through an anonymous letter.

The police were eager to have a plausible suspect in this perplexing string of vicious homicides, but a large obstacle remained in their way before they could investigate this man Rees any further: Rees, the footloose musician, had left the area, and no one knew his present whereabouts. For the rest of the year, the trail was cold. Then Moser received a letter from his musician friend, informing Moser that Rees was working as a piano salesman in West Memphis, Arkansas. Moser forwarded the letter to the police.

Through the FBI Rees was picked up on suspicion of murder. An eyewitness helped to make the charge more definite: a young man who had been with Margaret Harold the night she was killed—and had just managed to escape death himself—selected Rees out of a police lineup. A search of the home of Rees's parents in Hyattsville, Maryland, produced more damning evidence. In a saxophone case the police found a .38 revolver that was later determined to be the weapon used to kill Carroll Jackson. They also discovered a sort of murderer's journal, in the form of notes scribbled on pieces of paper, that provided a glimpse into the calculation and cruelty that went into Rees's crimes. Of the Jackson murders he wrote: "Caught on a lonely road. . . . Drove to a select [sic] area and killed the husband and baby. Now the mother and daughter were all mine. . . ." Still, the police had not unearthed all of Rees's misdeeds.

As the police continued to follow new leads, they concluded that the Jackson and Harold homicides were probably just the tip of the iceberg of Rees's murderous activities. The authorities came to believe that Rees was also the culprit behind the brutal murders of four teenage girls in Maryland that had taken place over the previous few years. As more became known about the case, the newspapers dubbed Rees "the Sex Beast."

The overwhelming evidence in the case of the Margaret Harold killing produced a conviction and life prison sentence in Maryland. After extradition to Virginia, Rees was then tried for the Jackson family murders. Here he was convicted again. This time he was sentenced to death. Rees was executed in 1961.

PENNY BJORKLAND

1941–

Penny Bjorkland had the sort of open, wholesome face that one would expect to find in the high school yearbook of a mythical Anytown, U.S.A. Blue-eyed and freckled, with blonde hair tied back into a ponytail, she seemed to be a perfect model of the squeaky-clean youthful

ideal of the Eisenhower era. Even years later in prison she would maintain to a reporter that she still considered herself "a normal, average girl." Those people observing her in high school might have noticed something slightly awry about her—she was highly nervous, a nail-biter, something of a loner, and was once disciplined for having a container of vodka and orange juice in her locker—but there was nothing about Bjorkland that was ominous, at least not without the benefit of hindsight.

At the beginning of 1959, there was little reason to suspect that, beneath the quiet, industrious appearance, something curious was going on with this eighteen-year-old girl. On February 2, 1959, local police discovered the ultimate consequence of her mind's secret workings.

On that day the body of a man named August Norry was found in the Daly City hills south of San Francisco. As far as the police could ascertain, Norry seemed to have been a harmless enough fellow. He was a twenty-eight-year-old landscaper, married, and was about to become a father for the first time. He had a reputation as a ladies' man, but other than that, the police could come up with little about the man that would indicate why anyone would have fired eighteen bullets into him.

The barrage of anonymous tips that the police soon received didn't shed any more light on what seemed to be a motiveless murder. The only useful clues were the testimony of a boy who had seen a "freckle-faced blonde" driving Norry's car "like mad" away from the hills, and the .38-caliber bullets found in Norry's body. After two months of exhaustive legwork, the police found their "freckle-faced blonde" by tracing the bullets—made from a highly distinctive mold—to the man who remembered selling a box of ammunition to Penny Bjorkland. When the police picked up Bjorkland at her parents' comfortable Daly City home, they may have had a prime suspect, but there were still many questions.

Bjorkland's confession the next morning provided some of the answers.

She had stolen a .38-caliber revolver from a friend's bedroom sometime in January, Bjorkland explained. When she left her house on the bright Sunday morning of February 1, with the army-issue handgun tucked into the waistband of her pedal pushers, her ideas about what she would do with the gun were still vague. They began to take more definite shape when she reached the Daly City hills and met August Norry.

Norry offered to give her a lift in his car. When she was in the passenger seat, Bjorkland came to a decision. She got out of the car, faced Norry, and fired five shots into him. Circling around the rear of the car, she took out fresh ammunition from her purse and reloaded. When she reached the driver's window, she emptied her chambers into Norry once more. Still she wasn't done. She returned to the passenger side and pumped more rounds into her victim before finally dragging him out of the car. In another moment she was behind the wheel, driving away from the hills.

One vital question remained: what reason could this pretty, polite teenager have had for firing eighteen rounds into a seemingly harmless gardener? From the beginning Norry's murder appeared senseless; Bjorkland's explanation made it seem even more so.

"For about a year or a year and a half I've had the urge to kill someone," she said—with some embarrassment, according to a reporter covering the case. "I'll admit that the motive sounds crazy," she went on. "But I wanted to know if a person could commit a crime like this and not worry about police looking for her or have it on her conscience." According to the ponytailed killer, there was something good, after all, to be found in this deadly affair: "I've felt better since I killed him," she said.

The police conjectured that August Norry's reputation as a ladies' man might have been a factor in the killing. Bjorkland told the police that, yes, she had met Norry once before. It seems that one day in January, while in the same Daly City hills where she would later commit murder, she ran into Norry while the landscaper was unloading some lawn clippings. They talked for a while, stopped off at a drive-in restaurant for some food, and then he drove her home. Consistent with his womanizing reputation, the married Norry had told her that he was single. Groping for some understandable motive, the police asked Bjorkland if Norry had sexually molested her in any way. She shook her head no.

Despite subsequent psychiatric examinations of Bjorkland, nothing more substantial was learned about her motivations.

Bjorkland's behavior during her trial only succeeded in making her seem more puzzling. Since she pleaded guilty, the only task before the court was to determine what sort of punishment would be appropriate. According to the *San Francisco Chronicle* reporter covering the trial, these proceedings didn't seem to concern Bjorkland a great deal; her conduct was described as one of "giggling disinterest." That behavior ended, though, when she heard the verdict. Judge Blum pronounced her guilty of murder in the first degree and sentenced her to life imprisonment. Bjorkland was stunned.

"I am unhappy," she informed reporters.

HEINRICH POMMERENCKE
1937–
"The Beast of the Black Forest"

In recent years much attention has been focused on the role movies and television play in the rising rate of violent crime. Many people have argued that horror films and action movies brutalize the minds of young people and perhaps even trigger real-life violence. "The Beast of the Black Forest" murders of the late fifties would seem to be a case that supports this point of view. It provided an example of a homicidal mind being set off by a night at the movies—but not necessarily in a way that

fits the usual pattern of cause-
and-effect cited by today's social
activists.

The killer in this case, a
young German named Heinrich
Pommerencke, did not have his
senses assaulted by a gory monster movie; neither did he have
his social inhibitions undermined
by the incessant violence of an
irresponsible crime melodrama.
On a February night in 1959,
Heinrich Pommerencke's murderous impulses were apparently
unleashed by an inspirational
biblical epic.

When twenty-two-year-old
Pommerencke went to see Cecil B. deMille's The Ten Commandments in
the West German city of Karlsruhe, he was already a drifter and
habitual criminal. But his crimes up until that point did not include
murder. Then something happened while he sat in that darkened theater. On the screen, Charlton Heston as Moses ascended Mount Sinai to
receive his God's laws, while in the valley below the Hebrews gave in
to temptation and began worshiping a golden calf instead of the true
deity. Their new religion was a hedonistic cult. Pommerencke watched
transfixed as women on the screen danced wildly, lost to sensual
abandon. He was overwhelmed by an obsessive thought. As he later
put it, "I saw women dancing around the golden calf and I thought they
were a fickle lot. I knew I would have to kill."

This sort of thinking about women, of course, did not actually
originate in that movie theater on that particular night. Pommerencke
had been a sex offender since the age of fifteen, first in a series of
attempted rapes in his native Mecklenburg, then later, between robberies, in a sequence of seven full-blown sexual assaults in Hamburg. But
as he watched The Ten Commandments in February 1959, his disordered mind took a quantum jump to a deeper, darker resentment of
females. He wasted no time in putting this new hatred to work.

Upon leaving the Karlsruhe theater, he bought a razor and walked the streets until he spotted a young woman whom he felt should be his first victim. He stalked her down a lonely street and attacked her, but when a taxicab came onto the scene, he ran off before he could finish the deadly job. Soon, however, Pommerencke found another victim to his liking. He knocked her down and dragged her to the dark corner of a nearby park. Then he ripped off her clothes, raped her, and slit her throat.

In the next few months Pommerencke proceeded with his insane revenge against women, roaming through the nearby Black Forest region as he picked out his targets. His basic method remained the same, a combination of ferocious rape and murder. In one case he cornered a young woman on an Italy-bound train and heaved her out of a doorway onto the side of the tracks. After pulling the emergency-stop cord, he bounded after her to complete the rape-murder on her then-unconscious body. Subsequent murder attempts, fortunately, failed, but kept the specter of "the Beast of the Black Forest" fixed in the public mind.

The police could find no useful clues for solving the savage killings. Ultimately, it was Pommerencke's compulsion to commit robbery that brought him to the attention of the law—that and what may have been a desire to get caught.

On a summer day in 1960, Pommerencke the drifter was passing through the town of Hornberg. He had previously placed an order with a local tailor for a new suit and now went to the tailor's shop to pick up the garment. Choosing to wear the new clothes, he arranged with the tailor to leave behind his old suit and his briefcase as he went off to take care of some errands. The tailor noticed something bulky in the briefcase and upon closer examination found that inside was a rifle with a sawed-off barrel. He contacted the police. Pommerencke was apprehended as he returned to the tailor's shop later in the day.

Pommerencke may have actually wanted the tailor to notice the customized weapon. As he later put it, he wanted some way to "undo" his sadistic crimes. But even so, he made some effort to conceal his worst offenses from the police.

The Hornberg authorities knew that a similar sawed-off rifle had been used in a railroad station holdup in a nearby town the day before. Pommerencke confessed to this robbery, as well as to three other holdups. But he denied any involvement in rapes and murders that had taken place in the vicinity of the robberies. He was eventually tricked into a confession when a policeman falsely claimed that bloodstains on Pommerencke's old suit had been matched with the blood of Black Forest murder victims. Convinced that he was trapped, Pommerencke decided the time had come to tell all, which he did in great detail. The murderous rampage that had begun with the showing of a Cecil B. deMille extravaganza had finally come to an end.

At his trial Pommerencke was convicted of four rape-murders, as well as twelve attempted murders and various other felony charges. He received a minimum prison sentence of 140 years.

ERIC COOKE
1931–1964

On January 27, 1963, a nightmare began for the Australian city of Perth. The sudden terror erupted on a dark, secluded road, where a businessman sat in his parked car with a young woman. They just happened to catch a glimpse of a man standing on the other side of the car window before the gun in the man's hand went off. Only one shot was fired. The bullet went through both of them, leaving them wounded but alive. In the next instant the attacker disappeared into the night. He had other deadly work ahead of him in other parts of the city.

People weren't safe in their homes that night. A young accountant was shot while lying in bed and was unable to get help for himself for several hours. His predicament was finally discovered the next morning. He would survive, but others would not be so lucky. Sometime in the night, a nineteen-year-old student named John Sturkey, also in his bedroom, was fatally shot in the head. At 4:00 A.M., George Walmsley was awakened by a knock at his front door. Groggy and baffled by this interruption in the middle of the night, he made it to the door and swung it open. A gunshot cracked from the other side of the threshold. The bullet smashed through his forehead and he dropped to the floor. He was soon dead.

Five shootings in one night. Two fatalities. All the wounds, the police determined, were made by bullets from a .22-caliber rifle. It seemed that the rampage had been carried out by one crazed assassin.

The description provided by the couple in the parked car wasn't detailed enough to significantly narrow the investigation's scope, so the police concentrated on what they knew about the murder weapon. They began tracking down .22 rifles and ran tests to see if any matched the ballistics report on the shootings. This was a long, tedious procedure that pulled in some sixty thousand rifles without turning up the weapon that the police were trying to find.

Months later, on August 10, the gunman emerged from the night to strike once more. True to unsettling form, a young woman was shot fatally through the head with a .22 round while baby-sitting some neighbors' children. And once again, the killer left the scene without a trace.

A week later, the police finally got a break. A rifle was accidentally discovered along a bush-lined walkway. It was matched to the murder of the baby-sitter seven days earlier, but not to the January 27 rampage. With nothing else to go on, the police operated on the assumption that the killer had not discarded the rifle, but had only left it to be retrieved later. Substituting another .22 rifle in the spot where the weapon had been found, the police began a stakeout of the area.

Two weeks went by, raising the frustrating possibility that the killer might have no further use for the gun after all. Then, on the fifteenth day, a young man showed up, went directly to the rifle's hiding place, and picked it up. The police had their man; a thirty-two-year-old truck driver named Eric Cooke. He wasted little time in helping the authorities. Not only did he confess to the baby-sitter murder, but he also led the police to the nearby Swan River, where they found the .22 rifle he had used for the five shootings on January 27.

But while he was helpful in assembling the evidence that would eventually convict him of three murders, Cooke was not especially illuminating when it came to explaining what was behind his seemingly random violence.

Not too surprisingly, Cooke grew up in Perth as a loner. Once, after learning that he had not been accepted into a congregational choir, he set fire to the congregation's church. In addition to arson, burglary also figured into his crimes over the years. As for his involvement with firearms, a hitch with the Australian army in the Korean War gave him practical experience. Other than these facts, however, not much else that seemed to bear any relation to his crimes came to light. When asked to explain what had turned him toward serial murder, he said, with a flair for understatement, that he "just wanted to hurt somebody."

After receiving the death sentence, Cooke injected some confusion into the case by admitting to a murder that dated back to 1959. This earlier killing involved the savage stabbing of a young woman named Jillian Brewster while she slept in bed. The authorities were put in a difficult position. A deaf-mute by the name of Darryl Beamish had already been convicted of the Brewster murder in 1961, despite his attempt to retract a confession that he claimed had been given under duress. After Cooke's confession to the Brewster murder, Beamish filed an appeal, but his conviction was still upheld.

On October 26, 1964, Eric Cooke was hanged. Seven years later, Darryl Beamish was released on parole.

ALBERT DESALVO

1931–1973

"The Boston Strangler"

Albert DeSalvo grew up with brutality. In his home in the Boston suburb of Chelsea, he, his five siblings, and his mother were victims of a reign of terror waged by his father. Once, Albert was clubbed across the back with a lead pipe for not moving fast enough. Another time, when Albert was seven, he watched as his father took a firm hold of his mother's hand and proceeded to bend back her fingers until they were all broken. Before long, Albert himself became a sadist. One game of his

was to put a starving dog and cat together in an orange crate so he could watch the cat scratch the dog's eyes out.

By the time Albert DeSalvo was a teenager, his career in crime had started with a series of arrests for breaking and entering. His sexual criminality, which would dominate his later life, came to the fore a few years later, when he was in the army. At that time he was indicted for allegedly entering a family home while the parents were out, and molesting a nine-year-old girl. He was released when the mother of the victim decided not to pursue the case.

Returning to Boston, DeSalvo made a living as a blue-collar worker, settled down with his wife and two children, and generally maintained a facade that concealed another, secret life. DeSalvo could be as charming as he was antisocial, and he used this ability to talk his way into women's apartments, where he would fondle them under the pretense of taking their measurements for a modeling agency. Known to the police as "the Measuring Man," he was arrested in 1960. Eleven months later he was back on the streets. Up until then, he had proven himself to be sexually out of control, but he had no violent criminal record. In 1962, when he was thirty-one, DeSalvo's tormented psyche took the next quantum leap.

On June 14 he talked his way into the apartment of Anna Slessers. That night her son found the fifty-five-year-old woman obscenely posed on the floor, practically naked, her legs apart. A bathrobe cord, which had been used to strangle her, was still around her neck, knotted into a crude, ornamental bow. This bow would prove to be DeSalvo's cryptic signature over the next eighteen months. In that time he would kill thirteen women.

As a rule, DeSalvo managed to get into his victims' apartments by claiming he was a handyman sent by the building superintendent to do some repairs. All the victims were strangled, usually with nylon stockings that were then tied into the characteristic bow, but DeSalvo wasn't always content with this. Some of the women were raped, others were sexually assaulted with bottles and broomsticks.

DeSalvo's first five victims were older women, one as old as seventy-five. Then, beginning in December 1962, five out of the next seven victims were young, between the ages of nineteen and twenty-three. Some psychiatrists who were recruited to assist the Boston Strangler investigation believed that the new victim profile meant that a second strangler was now at large. But according to one psychiatrist, this shift to young women was just the original strangler's deranged way of working through one sexual obsession to another. Whatever the psychological meaning of the new set of victims, the significance to Boston's general population was very clear and very frightening: all women were now fair game for the mysterious killer.

As DeSalvo started to prey upon younger women, his methods became more grisly. Twenty-three-year-old Beverly Samans, for instance, was stabbed twenty-two times. Nineteen-year-old Mary Sullivan, the final victim, was perhaps the most bizarre case. She was left sitting against the headboard of her bed, her knees up, with semen dripping from her face, a pink scarf tied in a bow around her neck, and a broomstick handle inserted into her vagina. Against her left foot DeSalvo had placed a Happy New Year card.

Around this time, DeSalvo was also indulging in nonlethal rapes. Once known as the Measuring Man, then "the Boston Strangler," he now cultivated a third identity, "the Green Man," because of the green work pants he wore during these attacks. Eventually one of his rape victims was able to give the police a description that led to his arrest. He was not, however, suspected of being a murderer at this time. Only when he began boasting about his strangling career to a fellow psychiatric inmate at Bridgewater State Hospital did the police finally realize they had accidentally caught Boston's most infamous killer.

Through an unusual arrangement engineered by famed trial lawyer F. Lee Bailey, DeSalvo was tried as the Green Man, rather than as the Boston Strangler, and was sentenced for life, thus avoiding the electric chair. Since DeSalvo was never convicted of murder, some have raised doubts about his being the true Boston Strangler. DeSalvo's confession, however, provided many details about the killings that would have been difficult, if not impossible, for anyone who had not been there to know. In any case, no other suspect has been seriously pursued. Any possibility of further information from DeSalvo was eliminated in 1973 when he was stabbed to death in Walpole State Prison. DeSalvo's killer was never found.

Ian Brady
1938–

Myra Hindley
1942–

"The Moors Murderers"

In 1961 Myra Hindley started work as a typist for Millwards, a chemical supply company in Manchester, the industrial center of northwestern England. The eighteen-year-old Hindley was an ordinary working-class girl, with ordinary boy troubles: despite her hopes for marriage, she had recently broken off an engagement because she had decided that her fiance was, in her words, "immature." Once at Millwards, though, she found the new love of her life, one that she would worship from afar for the next year.

Ian Brady, a Millwards stock clerk, bore the stamp of the angry-young-man-type that became a fixture of English life in the fifties and sixties. He wore black shirts. He slicked his hair back in an Elvis Presley pompadour. His mouth was down-turned and sullen. An illegitimate child born in the slums of Glasgow, he had a criminal record to go with the surly appearance. Starting at the age of thirteen, he had been arrested several times for petty theft and had been imprisoned for a year when he was eighteen. As a boy, he had also became known in his neighborhood as a sadist who liked to torture cats.

To Myra Hindley, however, he was irresistible. Her diary was filled with such sentiments as "I hope he loves me and will marry me some

day." After a year a part of Hindley's romantic daydream came true when Brady finally asked the heavy-featured young woman for a date.

Within a week they were having sex, and before long Brady was staying nights with Hindley at her grandmother's house. As the affair progressed, Hindley's infatuation with Brady deepened. Brady might not have reciprocated her starry-eyed devotion, but he recognized that Hindley certainly had her uses as far as he was concerned: the love-struck young woman was highly malleable. Brady tutored her in his chief interests: drinking, Naziism, and the philosophy of the Marquis de Sade. He convinced her to give up religion and made it clear that there was to be no marriage, which he considered "bourgeois nonsense." When he bought a camera and a timing device, they started taking pornographic pictures of themselves, sometimes with a flagellation theme.

In 1963 Brady decided that payroll robberies would be the best way to strike back at what he considered bourgeois society. The two began making preparations. Hindley even purchased a handgun for her lover, but the heists never happened. Instead, Brady and Hindley turned to another form of crime. They started killing people—very young people.

On the evening of July 12, 1963, sixteen-year-old Pauline Reade was on her way to a dance. Hindley pulled up beside the girl in a van and persuaded her to take a ride to Saddleworth Moor. Brady followed on his motorbike. Years later, when Reade's body was finally dug out of the moors, police discovered that the teenager had been raped and her throat had been slit.

Hindley had proved her devotion to Brady by rejecting her religious background, by adopting Nazi ideas, by submitting to pornographic photo sessions. Participation in the murder of Pauline Reade, it seems, was just another way to live her life for Ian Brady. And the partnership in murder would continue. In November 1963 John Kilbride, age twelve, disappeared following an afternoon at the movies. In June 1964 Keith Bennett, another twelve-year-old, vanished on the way to his grandmother's house. The day after Christmas of that year, ten-year-old Lesley Anne Downey dropped out of sight while spending the day at a fairground. Like Pauline Reade, they all ended up buried on the moor.

While Hindley's assistance helped Brady transform his twisted, murderous ideas into a grisly reality, he was not content with just one follower. Sometime in 1964, he came to know an impressionable six-teen-year-old named David Smith, recently married to Hindley's younger sister. A young man who already had a petty criminal record, Smith looked up to Brady, and Brady in turn began to teach Smith the way of the world as he saw it. A reflection of Brady's philosophy can be seen in the aphorisms that Smith jotted down in his diary at the time: "God is a disease, a plague, a weight around a man's neck." "People are like maggots, small, blind and worthless, fish bait."

By the fall of 1965, the time had come to make Smith an active partner. On the evening of October 6, Brady and Hindley met Edward Evans, a seventeen-year-old homosexual, at a Manchester pub and convinced him to come home with them for drinks. Hindley then went to get Smith. They arrived just in time to see Brady bludgeon Evans fourteen times with an ax and strangle the young man with an electric cord. "It's the messiest yet," Brady told Smith after the deed was done. "It normally takes one blow." Brady and Hindley got Smith to help them mop up the blood, but Smith's participation ended there. Sickened by what he had seen, he called the police the next morning. When they made the arrest, the police found Evans's body still in the house, along with other evidence linking Brady and Hindley to previous murders.

Public outrage over the heinous crimes was so great that the homicidal couple were protected during their trial by four-inch-thick bullet-proof glass. The horrifying highlight of the proceedings was the playing of an audiotape recorded while Brady and Hindley held Lesley Anne

Downey captive in their house. The ten-year-old girl could be heard screaming and begging for mercy as she was forced to pose for pornographic photos; sometime after this recording session, the girl was strangled. Later in the trial, when Brady was on the witness stand, he was asked how he reacted to the tape. He said it was "embarrassing."

Brady and Hindley, the lovers who loved to kill, were convicted of the murders of Edward Evans and Lesley Anne Downey, while Brady was found individually guilty for the killing of John Kilbride. They both received life sentences. In recent years Hindley has claimed that she had been Brady's unwilling accomplice and had never taken part in the actual killings. Brady countered by saying that Hindley had been an equal partner in murder, asserting that she had, in fact, been the one to strangle Downey with a silk cord. Later, he said, the ordinary working-class girl from Manchester would toy with the cord in public. According to Brady, this was her secret way of flaunting the ten-year-old's murder.

JACK THE STRIPPER
1964–1965

Like other unsolved serial murders, even the beginning of the Jack the Stripper case is open to question. Some writers point to a killing dating back to 1959. In June of that year, the body of a strangled woman was discovered floating in the Thames River in London. Another corpse, whose cause of death went undetermined, was uncovered four years later and represented the second of the murders, according to this theory. The official police version of the so-called Thames Nude Murders does not include these two victims, instead starting the grisly body count in 1964 when the corpses began to appear at a faster clip. Even if the more conservative assessment is accepted, Jack the Stripper's homicidal handiwork was frightening and frequent.

All the victims were young women, most of them between the ages of twenty and twenty-two, and all were prostitutes. The last fact invoked memories of the legendary Jack the Ripper, and the new killer consequently became his paraphrased namesake. True to his moniker, Jack the Stripper left most of his victims naked; contrary to the Thames

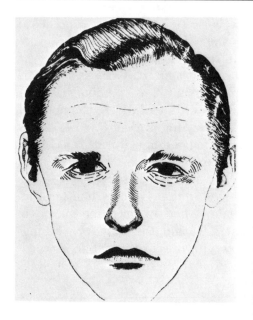

Nude Murders label, however, only three of the women were found in the river, and then only if one accepts the 1959 killing as part of the case. In most instances the cause of death was asphyxiation of some kind. Some of the women were strangled, but not all, leaving a question mark as to the murder method when strangulation was not apparent. Sperm was found in the throats of the last four victims, and based upon this discovery, a particularly grotesque *modus operandi* was theorized: the killer may have asphyxiated some of the women through forced, and especially violent, fellatio. In a year's time, starting in February 1964, Jack the Stripper was responsible for six deaths.

Early in the police's investigation, a man named Kenneth Archibald stepped forward to confess, but nothing came of this development. After he retracted the confession at his trial, he was acquitted, a sensible decision considering that the murders continued while Archibald was in custody. As with so many crank confessions that materialize during the investigation of well-known murder cases, Archibald had a flimsy motivation: he admitted to the Thames killing, he explained, because he was depressed at the time.

A rash of information from prostitutes about sexual deviants they had encountered didn't lead to anything either. Physical evidence found on some of the bodies, though, provided a clue of sorts. Flakes of paint were discovered on a few of the victims, and the police speculated that the bodies might have been kept near a spray-paint shop before they were discarded, and launched a massive hunt for this location. By comparing a chemical analysis of the paint flakes with paint used in all the London shops that were investigated, the location was finally pinpointed after the final murder in February 1965. The paint shop was near the site of the last killing.

For all their exhaustive work, the police did not get any nearer to an arrest. But the case may have been solved in another, roundabout way. The head of the investigation, a highly respected inspector named John Du Rose, kept the public abreast of the progress his team was making, going so far as to publicize the numbers of suspects and how short the list was getting. He was trying to get under the killer's skin; the more pressure he exerted, Du Rose figured, the more likely it would be that he would force the killer's hand. There is reason to believe he succeeded after announcing that the number of suspects had been narrowed down from twenty to three.

When it seemed like the murders might have stopped, Du Rose ran a check on all those men who had been arrested or had died since the last killing, thinking that Jack the Stripper might be out of circulation. One of the deaths that was uncovered was the suicide of a security guard who worked near the site of the last corpse discovery. The man also had access to the room alongside the paint shop located by the police. The man's suicide note stated that he couldn't "stand the strain any longer." The end of the Nude Murders, coinciding as it did with this suicide, supports the idea that the unnamed security guard might indeed have been Jack the Stripper. But a search of the man's home did not turn up any physical evidence that could further connect him to the killings.

The conclusion to the case would not get any more definite than that.

CHARLES SCHMID
1942–1975
"The Pied Piper of Tucson"

The phone call to the Tucson police came from Columbus, Ohio, more than fifteen hundred miles away, but the caller was Tucson native Richard Bruns, a young man with something to say about a local matter. Bruns had recently left his hometown with a problem weighing heavily on his mind, a problem he finally decided to reveal after reaching his grandmother's Ohio home. He wanted to tell the police about a friend of his.

Three months earlier, in August 1965, Bruns had been spending time with an older friend, twenty-three-year-old Charles Schmid, who started talking about the recent disappearance of two teenage girls.

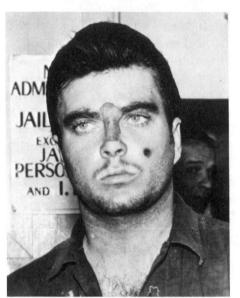 Schmid told a tall tale, as was his habit—or at least it seemed like a tale at first. As if he were bragging, Schmid told Bruns that he had killed the two girls. Bruns knew Schmid to be capable of all sorts of wildness, but he wasn't ready to believe the young man was *that* crazy. Then Schmid drove Bruns out to the desert and took him to a ditch where two decomposing corpses were sprawled. They were the bodies of Gretchen Fritz, age seventeen, and her thirteen-year-old sister, Wendy, the two girls who had vanished.

Calling from Ohio, Bruns now admitted to the police that, for the past three months, he had told no one in authority about what he had seen. As it turned out, Bruns had not been the only one to keep silent. Other young friends of Schmid had also known about the murders and had kept quiet. What prodded Bruns into finally coming forward now was his growing fear of Schmid. He was afraid that Schmid was going to kill again. Bruns's girlfriend had once insulted Schmid, and Bruns believed Schmid would consider that a killing offense.

Tucson police arrested Charles Schmid on November 11, 1965. As they gathered evidence and testimony, the authorities attributed a third murder to Schmid. The newspapers, meanwhile, latched onto the story, finding key sensational qualities in the case that were perfect for boosting newsstand sales: sex, wild rock 'n' roll youth, and a complete disregard for human life. As for Schmid himself, he became known as "the Pied Piper of Tucson," a man with a strange hold over a group of teenagers who were apparently willing to do anything for him. The story behind the bizarre murders had begun a few years earlier.

Schmid was a peculiar young man. After finishing high school, he had attracted attention by cultivating an irreverent, hedonistic image all his own. He dyed his red hair raven black (in the manner of Elvis Presley and other teen idols of the late fifties and early sixties), and applied cosmetic cream to his face in order to create an artificial complexion. He also spun yarns. The five-foot–three-inch Schmid boasted of fantastic sexual exploits; he claimed to be the kingpin of an enormous teen prostitute ring; he maintained he was a veteran of violent run-ins with mafiosi. He was determined to become a sort of underground youth hero, and in that he was certainly successful. A clique of Tucson teens collected around him, including a large number of infatuated girls, who would either go out with him individually or participate in orgies at his cottage bachelor pad. One of these girls, Mary Rae French, was so taken with Schmid that she handed over most of her weekly paycheck to him.

One night in 1964, while getting drunk with Mary Rae French and John Saunders, one of his male admirers, Schmid the thrill-seeker thought of a new way to get kicks and dazzle his followers. He made it known that the time had come to kill a girl. Apparently, French and Saunders didn't need much persuading. French convinced a fifteen-year-old girl in her neighborhood named Alleen Rowe to come out for a drive. Schmid and his two sidekicks drove Rowe to a lonely spot in the desert.

Schmid, accompanied by Saunders, took a walk with Rowe, away from the car. Schmid raped her. Then he picked up a heavy rock and smashed Rowe's head into a bloody pulp.

For over a year this thrill-killing satisfied Schmid's desire for new sensations. His second fling at murder came after some trouble cropped up in his relationship with Gretchen Fritz. The seventeen-year-old was one of Schmid's girlfriends. Some writers have suggested that Schmid decided to kill her because she was becoming too possessive; others have said that he murdered her because she had a sexual escapade with another young man. Whatever the motive, Schmid came upon Gretchen and her kid sister, Wendy, at a drive-in movie on the night of August 11, 1965, and used his considerable powers of persuasion to get them to take a ride out to the desert. After strangling both of them, he discarded their bodies in a ditch.

Once the grisly deed was done, Schmid's boasting about the double murder made it seem like this was yet another thrill-killing. But ultimately Schmid found he wasn't quite the cavalier killer that he claimed to be. One night, he started running wildly around his cottage, yelling again and again, "God is going to punish me!"

After Richard Bruns's call put the police onto Schmid, Mary French and John Saunders were also arrested for their part in the Alleen Rowe murder. The two accomplices supplied valuable testimony that helped ensure Schmid's conviction. For the Rowe killing he received a prison sentence of fifty years to life; for the double murder he got the death penalty. Thanks to a series of appeals, Schmid's execution was stalled long enough for the Supreme Court's 1971 decision against capital punishment to save his life. But prison proved to have mortal dangers of its own. On March 20, 1975, Schmid got embroiled in a fight among inmates and died of twenty stab wounds.

GERTRUDE BANISZEWSKI
1929–
"The Torture Mother"

The body of sixteen-year-old Sylvia Likens was brought to the attention of the Indianapolis police on October 26, 1965. After receiving an emergency call about a girl who had stopped breathing, the police went to the house at 3850 East New York Street and found Sylvia lying on a mattress in a second-story bedroom. It was immediately apparent that this was no ordinary death.

Even without the opinion of a forensic pathologist, the officers on the scene could make a good guess at what had probably caused the death of the half-naked girl on the urine-soaked mattress—she had been tortured to death. Scars, burns, and welts covered her body. The most bizarre of the wounds were the marks carved into her belly. The lines in the flesh formed the words "I am a prostitute and proud of it."

The police got an explanation for the condition of the girl's body from Gertrude Baniszewski, the divorced woman who owned the house and had placed the call to the police.

Sylvia Likens, Baniszewski said, had been living in the house for the summer, along with her fifteen-year-old sister, Jenny. Sylvia had brought torture and death upon herself, it seemed, by running away. While out on her own, Sylvia had been attacked by a wolfpack of boys and had died shortly after returning home.

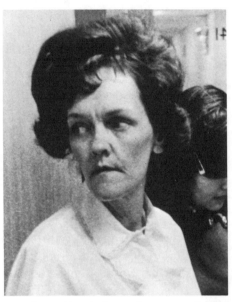

Any questions the police might have had about this explanation were soon answered when Jenny Likens was able to get one of the police officers alone. The terrified girl had a story to tell. After the police had the opportunity to investigate Jenny's account, the Gertrude Baniszewski case would shock the nation.

The story had its beginnings in the Baniszewski household's money troubles. With precious little wherewithal, Gertrude Baniszewski had the responsiblity of keeping up the family's home and feeding seven children. She made a meager living hawking soda pop at the Indianapolis Motor Speedway, supplemented by equally meager child-support payments from her ex-husband. In all, her income was barely enough to maintain the family's regular diet of canned soup. The soup was heated on an electric hot plate. The Baniszewskis had no stove.

Any chance to make some extra money was welcome, and such an opportunity landed in Gertrude Baniszewski's lap when the Likens couple offered her twenty dollars a week to look after their teenage daughters while the parents barnstormed with a Florida circus. Sylvia and Jenny Likens moved in with Baniszewski in July 1965.

Hard times can breed a profound sense of anger and frustration, but in the worn-looking thirty-six-year-old Baniszewski it triggered a volcanic fury soon after the two girls moved in. The immediate cause seemed to be Baniszewski's usual great concern: money, or rather, the lack of it, as the girls' parents failed to deliver the first week's payment on time. Baniszewski's response was to give Sylvia and Jenny a savage beating. While she battered the girls, she shouted, "I took care of you bitches for a week for nothing!" But if money matters were the start of it all, the arrival of the Likens' first payment the next day did nothing to appease the girls' caretaker.

Over the next three months Baniszewski's brutality escalated by terrifying leaps and bounds. From beatings by hand, she moved on to pummeling the girls with paddles, belts, and wooden boards. When these more prosaic forms of violence no longer kept pace with Baniszewski's rage, she came up with methods of torture that would have been worthy of the Marquis de Sade. For reasons perhaps known only to Baniszewski herself, Sylvia Likens became the one singled out for the most grisly treatment.

What is so especially unnerving about this case is not just the dementia that sprang up within Baniszewski, but the ease with which she recruited others into this hideous enterprise. The first to join in the beatings were two of Baniszewski's children. Next, some neighborhood boys were to be sicced upon Sylvia. One of them used her as a literal human punching bag; he flung her into concrete walls and down a flight of stairs as a way to perfect his judo throws. These boys would assist Gertrude Baniszewski with some of her most sadistic measures. At Baniszewski's direction the boys ground the glowing tips of cigarettes into Sylvia's flesh, inflicting more than 150 burns. Baniszewski's explanation for all this was simple: she was going to teach Sylvia a lesson. Still, however, the worst was yet to come.

Obviously, Baniszewski's maniacal rage was liable to be set off at any moment, and when Sylvia urinated on her mattress one night in October, her caretaker began what would be the final round of excruciating punishment. The cellar now became Sylvia's prison. While starved of any food, she was forced to eat her own feces and drink her own urine. Then Baniszewski brought in the boys. She commanded Sylvia to put on a performance for her teenage accomplices, a grotesque striptease that climaxed with the girl inserting a Coke bottle into her vagina. Then Baniszewski heated up a needle and, aided by one of the boys, used the white-hot tip to etch the words into Sylvia's belly.

When Sylvia later tried to attract the attention of neighbors, Baniszewski knocked the girl down; it was the last blow that Sylvia's body could withstand. She died when her head slammed against the concrete floor. Soon after that the emergency call was placed to the police.

At her trial Gertrude Baniszewski was given a life sentence. In 1985, despite public outcry, she was released on parole.

RICHARD SPECK
1941–1991

In 1966 a human time bomb by the name of Richard Speck came to the city of Chicago. The twenty-four-year-old man had already been arrested close to forty times in his boyhood home of Dallas, Texas, most recently for assaulting a woman with a knife. This latter crime would turn out to be a very small hint of what would come. Speck, who took work as a merchant seaman on the Great Lakes, harbored a growing urge to kill women. His murderous impulses detonated on July 13, 1966.

On that day Speck was waiting in Chicago for his next chance to ship out. He spent most of his time drinking beer and popping downers. Speck passed part of the day in the park behind Jeffrey Manor, a residence for student nurses working at South Chicago Community Hospital, where he tried to get a good view of the coeds while they

Nurse-killer Richard Speck following a suicide attempt.

sunbathed. At around eleven o'clock that night, he returned to the nurses' residence.

Answering the knock at the door, Filipino exchange student Co-razon Amurao was greeted by a pockmarked man holding a pistol and a knife. Speck rounded up the six young women in the house and put them all in a rear bedroom on the second floor, where he tied them up with strips of bed sheet. He did the same with the three student nurses who arrived at the house within the next hour. He kept saying he wasn't going to hurt them, insisting that all he wanted was money to get him to New Orleans. Taking him at his word, the young women didn't resist.

Despite his assurances he didn't leave even after taking their money. Before long he became agitated.

It has been suggested that this agitation was the result of brain damage caused by a series of head injuries that Speck sustained while growing up; among other incidents he had once hit himself accidentally with a hammer while pulling nails, and twice had fallen out of a tree. A stressful childhood and an extra Y chromosome have also been offered as explanations for the turn Speck's mind took on that July night. But no single factor has adequately explained why he decided to take twenty-year-old Pamela Wilkening into another room. All that the other nurses heard was something uttered by Wilkening that sounded like "ahhh," the only sound she made while she was stabbed in the chest and strangled with a strip of bed sheet.

Without any hurry, Speck took the young women, singly and in pairs, to other parts of the house. The nurses were methodically stabbed and strangled; one of them, Suzanne Farris, was stabbed as many as eighteen times. At first the young women who remained bound in the rear bedroom thought that any struggle on their part would provoke the stranger, but as their friends were taken from the room and did not return, it became clear that Speck already had senseless murder on his mind.

Corazon Amurao argued that they should untie each other and attack Speck at the first opportunity. Perhaps unable to do anything now because they were paralyzed by fear, the other nurses wouldn't go along with the plan. Left on her own, Amurao resorted to hiding under one of the beds. This relatively passive alternative was something the other women were willing to try. But they didn't hide as well as

Amurao did. One by one, Speck found all of them except Amurao, and the slow slaughter continued.

When Speck finally got around to Gloria Davy, he thought no one else was left. Taking even more time with her than the others, he raped Davy, mutilated her anus with a foreign object, then strangled her. He walked out of the house, confident he had left no survivors.

Corazon Amurao waited until after five in the morning before she finally emerged from her hiding place. At the second-story balcony she screamed, "They are all dead! My friends are all dead. Oh God, I'm the only one alive."

The police had several clues to aid their manhunt. Speck had left fingerprints all over the house, and the square knots used to tie the victims indicated that the killer was probably a seaman. This last clue was then coupled with Amurao's testimony that the murderer had talked about going to New Orleans. At a nearby Maritime Union hiring hall, the police learned of a man who had recently requested passage to New Orleans, and even obtained Speck's application form with ID photo attached. Four days after the murder of eight nurses, Speck was found in Cook County Hospital. He had slit his wrists after seeing his photo printed in the newspapers.

The jury that convicted Speck was very willing to complete the job that his suicide attempt had failed to do: he was sentenced to the electric chair. The mass murderer was spared, though, when the Supreme Court ruled that capital punishment was unconstitutional. Resentenced, Speck was given consecutive life terms amounting to a minimum of 400 years. He had served nineteen years of that sentence when he died of a heart attack in 1991.

CHARLES WHITMAN
1941–1966

For all his outward signs of conspicuous normalcy, a hidden strain of desperation resided within Charles Whitman from an early age. Growing up in the Florida resort town of Lake Worth, he took part in many activities emblematic of a Norman Rockwell boyhood: he was an altar boy in his family's church; he learned the value of honest, gainful enterprise by working his own newspaper route; he was an Eagle Scout by the age of twelve; he pitched for his high school baseball team. At the same time, though, he lived in a household marked by strife, where his mother was beaten by his father. Whatever else troubled Whitman as a boy, we'll never really know, but we do know that after he became a marine, in his late teens, his problems began to boil to the surface.

On one hand, he distinguished himself by earning sharpshooter status—he had always been unusually adept with firearms—and he would eventually leave the corps with an honorable discharge; on the

other hand, he had a few brushes with Marine Corps law. In one instance he was sentenced to thirty days' hard labor on an illegal firearms charge. After he left the service in 1964, his problems quickly got worse.

As usual, Whitman maintained a veneer of all-American virtue. Described as someone "more mature than most people his age," he got married and was working hard for his future, studying architectural engineering at the University of Texas in Austin. But he was also fighting a battle within himself, fighting against a growing rage. Like his father, he started to hit his wife.

In March 1966 Whitman's mother decided the time had come to leave her troubled marriage behind, and Whitman, the dutiful son, went back to his hometown in Florida to help her move out and relocate near him in Austin. His parents' breakup seemed to exacerbate his emotional condition. On March 29 he went to see the staff psychiatrist at his university.

Whitman told the doctor that he had become so consumed with rage that he was afraid he would snap. The manner of this feared breakdown had already taken shape in Whitman's mind. Referring to the university's thirty-story watchtower, he said he was "thinking about going up on the tower with a deer rifle and start shooting people."

The psychiatrist told Whitman he should come back for further sessions. The young man never did.

For the next four months Whitman's rage brewed. He also suffered splitting headaches. On the evening of July 31, 1966, he sat down at his typewriter, feeling an inexplicable compulsion to commit his thoughts to paper. He wrote of the same troubles that had prompted him to seek help from the campus psychiatrist, but now those thoughts were reaching their terrible, logical conclusion. "I am prepared to die," he wrote. "After my death, I wish an autopsy on me to be performed to see if there is any mental disorder." Later that night, he went to his mother's apartment, stabbed her in the chest, and shot her in the back of the head.

Back at home, he typed these words about his mother's death: "If there's a heaven, she is going there. If there is not a heaven, she is out of her pain and misery."

Around three in the morning, Whitman proceeded to his bedroom, where his wife was sleeping. He killed her by stabbing her three times in the chest. His continuing written record of what would be his last night alive stated that he wanted to spare his wife embarrassment.

A little after eleven o'clock the next morning, Whitman entered the university's watchtower building, wheeling a dolly upon which he had placed a foot locker and a duffel bag. He took the elevator up to the twenty-seventh floor—as high as it went—then lugged the bag and the locker up three more flights to the thirtieth. When he reached the reception desk at the tower's observation deck, he took out a rifle and slammed its butt into the receptionist's head. Then he shot her.

Once on the observation deck, he set himself up. In the duffel bag and foot locker were three rifles (one with a telescopic sight), three handguns, and one shotgun, along with food and water. He was interrupted by a family of sightseers trying to come out on the observation deck. Whitman killed two of them and wounded two others. At 11:48 Whitman set his sights on the people at the foot of the tower, some 300 feet below.

At first, the students and teachers crossing the campus mall could not comprehend what was going on as people started to drop. Then terror overtook the campus when it became clear that someone was shooting from the watchtower. With the aid of his telescopic sight, Whitman was able to cut down victims as far as three blocks away.

Around 130 law enforcement officers arrived on the scene, but Whitman was able to keep them at bay. Even a low-flying plane containing a police sharpshooter was not able to get to him. Only after an hour and a half was anyone able to reach the foot of the tower. Each maneuvering on his own initiative, four men reached the objective: three policemen and one armed civilian. The first two on the observation deck's square walkway were policeman Romero Martinez and civilian Allen Crum. After hearing footsteps around the near corner, Crum opened fire, distracting Whitman until Martinez could circle around the other side. Martinez shot Whitman six times.

Charles Whitman was dead at 1:24. His day of rage was over. Including his wife and mother, he had killed sixteen people and wounded thirty.

CHARLES MANSON
1934–

Charles Manson—the spellbinder, apocalyptic visionary, and ringleader of murder—began life as a virtual nonperson. He was officially designated at birth as "No Name Maddox." The negligence that his unwed sixteen-year-old mother displayed in naming him was an indication of what her idea of parenting would be. Her unnamed son would grow up without a home or any maternal care to speak of.

"No Name Maddox" acquired the first name Charles sometime during the first two years of his life, along with the surname Manson, which was bestowed upon him by one of his mother's succession of lovers. Whenever his mother was in prison or just more uninterested than usual, Manson was passed from one set of relatives to another. Among his surrogate parents were a religious-zealot grandmother, a meek, alcoholic grandfather who would eventually become psychotic, and an uncle who sent him to his first day of school in a dress as punishment for what the uncle considered Manson's sissy ways. Manson's mother finally tired of finding relatives to take care of her son and, in 1947, left him at the Gibault Home for Boys in Terre Haute, Indiana. This was the beginning of a twenty-year period in which Manson would spend the great majority of his time in one institution or another.

His brief interludes in the outside world would usually be spent

committing acts of theft or pimping, after which he inevitably ended up in an institution that was a little harsher than the one before. After suffering various forms of abuse, including head injuries that might have permanently altered the functioning of his brain, Manson completed the process of becoming a brutalized convict at the age of eighteen when he raped a fellow prisoner while holding a razor blade to his victim's throat.

When he was paroled in 1967, Manson was not willing to become a free man. Frightened at the prospect of reentering the outside world, a world he hardly knew, he insisted that he be kept inside California's Terminal Island Prison. But it wasn't to be. A few days after his release, thirty-three-year-old Charles Manson wandered into the Haight-Ashbury section of San Francisco. He arrived just in time for the Summer of Love.

Manson was transformed by his Haight-Ashbury experience, by the hallucinogenic drugs, by the free love, by his involvement in bizarre occult groups—and by a sudden sense of power. In the brutal environment of prison, the short, slightly built Manson had learned the value of ingratiating and manipulating others as a means of survival. Now, in a world of impressionable, flower-child runaways, he found that his way of dealing with people could not only ensure survival, but also ensnare devoted followers. He was no longer an ordinary psychopath. Before long, he accumulated a group of counterculture disciples, "the Family," with himself as the charismatic, quasi-religious, all-powerful father.

Popular music, so much a part of the late-sixties hippie scene, also became an important part of Manson's life. He was an aspiring singer/

songwriter who cultivated contacts in the Los Angeles music industry, but it wasn't just his own music that had meaning for Manson. The release of the Beatles' *White Album* at the end of 1968 opened his eyes to ominous visions of the future. Of special significance was the song, "Helter Skelter." The song's title was a British expression for a children's spiral slide, but to Manson "Helter Skelter" had a very different meaning. He believed the song was an allegory for an imminent race war in America. Blacks would rise up and exterminate the whites, Manson preached, but they would then find themselves incapable of running the country. In desperate need of help, the blacks would turn to the leader of a chosen tribe of white people who had hidden in the desert. The leader of that tribe would be Charles Manson.

After a while, Manson became impatient for the commencement of Helter Skelter. He decided to expedite matters in the summer of 1969 while living with the Family at the Spahn Movie Ranch, a riding stable and sometime film set north of Los Angeles. If Family members committed savage murders in such a way that black militants would become the prime suspects, Manson believed, then the race war would be ignited.

On August 9 three Family women, led by Manson's right-hand man Tex Watson, went to the home of film director Roman Polanski and his wife, actress Sharon Tate. There Manson's people found the pregnant Tate, Jay Sebring, Abigail Folger, Voytek Frykowski, and Steven Parent; they slaughtered them all. Parent was shot four times in the head, and Sebring and Frykowski received bullet wounds as well, but most of the attack was carried out with knives. With the exception of Parent, all the victims were stabbed repeatedly in a killing frenzy, Frykowski as many as fifty-one times. When Tate begged for the life of her unborn child, Susan Atkins, one of the Family women, simply told her, "Look, bitch, I don't care about you." Later, when Tate lay motionless with sixteen stab wounds, Atkins soaked a towel in the actress' blood and smeared the word *pig* on one of the doors, a message that was supposed to make the police suspect violent black revolutionaries.

The next night, Manson himself went inside the home of Leno and Rosemary LaBianca, tied up both the husband and wife, then ordered three of his followers to carry out the execution. Leno LaBianca was stabbed twenty-seven times, while Rosemary LaBianca was hacked to death with forty-one stab wounds. The word *war* was carved into Leno LaBianca's chest, and a serving fork was left sticking in his stomach.

The killers finished the job by writing more of their cryptic, bloody messages on the walls, among them, "Death to Pigs" and "Healter Skelter" [sic]. Their work done, the three Family members took showers and had a snack before leaving.

Feeling suddenly exposed to nightmarish assault in their own homes, wealthy Los Angeles residents took every conceivable precaution to protect themselves. The panic continued for over two months; then the police got a break. They learned the identities of the killers after Susan Atkins, in jail on other charges, began telling two of her fellow inmates about her murderous escapades.

Manson was eventually tried alongside his flower-child assassins, Atkins, Patricia Krenwinkel, and Leslie Van Houten, while Tex Watson, who had to be extradited from Texas, was tried separately. They were all sentenced to the gas chamber but then received life prison terms instead when, in 1972, the California State Supreme Court overruled the death penalty.

As hair-raising as the Tate/LaBianca killings were, some believe that they constituted only a portion of the murders committed in the name of Manson's Family. Police were able to prove that Family members killed musician Gary Hinman two weeks before the Tate slaughter, and the Family may have also been responsible for the deaths of Spahn Ranch cowboy Donald "Shorty" Shea, who knew too much, and Leslie Van Houten's lawyer, Ronald Hughes, who didn't go along with Manson's defense strategies.

ZODIAC

1968–1969

Unidentified Serial Killer

During the sixties the American public's sense of safety was increasingly battered by a trend of random, deadly violence. Perhaps no other case so epitomized this unnerving trend than a series of seemingly arbitrary killings in the San Francisco Bay Area at the close of the decade. Little was ever found out about this murderer. He would come out of nowhere, kill his victims for no apparent reason, then disappear. To this day the only name we have for the assassin is a cryptic, astrological moniker, Zodiac.

At first the killer's preferred target seemed to be young couples parked at night in secluded lovers' lanes. David Faraday and Bettilou Jensen were parked in just such a place north of San Francisco on December 20, 1968, when a man appeared at the driver's-side window. A .22-caliber bullet through the head killed Faraday immediately. Faraday's date, on the other hand, had some time to react before the gunman turned on her, but not very much. Bettilou Jensen scrambled out of her side of the car and ran some thirty feet, at which point five shots in the back knocked her down.

Seven months after this double homicide, a telephone call to the police established what sort of murderer was at work here. The male caller supplied information on where to find another young couple in a parked car. Arriving at the scene, the police discovered Michael Mageau, shot four times with a 9mm pistol, and Darlene Ferrin, shot nine times. Mageau, as it turned out, would live, but Ferrin would not. The mystery phone call had made it clear that a habitual killer was on the loose, because the caller's statements hadn't related only to the events of that night. "I also killed those kids last year," he had said.

The case took an especially bizarre turn a few weeks later when letters from the killer appeared simultaneously in three Bay Area newspapers; the letter-writer had threatened to add to the murder total if the letters weren't published. Each note contained a coded section. Taken together, the ciphers in the three letters constituted one complete message. The police weren't able to break the code, but a local high school teacher and his wife managed to unscramble the message's meaning. People in the San Francisco area now had a better idea of just how deranged the mystery killer was.

"I like killing people because it's so much fun," the deciphered message declared. In addition to homicidal pleasure, there was also another, deeper motive. The message made it clear that the killer believed he had somehow taken possession of his victims' souls by killing them. When he died, his victims would be his slaves. The notes also provided a name for the murderer: the letters were signed with a cross drawn over a circle, the Zodiac symbol, representing the spectrum of astrological signs.

Now the killer began to change his methods. His next victims, another young couple, were not shot but were instead tied up and repeatedly stabbed. The young man managed to live, but his date died of her twenty-four knife wounds. The next attack departed even further from the original Zodiac pattern. Rather than a couple, the victim was one lone man, a San Francisco cabdriver named Paul Stine. While seated in the backseat of the taxi, Zodiac shot him through the head with a 9mm pistol, then fled from the scene on foot. Before leaving the cab, though, he tore off a section of Stine's bloody shirt. He enclosed patches of the shirt with some of his subsequent letters to demonstrate that the author of the notes was truly the killer he claimed to be. One of those letters triggered a new wave of hysteria in the Bay Area: Zodiac now said he would "wipe out a school bus some morning." Fortunately, he never carried out the threat.

Based upon a description provided by a witness to Zodiac's flight from the Stine murder, the police circulated a description and sketch of the killer. They were looking for a somewhat heavyset man in his early twenties with a reddish crewcut who wore thick glasses. At this point the police also speculated that Zodiac might have been responsible for the unsolved murder of a young woman committed in 1966. But this would be as close as the police would ever get to identifying the Zodiac killer. Paul Stine would be the murderer's last confirmed victim. Whether Zodiac died or was incarcerated in a mental institution or mysteriously moved on to other killing grounds or simply stopped, his one-man reign of terror was officially at an end. His brief, ghastly career would set the pattern for all too many other senseless killing sprees to come.

JOHN LINLEY FRAZIER
1946–

In the late sixties and early seventies Charles Manson and his Family of hippie assassins were not the only ones to exacerbate fears about the drug culture's dark side. From the backdrop of California's flower-child scene emerged another long-haired young man who, like Manson, was driven by apocalyptic visions. In the fall of 1970, after he decided the time had come to transform counterculture rhetoric into harsh reality, he left the bodies of five people floating in a swimming pool.

For his first twenty-three years John Linley Frazier gave little indication that his life would climax with an act of cold-blooded multiple murder. Unlike Manson, whose traumatic early experiences were an

unrelenting breeding ground for psychopathic disorders, Frazier led a fairly ordinary existence. After dropping out of high school, he took up a trade as an auto mechanic and worked steadily at it in the northern California town of Santa Cruz. His wife described him, in the vernacular of the times, as a "beautiful person." The marriage broke up, though, sometime after he started taking drugs in the spring of 1970.

As he adopted the ways of the counterculture, Frazier became especially zealous about ecology. He became so ardent about this that he decided to quit his car-repair job and drop out in general, explaining to his boss that he refused to "contribute to the death cycle of the planet." Leaving his wife, he set out for the hippie communes in the hills outside town.

Frazier became increasingly fascinated with the mystical meaning of tarot cards, and his concern for the environment grew into a full-blown obsession. As a result, he didn't always fit in with his newfound hippie friends. He was considered fiercely paranoid, a style that did not sit too well with the mellow commune dwellers. After a while he drifted away from the communes and became more of a self-styled, Aquarian Age hermit, taking up residence in a six-foot-square shack in the woods. About a half-mile away, in the rich residential area of Soquel, California, was the home of an eye surgeon named Victor Ohta.

One day, while the Ohta family was out, Frazier broke into their home and left a little while later with a pair of binoculars. He also left with a distinct impression of the people who lived in the luxurious, hilltop house. As he later told a friend, he considered the Ohtas to be "too materialistic." His solution to this social sin was simple: the Ohtas "should be snuffed."

On the afternoon of Monday, October 19, 1970, Frazier returned to the Ohta house. Victor Ohta's wife, Virginia, was the only one there. Holding a .38 revolver on her, Frazier tied her wrists with a scarf, got ahold of the woman's .22 pistol, then waited for the rest of the family to show up. Before long, Dorothy Cadwallader, Ohta's secretary, arrived with one of the two boys in the family, whom she had driven home from school. Then Ohta himself brought home his second son. As each of them arrived, Frazier tied their hands at gunpoint.

By the side of the Ohtas' lagoon-shaped pool, Frazier began lecturing his captives about the evils of materialistic society and the ways in which it destroyed the environment. According to accounts later related by Frazier to a psychologist, Ohta got into an argument with his captor, which prompted Frazier to shove the man into the pool. Ohta tried to scramble out of the water. Frazier shot him three times.

One by one, Frazier killed the rest of his captives, shooting each of them in the head, as if performing an execution in the name of his ecological cause; first Virginia Ohta, then Dorothy Cadwallader, then the two boys, Derrick and Taggart, ages twelve and eleven respectively. That done, Frazier went into the house, typed a note, and set the house on fire.

When fire fighters showed up later, they found the five bodies in the pool. They also found Frazier's typewritten note under the windshield wipers of the Ohtas' Rolls-Royce. The message announced that the killings were the start of "World War 3." In the name of the "People of the Free Universe," the note promised death to all who would ruin the environment. It was signed with the names of Tarot cards: "Knight of Wands, Knight of Cups, Knight of Pentacles, and Knight of Swords."

The surrounding community was gripped with fear. The Tate/ LaBianca murders, committed by the Manson Family, had occurred just a little over a year before, and now, it seemed, the people of California could expect more of the same. The nearby hippie communes immediately became the target of suspicion. The police quickly learned, however, that the hippies were also spooked by the Ohta slaughter. Not only that, they were willing to cooperate.

When the contents of the murder-scene note were published, a group of commune residents went to the district attorney. They recognized the note's ideas as those of John Linley Frazier, and they supplied information that led the police to Frazier's shack. Frazier went back there a few days after the murders, and the police were waiting for him.

Frazier's fingerprints, lifted from the Ohtas' Rolls-Royce and from a beer can found in the remains of the Ohta house, provided compelling physical evidence. When Frazier was convicted in November 1971, a sanity hearing followed to determine what sort of punishment would be appropriate. To say that Frazier displayed a flair for courtroom theatrics at this hearing would be a considerable understatement. One side of his head was completely shaved, while his long hair and beard still sprouted on the opposite side.

Frazier's reasons for this stunt were quite convoluted. While it appeared he was simply putting on a crazy act to win an insanity plea, Frazier's psychologist maintained that Frazier had something altogether different in mind. Actually, the psychologist said, Frazier was trying to *appear* like he was faking insanity. In that way, the convicted murderer reasoned, the jury would feel obliged to dismiss the insanity argument. In the end Frazier really did seem to be crazy—like a fox. He got exactly what he wanted: a sanity ruling and a death sentence. As Frazier put it, he regarded the gas chamber as preferable to "having any fascist pigs working on my head."

Frazier's wish was subsequently denied when the California Supreme Court abolished capital punishment. His sentence was commuted to life imprisonment.

JUAN CORONA
1934–

At the time of his trial in the early seventies, Juan Corona was convicted of more murder counts than any other defendant in American history. But the case against him could not be characterized as clear-cut. The evidence presented was circumstantial, and unlike many other serial-murder cases there was never any confession. Further complicating matters were controversial racial, political, and legal issues. Juan Corona might very well have been the perpetrator of the twenty-five grisly murders of which he was convicted, but the case was never truly settled in the minds of many people.

One of the factors that weighed significantly in favor of Corona's guilt was a background of mental illness. In late 1955, after leaving his native Mexico to work as a seasonal fruit picker in California, the twenty-two-year-old Corona was seized by delusions. He believed that a recent flood had completely depopulated the entire surrounding area. At the request of his half-brother Natividad, Juan Corona was institutionalized. Psychiatrists diagnosed him as schizophrenic, but he recovered rapidly and was released after only a few months.

Or did he really recover?

Corona's subsequently successful, orderly life certainly suggested that he was a readjusted young man. The jury at his 1973 murder trial, though, apparently believed that madness still lurked somewhere in his psyche.

After he was released from psychiatric care in April 1956, Corona remained near the northern California town of Yuba City, where his brothers were planting family roots. Following his brothers' example, he declined to follow the migration patterns of other itinerant Mexican

workers—a meager existence at best—and aimed for the management
side of California farming by becoming a labor contractor. He persuaded a rancher named Jack Sullivan to let him bring in workers for a
commission. He was on his way to living the American dream of the
immigrant turned self-made man.

He made arrangements to board his workers on Sullivan's ranch,
occasionally contracting out to other farmers in the region as well, and
by the time he was in his thirties, Corona was established as a successful businessman. Completing the picture, he also got married and raised
a family. Even in the early seventies, when bad weather and increased
mechanization conspired to make times hard for Corona and other
contractors, he was still regarded as a solid, hardworking man. If there
were any suspicions about him, they were not made known.

Not until May 1971 was there even a hint that a series of murders
were taking place in Yuba City. An indentation in the ground was
discovered one day in the middle of a peach orchard along the Feather
River. Below the ground's surface was the body of a man. The victim
had been stabbed, and his head slashed and battered. Later that month,
another buried body was uncovered on the Sullivan ranch, home for
Corona's labor crews. A methodical two-week search of the area then
revealed that many of the orchards surrounding Yuba City were being
used as graveyards. In all, twenty-five male corpses were found. The
murder method was consistent: the men had been stabbed in the chest
with a knife, and their heads had been ferociously mutilated by some
larger instrument, such as a machete. In many cases the lower half of
the victims' bodies were naked, indicating sexual assault as well. The
murderer's targets were either migrant workers or other transients, men
who could go missing for a long time without being noticed.

Corona was implicated in the murders when receipts bearing his
name were found on two of the bodies. The police then learned that
another victim had been seen, shortly before his disappearance, riding
in Corona's pickup truck. A search of Corona's house and his workers'
barracks on the Sullivan ranch uncovered two knives and a bolo machete, while bloodstains were found in his car. Also collected from the
house was a notebook that the police suspected was a ledger of victims.
Corona was placed under arrest and was accused of waging a secret
campaign of terror and murder against Yuba City's transient population.

At his trial Corona became a *cause celebre* for Mexican-Americans who believed he was a victim of Anglo bigotry. His defense attorney, meanwhile, claimed that not only was the prosecution's evidence purely circumstantial, but the burden of proof in the case had improperly been placed on the defendant. He also argued that the true culprit in the case was more likely to have been Corona's half-brother Natividad.

It turned out that Natividad, the half-brother who had had Juan Corona committed to a mental institution in the fifties, had been involved in an incident that bore some similarity to the twenty-five murders being considered at Juan Corona's trial. In 1970, a year before the first murders took place, Natividad had been running a cafe near Yuba City, where he had gotten into some sort of argument with a young Mexican. When the fight was over, the young man was lying on the bathroom floor, his scalp sliced open by a machete. Natividad wasn't criminally charged for this attack, but he later ran off to Mexico when the assault victim won a $250,000 lawsuit against him.

The jury in Juan Corona's trial took a long time to reach a verdict—nearly a week—but the jurors were not persuaded by the defense's claims. Corona was convicted of twenty-five counts of murder, each carrying a consecutive life sentence. His lawyers succeeded in obtaining a retrial in 1982, at which Natividad was again offered as an alternative suspect, but Corona was found guilty once more. Since then, there has been no further official reassessment of the case.

EDMUND KEMPER III

1948–

"The Co-Ed Killer"

At a phone booth in Pueblo, Colorado, twenty-five-year-old Edmund Kemper got out of the car and placed a call to the police in his California hometown of Santa Cruz. He told them about eight women, six of them of college age or younger, two of them older—all of them dead. But the policeman on the other end of the line wasn't interested, as if this were some kind of crank call. He suggested that Kemper try phoning back later. Kemper did as he was told, but didn't have any more success in convincing the officer of his story's authenticity, so he called back again, and again. Each time he supplied more details about how he had killed his victims and what he had done with the bodies, until finally Santa

Cruz officers went across three states to retrieve him. Kemper sat and waited for his arrest.

This was not the first time authorities had failed to respond quickly to this tormented young man and his potential for turning that torment on others. Since Kemper's teens, if not earlier, there had been critical opportunities to take action that might have saved lives. In one sense the inability to perceive the true danger is understandable. Who, after all, could have really foreseen the horrifying extent of the crimes Kemper would commit in 1972 and 1973? Who would have guessed that he was capable not only of murder, but of necrophilia and cannibalism as well?

According to Kemper he was emotionally savaged by his mother at an early age. Estranged from her husband, Clarnell Kemper raised her son and her two daughters on her own, and she compensated for the absence of a paternal influence by subjecting Kemper to severe discipline. Kemper claimed he was constantly belittled. His later crimes have been characterized by psychiatric examiner Dr. Donald Lunde as an act of revenge against his mother.

In his early teens Kemper killed two of his family's cats. His mother found the remains of one, minus the head, in the garbage can, while Kemper kept dismembered pieces of the other in his closet. Along with this early sadism came a glib ability to explain away his actions and deflect blame onto others. And under this disconcerting surface lurked an even more disturbing fantasy life. He was already pining for women sexually by the age of ten but was convinced that as long as they were alive, they would inevitably rebuff him. He daydreamed, as he later put it, of "making a doll out of a human being."

Kemper committed his first murder at the age of fifteen, after he had been sent to live with his grandparents. He murdered them both in August 1963. His explanation to the police for the double killing: "I just wondered how it would feel to shoot Grandma."

As shocking as this crime was, the authorities felt that putting Kemper in a prison mental hospital for just six years was a sufficient response. Psychiatric treatment during this time was negligible, and it was nonexistent after his release. He was sent to live with his mother in Santa Cruz, not exactly the most therapeutic setting for him. Three years later, he started killing female college students.

In the early seventies, hitchhiking was an accepted part of the youth culture, even for unaccompanied young women. Kemper took advantage of this. Between May 1972 and February 1973, he picked up and murdered six young females. Once he had them on a secluded stretch of road, he would typically shoot or stab them to death, then store them in the trunk for the ride back to his house. When his mother was either away or asleep, he would bring the bodies inside; then, living out his boyhood fantasies about human dolls, he would sexually violate the corpses. Sometimes he cut the heads off, and sometimes he cooked and ate the flesh of victims as part of a casserole.

Even after the murders started, Kemper was still within reach of the authorities. In September 1972, as a follow-up to his earlier psychiatric treatment, Kemper was examined by a panel of psychiatrists representing the state. After he was judged by the panel to be no threat to society, Kemper drove away in a car that contained the head of a fifteen-year-old girl in the trunk.

Kemper's string of murders reached a climax on the day before Easter, 1973, when he turned to what may have been his real target all along. He went to his mother's bedside while she slept, then bashed in her skull with a hammer and decapitated her. As an act of revenge against all the tongue lashings he got from his mother, he cut out her larynx and shredded it through the garbage disposal. He killed one more woman in a similar manner that day—one of his mother's friends, whom he invited over for dinner—before he set out for his last car ride as a free man. The drive would eventually take him to the phone booth in Pueblo, Colorado. The news reports he heard on his car radio gave no indiction that the police were searching for him. His call to the Santa Cruz police rectified the situation.

After providing a highly detailed confession, Kemper was convicted of eight murders. At the end of his trial, before receiving his sentence of life imprisonment, the judge asked Kemper what he thought a suitable punishment would be. This turned out to be a potent question for the prisoner.

As a child, one of Kemper's favorite games had been to make believe he was going to the gas chamber. One of his sisters would lead him down the proverbial last mile, place him in his chair, then pretend to throw the switch. Kemper would then enact his own agonized death by asphyxiation. Over the years, it seems that Kemper's fantasies about his own execution had been embellished. In response to the judge's question at his 1973 trial, he said he believed he should be tortured to death.

DEAN CORLL
1939–1973

In the early seventies, teenage boys in Houston, Texas, began to disappear. As far as the police could ascertain at the time, no foul play was involved. Runaways were common, after all, and the missing boys had probably just left home. There was certainly no substantial reason to suspect that a man named Dean Corll might be the person responsible for these disappearances—not while he was alive, anyway. Only when Corll was reported killed and his apartment searched did the story emerge, suddenly, and with stomach-churning impact. In a very short time twenty-seven of the missing teenagers were accounted for. Others, whose bodies were never found, may have shared the same horrifying fate in the apartment that Corll had turned into a torture chamber.

Dean Corll had been living in Texas since 1954 when, at the age of fifteen, he had relocated to the Lone Star State from Indiana with his divorced mother. Like many serial killers, he was virtually an invisible person while growing up; if noticed at all, he was described by teachers as quiet and polite. In the sixties, before and after a stint in the army, he worked with his mother in the family business, the Corll Candy Company, headquartered in Houston, and as far as most people could tell, he was simply a hardworking young man. He started as vice president of the Corll enterprise and later added the duties of general manager to his responsibilities. One thing about him, though, struck some people as peculiar. Corll, in his midtwenties at the time, seemed to take an unusual interest in young boys. He cultivated their friendship by handing out free candy. For the time being, at least, this interest didn't extend to any behavior that would have been regarded as outright alarming.

But Corll turned a corner sometime after his mother de-

This fuzzy snapshot is the only photograph made public of the adult Dean Corll. His violent death at the hands of one of his accomplices precluded any official photographic record of him while alive.

cided to disband the family company in 1968. Set adrift, Corll seemed to become another person, or rather, he developed another, alternate personality. The police would never have the chance to question Corll about his crimes, and psychiatrists would never have the opportunity to explore his motivations, so we know little about the process of this change. But we do know that this thirty-year-old man with the mild-mannered exterior became capable of monstrous savagery.

Going far beyond enticing youngsters with candy, Dean Corll now lured teenage boys to his apartment for wild parties in which he and his underage friends got their kicks inhaling the fumes of paint and glue out of paper bags. The most important of his new young acquaintances were David Owen Brooks and Elmer Wayne Henley, who became his lovers as well as his accomplices in murder. Corll required a steady stream of teenagers to satisfy the demented tastes he had developed, and he relied on Brooks and Henley to recruit victims for him.

The glue-sniffing sessions were a vital part of the procedure for murder. Once his senses were sufficiently deadened by the noxious fumes, the victim could easily be made incapable of resisting. Corll, the man who had grown up so quiet and polite, would tear off the victim's clothes and tie him down to a wooden board outfitted with handcuffs and ropes. With the boy lashed into place, Corll would then take his time. Sodomy was part of the procedure. So was sexual mutilation. The abuse and torture could last for days. The end of the ordeal would come via strangulation or a pistol shot to the head.

In addition to supplying victims, Brooks and Henley helped dispose of the bodies. They were also involved in some of the murder acts themselves. There seemed to be nothing they wouldn't do for Corll, their master, but in the end Elmer Wayne Henley would stray from the path laid out by his mentor. His disobedience would bring the secret reign of terror to an end.

On August 8, 1973, Henley committed the unforgivable offense of bringing a girl to one of Corll's all-male paint-sniffing parties. He discovered just how much he had disappointed Corll when he emerged from his paint-sniffing stupor: Corll had tied Henley up while he was unconscious; Henley was to get a taste of the terrors endured by other boys trapped in Corll's apartment. But unlike other victims, Henley knew how to talk Corll's language, and promising to help rape and kill the girl and the other boy at the party, he persuaded the man to untie him. After he was set free, though, Henley was to prove disobedient again. No longer a willing accomplice, he wanted to let the girl go. As he argued with his master, Henley got a hold of Corll's .22 pistol. The time had come to free himself from the torture madness. He shot Corll six times.

Henley gave himself up to the police and told them the story of Corll's atrocities. He led the authorities to three shoreline graveyards in the Houston area. In all, the police dug up twenty-seven bodies. One of the victims was only nine years old. There may have been other victims that weren't discovered.

Both Henley and Brooks were arrested and convicted for their participation in the murders of their fellow teenagers. They are now serving life sentences.

PAUL JOHN KNOWLES
1946–1974

"The Casanova Killer"

Paul Knowles had a way of getting people to trust him. He could be so winning, in fact, that he was able to successfully court a woman while in prison. In the early seventies, when he was serving a stretch at the Raiford Penitentiary in Florida, he became pen pals with a San Francisco woman named Angela Covic and eventually got her to agree to marry him. With his charm he managed to gloss over the fact that he was serving time for burglary and kidnapping, among other crimes, and had spent approximately half of the last seven years behind prison walls for one offense after another. Somehow, young Knowles made Covic believe in him. She even hired an attorney who was able to arrange parole for her convict fiance.

On May 14, 1974, Paul Knowles was released from prison. He was now twenty-eight years old. His actions over the next few months would guarantee that he, as well as many other people, would not get the chance to get any older.

When Knowles came to San Francisco, Angela Covic found that her fondness for him, which had developed through letters and prison visits, began to unravel upon closer examination of her husband-to-be. There was, it seemed, a dark side to this habitual criminal, after all; there was something about him that made it impossible to view him merely as a young man dogged by hard luck. That disturbing quality became the master of Knowles's life after the increasingly jittery Covic broke off their engagement. In his later confession, recorded on audiotape shortly before his death and left with his lawyer, Knowles said that his reaction to this bitter disappointment was to roam the San Francisco streets and arbitrarily pick out three people and kill them. As writer Colin Wilson points out, this explosively violent response to rejection was typical of Knowles. The San Francisco killings were not verified, but the confirmed murders began soon enough.

In late July Knowles was back in Florida, his native state, where he broke into the home of a sixty-five-year-old woman. This might have been planned as a simple robbery—he took both cash and a car—but the gag he left in the bound woman's mouth soon cut off her air and suffocated her. His next homicides just a few days later, on the other hand, were clearly intentional. He strangled two girls, sisters aged seven and eleven, for no reason other than the fact that they knew him and his family and might tell police they had seen him. Knowles now became a one-man murder plague, bringing sudden death wherever he went, first in the Jacksonville area, then north through Georgia, up to the Midwest, then cross-country and back.

Sometimes he would force his way into a house, as he had with the Jacksonville woman; sometimes he would find his victims at randon, as they hitchhiked along his nomadic route. In one case he got into a Connecticut house and raped and strangled both a woman and her teenaged daughter; in another instance, while passing through Nevada, he stumbled upon, and killed, an elderly couple out camping. In still other cases, he used his amiable gift of gab to get close to strangers before murdering them. In Lima, Ohio, he struck up a barroom friendship with a local businessman. A short time later, the man was lying in the woods, strangled, his car on the highway, heading west, with Knowles at the wheel. Three weeks later, Knowles was in Alabama, traveling in the company of a Birmingham beautician who had taken a liking to him. For his part Knowles had taken a liking to the ready cash the woman was willing to spend on him. When that was gone, she was dead.

For four months Knowles continued his homicidal drift. By November 1974 he was in Atlanta, drinking in the Holiday Inn bar, where he hit it off with a woman named Sandy Fawkes, a British journalist. He liked her enough not to end her life, and as a result he achieved a certain immortality, as Fawkes would later turn this experience into a book called *Killing Time*. Knowles and Fawkes had a six-day fling. Due to Knowles's impotence, it was not a sexually successful affair, but that was not the compelling reason why Fawkes decided to bring the relationship to an end. Like Angela Covic, she discerned the evil within him, even when he was doing his best to be likable.

The disappointment of this breakup refueled Knowles's rampage. He tried to rape one of Fawkes's friends, but the woman managed to get away and told her story to nearby patrolmen. The police officers made an unsuccessful attempt to capture Knowles. Even though the mad-dog killer was on the loose again, the police had picked up his trail. Knowles didn't have much time left.

In Georgia he hijacked two vehicles, one belonging to a police officer, the other a civilian's. He shot both drivers in the back of the head. That same day, after trying to run a roadblock, he plowed the car he was driving into a tree and was forced to attempt a getaway on foot. Soon, the two hundred pursuing policemen unintentionally drove him into the path of a shotgun-toting hunter, who finally took Knowles captive.

The four months of murder were over. In that time Knowles had killed at least eighteen people.

But he wasn't quite done yet. The next day, while being transferred to a maximum-security prison, he tried one last mad, violent act. With a sheriff to one side of him and an FBI agent to the other—and with no reasonable chance to escape—he made a grab for the sheriff's sidearm. The FBI agent shot him dead.

JOACHIM KROLL

1933–

"The Ruhr Hunter"

On a summer day in 1976, a report of a missing four-year-old girl was received by police in Duisburg, at the heart of West Germany's industrialized Ruhr District. A painstaking search was immediately launched. From time to time sex criminals had plagued the region, and now the police had an opportunity to swing into action soon after a disappearance had taken place. Perhaps some unspeakable crime could be prevented, or perhaps the girl was simply lost. The police moved quickly, prepared for anything. Beginning with the area surrounding the playground where the girl had last been seen, they searched alleyways and knocked on every door, requesting any information that might steer

them in the right direction. In the course of interviewing an old man at one of the nearby apartment buildings, police officers heard a crazy story, one that was too crazy to ignore.

The old man mentioned that a fellow tenant in the building by the name of Joachim Kroll had told him not to use the communal bathroom on their floor. It seemed that the toilet was backed up. The only reason the old man brought his building's plumbing problems to the attention of the police was the explanation offered by his neighbor for the difficulties: Kroll had said, rather offhandedly, that the toilet was clogged "with guts." Following up on this, the police had the toilet plunged. Up came human entrails. The entrails were small, about the size of a small girl's.

The next stop was the apartment of the neighbor named Joachim Kroll. The occupant was a men's room attendant in his forties—somewhat dim, it seemed—whose bald head was flanked by big ears and whose eyes were partially obscured by tinted glasses. There was nothing about Kroll's manner to suggest that he had anything to hide. He did nothing to prevent the officers from opening the freezer to find plastic bags filled with human flesh, or to steer them away from the stove where a child's hand simmered in a saucepan with some sliced potatoes and carrots.

The sickening discoveries suggested that the police might be about to solve a case that was seventeen years old. Finally they had in their grasp the man who could be the roving cannibalistic killer known as the "Ruhr Hunter."

At the police station Kroll continued to be obliging. Yes, he admitted, he was the Ruhr Hunter. He was the man who had strangled and raped sixteen-year-old Manuela Knodt in 1959, thirteen-year-olds Petra Giese and Monika Tafel in 1962, and five-year-old Ilona Harke in 1966. And yes, it was true, from all of them he had carved off chunks of flesh to be eaten. The four-year-old child butchered today made it five girls murdered and ravaged in five different Ruhr towns.

The outcome of the day's search had been absolutely horrifying, but at least the police could take some comfort in bringing a long-standing, grisly case to a close. Loose threads from seventeen years of sporadic serial homicide were now finally entwined in a neat knot.

Almost.

Kroll had more to tell, if the police were interested. It was difficult for Kroll to remember exactly—there was so much to recall from so many years past—but the details emerged as he warmed to the task. There was the nineteen-year-old girl in the town of Walstede, way back in 'fifty-five it was; and the twelve-year-old a year later in Kirchhellen; and the girl in Burscheid in 'sixty-two; and the other one in Grossenbaum; and the one near the town of Marl sometime around 'sixty-six. . . .

The horrible list grew longer and longer.

When Kroll was finally done, and the police confirmed his stories, nine more unsolved murders were accounted for, killings that had never been attributed to the infamous Ruhr Hunter. Cannibalism was not a feature of these deaths, but the *modus operandi* of strangulation and rape was unsettling enough. In all, the seemingly dim lavatory attendant was responsible for fourteen murders, twelve of them of girls and young women, one of them a sixty-one-year-old widow, and one a young man. The latter was stabbed to death while out parking with his girlfriend.

Kroll had a special reason for being so cooperative with the police. Apparently, he didn't believe he would necessarily go to prison for his crimes. He thought a brain operation would remove all his antisocial thoughts and would allow him to remain at large. Thanks to his confessions, though, he now serves a life sentence.

David Berkowitz

1953–

"Son of Sam"

In the gruesome history of modern serial murder, there have been killers who have accounted for more victims than David Berkowitz. There have also been many others whose methods have been far more sadistic. But few criminals have cast such a spell of palpable fear over so many people as this chubby postal worker did in New York City during the midseventies.

On a residential street in the Bronx, a little after one o'clock on the morning of July 29, 1976, five gunshots crashed through a car windshield. Inside the car eighteen-year-old Donna Lauria was already dead by the time the shooting stopped, while Jody Valenti, wounded in the

thigh, started to scream and leaned on the car horn to sound an alarm. Before anyone could arrive on the scene, though, the killer had disappeared. In the following fall and winter the mystery gunman emerged out of the city night four more times.

The public became aware of an unnerving pattern. Some of the details would differ from one attack to another, but two things tied them all together. One was the type of bullet used by the gunman—.44 caliber—and the other was the fact that the victims were taken completely by surprise; the killer might strike anytime after dark and anywhere within the city limits. He might have had a preference for young people in parked cars, but even if a person avoided being caught in that sort of situation, he or she was still not necessarily safe. In one instance two young women were shot while sitting on a stoop in Queens; both of them were wounded, one of them paralyzed by a bullet in the spine. In another case a young woman was confronted by the gunman while walking along one of her neighborhood streets. In a desperate attempt to protect herself, she held a book in front of her face. The .44 slug went through the book and killed her immediately.

The words ".44 CALIBER KILLER" screamed from newspaper headlines on a regular basis, and New York City nights were filled with fear. At a time when disco fever would normally have kept night spots bustling, business dwindled at New York dance clubs as many people chose not to risk a night on the town. According to some sources, the Mafia was so concerned about declining receipts at mob-associated clubs that they conducted their own private investigation into the murders. More respectable citizens, meanwhile, became so jittery that they were known to chase possible suspects in the streets at the slightest pretext; in one instance citizens attempted a lynching. Throughout all of this, the police department was unable to make any headway in finding the mad gunman. Aside from the .44-caliber link the only thing that was known about the killer was that he seemed to prefer female victims with long, dark hair. Women fitting that very general description flocked to beauty salons to get their hair shortened and colored.

While the city seemed helpless, the .44 Caliber Killer struck again in April, murdering a dating couple parked in the Bronx. The mysterious gunman provided police and the press with a new moniker for himself in a note he left in the street:

I am the "Son of Sam." I am a little "Brat". . .
POLICE—let me haunt you with these words:
I'll be back!
I'll be back!
To be interpreted as—Bang, bang, bang, bang, bang—Ugh!!

The citywide panic escalated. But still the police had no idea how to close in on the madman now known as Son of Sam. The killer wounded Salvatore Lupo and his girlfriend Judy Placido while they were parked in Queens, and shot both Stacy Moskowitz and Robert Violante through the head as they sat parked near the Brooklyn shore. Moskowitz was killed instantly. Violante lived but was blinded.

In the end the breakthrough for the police proved to be a thirty-five-dollar parking ticket.

On the night of the Moskowitz murder, a woman noticed a man drive away from the vicinity of the crime in a car that had been given a ticket. With the vehicle's license plate number now in their possession, the police learned that the car belonged to twenty-four-year-old David Berkowitz of Yonkers, just north of New York City. When they arrested him, they found a .44 Bulldog revolver inside his car, along with a semiautomatic rifle and a note outlining Son of Sam's plans to cut loose with the rifle in a chic Hamptons disco.

David Berkowitz, the pudgy postal worker, was described by his fellow workers as courteous and dependable. Once he was arrested, though, he revealed the twisted, darker side that had compelled him to kill six people and wound seven others. He said that his first attack had been on Christmas Eve, 1975, seven months before Son of Sam's first fatal shooting. On that night Berkowitz had tried stabbing two women, but their screams had rattled him. "I didn't want to hurt them," he said. "I only wanted to kill them." As for the .44-caliber shootings, he provided a headline-grabbing motivation. Son of Sam claimed that he got his orders to kill from a demonic neighbor, Sam Carr; the commands were transmitted to Berkowitz through Carr's dog.

This bizarre story would seem to be the basis for an insanity plea, but the court decided Berkowitz was competent to stand trial. After pleading guilty, Son of Sam was sentenced to consecutive terms totaling over 300 years. In 1979 the court's position was vindicated. Berkowitz called a press conference and admitted that his demon-and-dog story had all been a hoax. According to Dr. David Abrahamsen, a psychiatrist who interviewed the killer extensively, the invented story was Berkowitz's way of shrugging off blame for crimes that even he knew were unforgivable.

TED BUNDY
1946–1989

So much about Ted Bundy seemed so normal. By the time he was a psychology major at the University of Washington, he was, to all appearances, an intelligent, likable young man, active in conservative politics and destined for success. But as it turned out, there was more

than one Ted Bundy dwelling inside the young man's pleasing exterior. Like Dr. Henry Jekyll, Bundy was plagued by an alternate self, a Mr. Hyde that embodied all the conniving, monstrous impulses that arguably lie within all of us to one degree or another. As was the case with Robert Louis Stevenson's fictional creation, Bundy's second, fiendish personality, once it was unleashed, became more and more powerful, more and more out of control.

An illegitimate child, Bundy lived the first four years of his life with his mother and grandparents in Philadelphia, where he was passed off as his grandparents' adopted son. His mother provided him with a more normal home situation when she moved to Tacoma, Washington, and married a man named John Bundy. Still, Ted became known as a liar and petty thief. Something was simmering beneath the surface, something that would eventually erupt when Bundy was in college, driving him to ferocious sexual violence.

While pursuing an orderly academic career at the University of Washington, Bundy was also becoming a Peeping Tom and was fantasizing about assaulting young women. On the night of January 4, 1974, Bundy's secret self came fully to the fore as he slipped into the Seattle basement apartment of a young woman living near the university. Bundy pounced upon his victim while she lay in bed and, with a metal rod yanked from the bed frame, clubbed her over and over again, leaving her face a bloody mess. He then forced the metal rod into her vagina. This, the first of Bundy's victims, would survive—after a fashion. The trauma of the attack produced brain damage and the woman was unable to provide a description of the man who had assaulted her. Bundy was free to strike again.

His next attack would prove to be more typical of the Bundy horror to come: the young female victim was abducted, never to be seen alive again. By summer five more young women disappeared from the Seattle area. Bundy was no longer sneaking into apartments and surprising his victims; he was luring them, using his good looks and amiable manner to persuade them to get into his car. Sometimes he wore a sling around his arm and pretended that he needed help. On July 14, when he kidnapped two women in broad daylight from a crowded picnic area, witnesses remembered seeing one of the abductees talking to a man wearing a sling, a man who called himself Ted.

Using the name Ted as a guide, the police compiled a list of two thousand possible suspects. On this list was Ted Bundy, but the police didn't rate him a serious suspect. Like Bundy's victims, the police just could not believe that there could be an evil side to this model young man. By the time the discovery of decomposing female bodies prompted officials to classify the string of abductions as a bona fide murder case, the Seattle police had lost their chance to find the killer. By then Ted Bundy had moved on.

He was now a promising law student at the University of Utah in Salt Lake City. His horrific double life continued. Young women in the area began to disappear. The discovery of one of the victims, the daughter of a police chief, revealed that she had been sexually assaulted and bludgeoned so badly that her face was reduced to a virtually unrecognizable pulp. Bundy's next stop, in early 1975, was Colorado, where, it is believed, he preyed upon five more victims before returning to Salt Lake City.

Bundy had proven himself deft at keeping one step ahead of the law, but now evidence against him began to accumulate. The turning point was August 16, when his reckless driving led to a police search of his car. Uncovered in the search were human hairs that were matched to those of one of the murder victims. Bundy was then identified by a woman who had barely escaped abduction the year before. A picture of Bundy, the secret, vicious killer, began to come into focus. He was convicted in Utah of attempted kidnapping and was extradited to Colorado to stand trial for murder. But he wasn't the docile, cooperative prisoner he appeared to be. He was able to wangle permission to use the law library in the Aspen courthouse and managed to jump out the second-story window and run off. His recapture eight days later didn't discourage him. On December 30, 1977, he slipped out of custody again by sawing a hole in his jail-cell ceiling. This time he eluded authorities and left the state, ending up in Tallahassee, Florida.

Bundy might have escaped detection if he could have held himself in check, but his Mr. Hyde was not to be denied, as if that part of him was becoming his master. On January 15, 1978, on a night of berserk attacks, Bundy slipped into Florida State University's Chi Omega sorority house, raped and killed two women, and savagely assaulted two others. In the case of one of his murder victims, Lisa Levy, Bundy nearly bit off a nipple and bit her buttocks so deeply that he left teeth marks. A short while later, he got into a second sorority house and fractured the skull of another student. This night of bestial violence was followed up a month later by the abduction, rape, and murder of a 12-year-old girl.

Eventually, Florida police apprehended Bundy for driving a stolen vehicle. Following this minor arrest, a thorough investigation into his other activities in Florida led the police to file murder charges against Bundy. The most damning evidence against him were the bite marks on Lisa Levy, which were matched to an impression of his teeth.

Bundy was convicted on two counts of murder on July 23, 1979, and was sentenced to the electric chair. The smooth-talking, manipulative Bundy was still not through, however. Acting as his own attorney, the former law student stalled his execution for ten years through one appeal after another. When it became clear that the usefulness of this tactic had been exhausted, Bundy then tried cooperating with the authorities; after years of denying all murder charges, he finally confessed, admitting to twenty-eight killings. This belated turnaround did nothing to change the state's plans for him.

In a last-minute interview before his execution, he grasped at a final, desperate ploy. Bundy, always ready with a glib explanation, now claimed that his hideous acts were caused by violent pornography. Some anti-media-violence activists took Bundy's final statement to heart, but the three hundred demonstrators outside the prison at the time were clearly unimpressed. They hoisted champagne glasses and cheered a short time later when they heard that Ted Bundy had just been electrocuted.

JOHN WAYNE GACY

1942–

"The Killer Clown"

The last chance to stop John Wayne Gacy before he turned serial killer came in 1971—it was a chance that came and went without any action being taken. Gacy was on parole at the time as a result of an Iowa conviction for sexual assault against a teenage boy. The Iowa Parole Board would have had reason to reevaluate their opinion of him if they had been apprised of what was going on in Chicago. Gacy had just been arrested there. The charges were dropped, due to a failure to testify by the complainant, but the nature of one of the charges should have been of interest to the Iowa authorities: Gacy, the convicted sex offender, had been accused of attempted rape, once more against a young man. As it

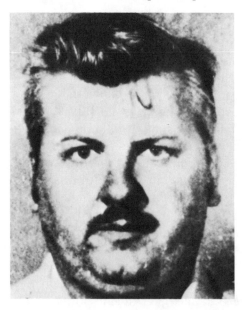

turned out, no information about the Chicago arrest reached the parole board. When Gacy's case subsequently came up for review, the board was under the impression that their charge was turning himself into a productive, law-abiding citizen.

There certainly was reason to think Gacy had reformed. The persona he projected was that of a model citizen. He was becoming a successful building contractor, he was heavily involved in community affairs and Democratic politics, and most incongruous of all, he would often dress up as Pogo the Clown and devote spare time to making children laugh. In a few years the image of this model solid citizen would even be captured in the now well-known photograph of him shaking hands with First Lady Rosalyn Carter. With no information to the contrary, the Iowa Parole Board had no reason to doubt the respectable front put forward by Gacy. As a result, later in

1971, Gacy was discharged from parole status, allowed to carry on without official monitoring. Two-and-a-half months later, he committed his first murder.

He would keep murdering for six years, preying upon boys and young men with sadistic ferocity.

For Gacy murder was a matter of sexual fulfillment, and he made a point of prolonging the process. After he brought the young males to his house—often under the pretense of being a plainclothes policeman— he would handcuff them, then rape and torture them for hours. Only after inflicting untold agony would he kill them by strangulation, a method of murder that Gacy called the "rope trick." His sexual climax would coincide with the victim's final breaths.

The years of killing went by without any serious suspicions being directed at Gacy. The idea that such a substantial member of the community could be a mass murderer was inconceivable. Still, there were reasons to have doubts about this man. Unfortunately, the law enforcement system at that time was not especially well geared toward detecting Gacy's sort of behavior.

Well before Gacy's final arrest for murder, evidence existed that he had had contact with boys who had been reported missing. But then, the Chicago Police were flooded with missing person reports of all kinds, and the particular data concerning Gacy weren't followed up as a possible lead.

In December 1978 the connection was finally made between the missing boys and one of the ominous indicators from Gacy's past. Fifteen-year-old Robert Piest dropped out of sight on his way to talk to Gacy about a construction job, and the police, running a check on the building contractor, found out about Gacy's sodomy conviction in Iowa ten years before, a conviction for a crime committed against a boy who had been the same age as the missing Robert Piest. The time had come to search Gacy's house.

Soon it became clear that this move was several years too late. In the crawlspace beneath the floor, the bodies of twenty-nine boys were found. Several more would be dragged out of a river.

Following Gacy's arrest, the hidden story of his past began to come out. An examination of his childhood revealed that his early years were fairly typical of many serial murderers. He had been brutalized and relentlessly demeaned by an alcoholic father, made to feel useless and insufficiently masculine. In addition to this emotional torment, he also may have suffered some sort of brain damage. When Gacy was eleven, a playground swing had slammed into his head and created a blood clot in the brain. Once all the information about his past was recorded, the question of his legal sanity naturally arose at his trial. Gacy maintained that he was a multiple personality and that an alter-ego named Jack was the real culprit behind the torturous deaths of thirty-three young men.

The jury decided Gacy was legally responsible for his actions. He was convicted in 1980 and sentenced to the electric chair. He waits on death row as the appeals process runs its course.

KENNETH BIANCHI
1951–

ANGELO BUONO
1934–

"The Hillside Stranglers"

Kenneth Bianchi had ambitions to become part of a helping profession. In his native Rochester, New York, he tried to join the local police force, but he wasn't able to pass the required exams. When he moved to California in his midtwenties, he made similar attempts with both the Glendale and Los Angeles police. In both cases he was rejected again. He then pursued other avenues; if the police wouldn't have him, perhaps he could become a psychologist. With the skill of a scam artist— he was already a practiced liar and thief at this point—Bianchi assembled convincing, if completely fraudulent, credentials and was able to secure office space for himself in the suite of a legitimate Los Angeles therapist. But his bogus counseling practice was short-lived. Involvement with his cousin Angelo Buono led to other, darker pursuits.

Bianchi had roomed with his older cousin when he had first moved to Los Angeles in 1976. A former thief, Buono now had his own auto upholstery shop in Glendale. His three ex-wives knew him as a brutal

Kenneth Bianchi   Angelo Buono

man. On one occasion he was alleged to have sodomized one of his wives in front of his children. When Kenneth Bianchi moved in with him, Buono was living a sexually active life, specializing in teenage girls. Bianchi admired cousin Angelo. For now, he abandoned his ambitions to serve the public through the police force or to counsel troubled people; instead he joined Buono in a new enterprise: running a prostitution ring.

Their pimping business was a vicious one. Some of the prostitutes have said that Buono enjoyed inflicting pain. In particular he is said to have taken pleasure in making the young women force unlubricated dildos into their anuses. Young Bianchi, who had been prone to violent rages himself from time to time, went along with this sort of behavior. When they later made the transition from brutal pimping to serial murder, Bianchi was an enthusiastic participant.

According to one version of the case, the first killing was committed on a sort of psychopathic whim. Writer Colin Wilson, on the other hand, suggests that the turning point for Bianchi and Buono may have been a business deal that went sour. When Buono discovered he had bought a worthless list of johns from a veteran prostitute, he decided to get revenge. He and Bianchi couldn't track down the prostitute, so they got ahold of one of the woman's friends instead, another prostitute named Yolanda Washington. They raped her, strangled her, and dumped her nude body near the Forest Lawn Cemetery.

A floodgate of homicidal impulses seemed to have been flung open. In a period of four months, ten strangled female bodies were found on hillsides in the Los Angeles area. In the month of November 1977 alone, six young women were killed. And strangling was only one element in these crimes; rape and torture were often a prelude to death, the killers becoming more and more sadistic as their spree progressed. In one instance, after sexually violating a victim with a soda bottle, Bianchi made a point of prolonging the strangulation. Several times, he choked the young woman until she passed out, then let her regain consciousness, then cut off her oxygen again before finally completing the murder.

In February 1978 the Hillside Stranglings came to a halt. It was not that the police had been able to make any headway in solving the case; the killings just stopped. Buono tended to his auto upholstery business, and Bianchi left the state and resettled in Bellingham, Washington.

As if his career of unspeakable murder was a thing of the past, Bianchi took up what seemed to be a normal life. With his loving common-law wife, he had a child, and he supported his family by taking a job as a security guard. But the other side of him was not completely forgotten. In January 1979 the smooth-talking Bianchi persuaded a young woman named Karen Mandic to take an overnight house-sitting job, supposedly in connection with the security company for which he was working. That night Mandic showed up at the house with a friend, Diane Wilder. Bianchi raped and strangled them both.

After the bodies were discovered, the Bellingham police learned that Bianchi had been the contact for the house-sitting job. They also came up with physical evidence—such as specimens of Bianchi's pubic hair at the scene of the crime—that made it even clearer that Bianchi was their man. Bianchi's claims of innocence quickly unraveled. When the police discovered that Bianchi had been a resident of Los Angeles, they contacted authorities in that area, who in turn uncovered evidence implicating Bianchi in the Hillside Stranglings. The Bianchi case now took a new turn.

While apparently under hypnosis, Bianchi revealed that he had dual personalities, one good, the other homicidal. Some experts believed this psychosis to be genuine; others maintained that Bianchi's revelations were actually a self-serving ruse. In the end the court agreed with the skeptics. Bianchi was scheduled for trial as a legally sane defendant. With no other way out, Bianchi now decided to cooperate with the prosecution in order to avoid the death penalty. He pleaded guilty to the Bellingham double murder and five of the Hillside Stranglings and testified against his cousin Angelo Buono.

The Buono trial dragged on for two years, ending in convictions on nine murder counts, despite Buono's denial of all charges. The cousins are now both serving life sentences, Buono in California for the Hillside Stranglings and Bianchi in Washington for the Bellingham murders.

PETER SUTCLIFFE
1946–
"The Yorkshire Ripper"

The Ripper moniker that was attached to English killer Peter Sutcliffe was no careless tabloid label. In many ways he seemed to be a true reincarnation of the original Jack the Ripper, who terrorized London in 1888. Like his murderous predecessor, Sutcliffe, the Yorkshire Ripper, roamed city streets known for vice and preyed upon the prostitutes who made their living there. Also frighteningly reminiscent of the Victorian Age serial killer was the ferocity of his attacks. Sutcliffe differed, however, in one respect. Although he originally targeted prostitutes, as though he were possessed by a puritanical religious mania, the last six women he killed or assaulted didn't fit that description at all. The longer he killed, the wider the scope of his victims became. In some cases his methods became more savage as well.

Whatever may have been the original source of his obsessions, Sutcliffe started showing blatantly morbid habits in the early sixties while in his late teens. After dropping out of school at fifteen, he took a job as a gravedigger and mortuary attendant. Fellow workers reported that he often pilfered jewelry from the bodies with which he came into contact. He was also known to manipulate corpses as if they were

puppets and put on little ventriloquist parodies.

Sutcliffe's next occupation, one that would last until his arrest, was as a truck driver. He seemed to adjust well enough to this job, but people did notice one peculiarity. He had a card in plain view inside his truck that had a strange message written on it: "In this truck is a man whose latent genius, if unleashed, would rock the nation, whose dynamic energy would overpower those around him. Better let him sleep?" Only later would people understand exactly the gruesome nature of this "latent genius."

In later psychiatric interviews Sutcliffe would attribute the origin of his homicidal impulses to a traumatic head injury suffered in a motorcycle accident. As for the targeting of those impulses, he would pinpoint the origin to the humiliation he suffered in 1969 when he was ripped off by a prostitute. The timing of this experience supports Sutcliffe's contention: soon afterward he attacked a prostitute with a weighted sock.

His first murder came six years later, by which time he had discarded the weighted sock as part of his arsenal of weapons. When he attacked prostitute Wilma McCann on October 29, 1975, in the Yorkshire town of Leeds, he smashed the back of her head with a ballpeen hammer, then took hold of a knife and thrust it fourteen times into her torso and neck. He killed again just three months later, but laid low for a year after that before going on a feverish spree of murder that claimed seven victims in the fifteen months between February 1977 and May 1978. He continued with his pattern of first bludgeoning the women with a hammer, then indulging in an orgy of slashing. One victim he stabbed as many as fifty times. In some cases he mutilated the genitalia. Eight of his first nine murder victims were prostitutes.

The police in England's northern counties were at their wit's end in their attempt to catch the man known as the Yorkshire Ripper. In all, they would expend £4 million on the Ripper manhunt, but nothing they did could bring an end to the terror. The killings continued into 1979.

In April of that year, Sutcliffe's sights drifted away from his usual prostitute victims, and he began to prey upon female college students and young working women. His last four murders and last two murder attempts were directed at women in this group. He also began to rely on a different weapon. Instead of a knife, he started stabbing women with a screwdriver. In the case of the last of his murder victims, he found himself taken aback for a moment when he looked into the dead girl's open eyes. To his mind, there was something reproachful about them. As he later put it at his trial, "This shook me up a bit." He stabbed one of the eyes with the screwdriver.

When Sutcliffe was finally caught in January 1981, his arrest came about by happenstance. Two patrolmen spotted Sutcliffe sitting in a parked car with a prostitute and, as a routine check, asked him what his business was. Sutcliffe tried to tell the policemen that the woman next to him was his girlfriend, but his inability to think of the woman's name prompted the policemen to pursue their routine suspicions further. Eventually they discovered that Sutcliffe had in his possession two knives and a ballpeen hammer. Confronted with this discovery of an obvious link to the Ripper murders, Sutcliffe stopped trying to talk his way out of the situation. He started to confess. He confessed for sixteen hours.

At his trial the defense tried to convince the court that Sutcliffe was legally insane, that he had committed the Ripper murders because he believed he had been ordered by God to do so. The court believed instead that Sutcliffe's lawyer was making a sane attempt to win a lenient sentence. The Yorkshire Ripper was sentenced to life in prison.

ARNFINN NESSET
1935–

When the Orkdal Valley Nursing Home was opened in 1977, Arnfinn Nesset was a logical choice for the Norwegian institution's directorship. At the age of forty-two, he was a seasoned professional with fifteen years' experience in health-care establishments. In addition, the balding, bland-looking administrator was also known for his altruism, often involving himself in charity work, particularly with the Salvation Army. On all accounts he was exactly the sort of person to take on a responsible job helping and housing elderly people, and for four years director Nesset did indeed carry out his duties to the satisfaction of all concerned. In any case, the only ones with a complaint were beyond objecting to anything.

Between 1977 and 1980 thirty patients at the nursing home died. The total was high, but then again the patients were elderly and often enfeebled to begin with, so there was no reason for alarm. Not, at least, until 1981, when an employee at the home noticed something peculiar about the drug requisitions.

Along with all the standard medications, a great deal of curacit had been acquired. A derivative of curare, this drug can be used as a muscle relaxant during abdominal surgery and as a way to keep throat muscles from constricting during throat examinations. Neither application would be in great demand in a nursing home. When used improperly, curacit can also be as deadly as the arrowheads poisoned with curare by South American Indians.

The person responsible for ordering the drugs was Arnfinn Nesset.

After the information about the curacit was relayed to the police, the nursing home director was brought in for questioning. He admitted to wangling the acquisition of the drug: after getting a physician's signature of authorization for a list of medications, he would add a request for curacit to the order. But there was nothing sinister about all this, Nesset assured the police. He had simply ordered the dangerous drug to take care of a pack of wild dogs in the neighborhood.

The police were not convinced. The poisoning of a few unruly dogs would not have required the 11,600 milligrams of curacit that Nesset had obtained. If someone wanted to, he could use an amount of that size to kill as many as 300 people.

After a while, Nesset himself saw the hopelessness of standing by his dog story; he about-faced and started to confess. He admitted to killing twenty-seven nursing home patients. Death was not easy for the old people Nesset preyed upon. An improper injection of curacit paralyzes the nervous system and makes it impossible to breathe. Nesset's victims died while desperately, and futilely, gasping for breath.

Nesset's admissions were ghastly enough, but when pressed for more information about what he might have done at previous jobs, he made the chilling remark: "I've killed so many I'm unable to remember them all." When the police were done poring over Nesset's past, they estimated that he might have been responsible for 138 deaths in a little less than twenty years.

The charges presented at Nesset's trial were not quite so spectacular. Nesset about-faced once more and denied everything, claiming that his confession had been bullied out of him. The prosecution had to limit its case to twenty-five murder counts involving Nesset's most recent alleged crimes, to which witnesses could testify. Even there, the prosecution faced some difficulties.

Prosecutors usually handle poisoning cases by using autopsy reports to show traces of the poison in the victims' bodies. But curacit can be impossible to detect even a short while after it has been injected, and no suspicious traces of the drug could be produced for the trial. The case rested instead on circumstantial evidence: the testimony of people who saw Nesset with the victims shortly before their deaths (sometimes with a syringe in his possession), coupled with injection marks found on victims' arms. With 150 witnesses supplying the circumstantial evidence, though, the jury found the prosecution's case persuasive. In March 1983 they convicted Nesset of twenty-two of the twenty-five alleged murders. He was given the maximum sentence allowed by Norwegian law, twenty-one years, which could be extended to thirty-one if it is judged that Nesset requires what is called additional preventive detention.

As Nesset continues to serve his time, the reasons behind his mass murder of completely helpless victims remain a mystery.

PEDRO ALONZO LOPEZ
1949–

"The Monster of the Andes"

The police in central Ecuador had no concrete evidence of a serial killer in their midst until an act of nature suddenly uncovered some grisly secrets. In April 1980 a torrential rain forced a river outside the city of Ambato to overflow. Water flooded across the valley and swept away the topsoil in its path. The flood also opened up four shallow graves, each holding a girl who had been raped and strangled.

On the alert now for a mad killer, the police had no leads to follow and could do little else but be watchful for suspicious characters. They didn't have to wait very long. Just a few days after the flood, civilians captured a man in an Ambato marketplace. The man had been spotted leading away a twelve-year-old Indian girl. His name was Pedro Lopez.

Police questioning got nothing out of the tight-lipped suspect, but when a man posing as a fellow prisoner tricked him into talking about himself, Lopez began to relate a story so horrible that it defied belief. After he found out he had revealed himself to a police confederate, Lopez saw no point in holding back anymore and decided to

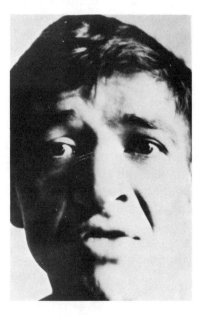

make a complete statement for the record. The more he talked, the more gruesome the story got.

Lopez confessed to raping and murdering 110 girls. And that was only in Ecuador. He also said he had killed another hundred in neighboring Colombia and more than a hundred more in northern Peru. To establish the seriousness of his claims, Lopez took police to nearby spots where he was supposed to have buried some of his victims. The bodies of fifty-three girls between the ages of eight and twelve were uncovered.

In subsequent investigations the police were not able to verify the remaining fifty-odd murders allegedly committed in Ecuador. Some investigators believe, however, that Lopez's total claim of some 350 victims may very well be true.

Corroboration of Lopez's story is difficult because of his ability over the years to avoid detection, and also because he tended to prey upon Indians, whose problems often did not get sufficient attention from the authorities. What we do know about Lopez is based primarily upon an interview he gave to an American journalist named Ron Laytner.

Lopez's story begins with a harsh early life in an eastern Colombian town. His childhood effectively ended at the age of eight. One of thirteen children of a prostitute, he was already far enough beyond innocence at that point to sexually molest one of his sisters. As punishment, his mother kicked him out of the house. The eight-year-old Lopez was raped by a man while living on the streets in the next town.

Lopez was sexually assaulted again when he was eighteen, while serving a prison sentence for car theft. This time he was gang-raped by four older convicts. The incident led to his first murder conviction as, within two weeks, he had killed three of his four attackers. He received a two-year sentence for this triple homicide, in light of the provocation that had triggered the killings. By the time he was released from prison in the seventies and drifted across the border into Peru, he was nurturing an impulse to kill that required no provocation at all. In fact, as far as he was concerned, the more innocent the victims were, the better.

His usual method was to wander through a marketplace until he found a girl whom he could lure to an isolated spot. First he would rape his victim, then strangle her. He said he preferred killing in the light of day so that he could watch his victims die more clearly.

By 1978 he may have killed a hundred Peruvian girls. Then he was caught—but only temporarily.

In an Ayachuco Indian village Lopez was apprehended trying to snatch a nine-year-old girl. The Ayachucos' concept of justice was apparently not tempered by modern constitutional ideas of due process and restraint. Their first response was to pummel Lopez, and then, when he was sufficiently subdued, they tortured him. An American female missionary drove up in her jeep in time to see the villagers about to toss their savaged captive into an open grave where he would be buried alive. After a long, difficult argument, the missionary managed to persuade the Ayachucos that she should be allowed to take Lopez to the authorities.

As a result of this act of mercy, Lopez was able to continue his murders. The fault, though, was not with the missionary, but with the authorities who took Lopez into custody. The kidnapping of an Indian girl apparently did not trouble them very much. Their idea of appropriate punishment was simply to escort the prisoner out of the country. Lopez was not greatly disturbed by this; in fact, he came to prefer operating in Ecuador because he considered the girls there to be "more gentle and trusting, more innocent."

It was after raping and killing perhaps as many as 110 Ecuadoran girls that he was finally trapped in the Ambato marketplace in 1980. Following the initial unearthing of fifty-three victims, the police were led to twenty-eight other alleged burial sites but were not able to uncover any more bodies. As reported by Michael Newton in *Hunting Humans*, an official at Lopez's prison does not believe that this means there are no more murder victims to be found. His theory is that the later searches failed because Lopez had second thoughts about cooperating and had decided to lead the police on wild goose chases instead.

An Ecuadoran court convicted Lopez and sent him to prison for his mass murders, but the laws of the country may allow him to win parole. Still to come, however, once the current prison term has been served, are trials in Colombia and Peru.

DENNIS NILSON
1945–

The young men were lured to an apartment. When their defenses were down, they were murdered and their bodies dismembered. Parts of the corpses were kept in the apartment as if they were ghastly mementos. This unsettling scenario brings to mind the case of Jeffrey Dahmer, whose gruesome exploits shocked America in the early nineties. But it also happens to fit a harrowing precursor that unfolded in London some ten years before the Dahmer horrors. The murderer in this case was a British civil servant named Dennis Nilson, another homicidal lost soul who, as his biographer Brian Masters put it, killed for company. All told, Nilson killed for company fifteen times.

When he was growing up in Scotland, Dennis Nilson was hard up for company of the intimate family variety. His father was rarely around, then left entirely as a result of a divorce when Nilson was four. Nilson's mother also abandoned him in effect: she sent him off to live with his grandparents. This actually turned out to be amenable to young Nilson because he loved his grandfather dearly, but the man died when Nilson was only six.

Eager to leave behind what he considered an unsatisfactory family, he enlisted in the Junior Leaders' Regiment at the age of sixteen and went on to make the army his home for eleven years. He served a stint with London's police force once he was a civilian again, then settled into the life of a confirmed civil servant.

Like Dahmer the turning point for Nilson seemed to have been the experience of suddenly finding himself alone. Dahmer began his plunge into homicidal madness when his parents got divorced and left him alone in the family house at the age of eighteen. Nilson may have experienced something similar at the age of thirty-two when a male roommate, and sometime lover, moved out. A year and a half later, Nilson brought home a young man who turned down an offer to stay on at his apartment for the next week or two. Nilson made it impossible for him to leave by killing him.

The way Nilson murdered and disposed of this first victim would prove to be typical. He met the young man in a pub and brought him home for some more drinks and a place to stay for the night. When the young man was asleep, Nilson strangled him with his necktie. He then scrubbed the body clean, wrapped it in plastic sheets, and stored it under the floorboards.

In some cases Nilson may have masturbated on the corpse. Often he chopped up the bodies to make it easier to store the remains in confined spaces. Some of the body parts he boiled and flushed down the toilet. The disposal of the body would not always be immediate: he might leave the corpse in one of his rooms for a couple of days as a sort of hideous, mute companion.

One of the reasons Nilson was able to keep murdering as long as he did was that he periodically removed the human remains from his apartment and destroyed them. He did this by secretly putting the corpses and various body parts into a bonfire that he would build at night in his house's yard. He would put pieces of rubber into the blaze as well to create an odor that would camouflage the stench of burning flesh. When he moved out of his apartment in Cricklewood for another flat in Cranley Gardens, he used a bonfire to incinerate all the incriminating evidence still being stored in the older residence.

He went on to kill and butcher three more young men in the Cranley Gardens apartment, but his disposal methods finally caught up to him.

Some of the remains of a victim killed in February 1983 were flushed down the toilet and ended up blocking the plumbing for the entire house. Neighbors complained of toilets that wouldn't flush. The backup also produced a stench. The plumber who opened the manhole at the side of the house came upon human finger bones and decomposed flesh clogging the lines.

The police came on the scene to question the house's tenants, and as it turned out, they didn't have to perform any great feat of interrogation when they got around to Nilson. He directed them to a closet where they could find additional, physical evidence.

The discoveries made in Nilson's apartment might not have been quite as overwhelming as those made ten years later in Jeffrey Dahmer's rooms, but they were more than grisly enough. In the closet that Nilson pointed to were two plastic garbage bags containing two human heads (one boiled, the other parboiled), two torsos, four arms, and various internal organs. In a tea chest were another torso and an assortment of bones that Nilson had still not parted with. The story behind this gruesome collection was supplied very willingly by Nilson. He confessed in detail to all fifteen murders.

At his trial the jury determined that Nilson had not suffered from diminished responsibility at the time of his crimes. He was sentenced to prison for life.

HENRY LEE LUCAS

1936–

"Killing someone is just like walking outdoors. If I wanted a victim I'd just go to get one." These are the words of Henry Lee Lucas, drifter, occasional construction worker, and perhaps, the most prolific serial murderer America has ever known. When he was arrested in 1983, on a relatively minor charge, he felt compelled to start talking about his past, about "bad things" he had done, as he put it. Stories of killings began to emerge, then came a torrent of confessions that amounted to a horrifying saga of mass murder stretching across twenty-seven states. At one point, Lucas offered a victim count as high as 360. Law enforcement officials, however, have come up with much more conservative

estimates. The problem in getting at the truth is that the only evidence for many of these murders is the word of Henry Lee Lucas, who is often characterized as a pathological liar.

Lucas's first murder arrest came in 1960. Arguably he was guilty at the time of what might be called justifiable homicide. His victim was his seventy-four-year-old mother.

Viola, Lucas's mother, had raised her children while supporting herself as a prostitute in Blacksburg, Virginia. Lucas has said that his earliest memory of her was the time she blasted a customer in the leg with a shotgun. From then on, Viola would have sex with her clients in front of Lucas on a regular basis. She also beat Lucas; in one instance Viola's idea of parental discipline was to slam the back of his head with a two-by-four. Among other incidents that stood out in Lucas's childhood was his first day of school. In honor of the occasion, his mother fashioned his hair into girlish ringlets and put him in a dress.

By 1960, when Lucas was twenty-three, he had allegedly committed his first murder—a teenage girl who had resisted his attempt to rape her in 1951—but had never been arrested for the crime. He had, however, been in and out of reformatories and prisons on various lesser charges. On January 11, 1960, he was drinking with his mother in his new home of Tecumseh, Michigan, when the two of them got into an argument. Reverting to old habits, she hit him with a broom. Soon after that, she was sprawled on the floor, a knife wound in her chest, mortally wounded. But Lucas was not through with his mother. While in prison, serving a twenty-to-forty-year sentence for this murder, he could still hear her voice which plagued him with commands to defy the authorities' orders and to commit suicide. In all, he served only ten years of his sentence, at which time he was judged fit to reenter society despite his protests that he belonged in prison and that his murderous urges would overcome him if he were set free. According to one of his later statements, Lucas killed a woman in Jackson, Michigan, on June 3, 1970, the day of his release.

As Lucas's story goes, this killing initiated his life as a nomadic murderer, wandering from place to place, finding his victims along highways and interstates and near the temporary homes he inhabited along the way. He married a woman in Pennsylvania in 1975 and took on the responsibility of her two daughters from a previous marriage, but this did not slow him down for long. His wife divorced him in less than two years. Around the time Lucas was losing his wife, he acquired another companion, one who would pass in and out of his life for close to seven years and who would play an important part in his homicidal pursuits. Lucas met a man named Ottis Toole in Jacksonville, Florida, in 1976. Kindred spirits, they would often go out in search of murder victims along Florida's highways. To Lucas's penchant for rape, murder, and dismemberment, his sometime lover Toole added a taste for human flesh.

There was also to be another woman in Lucas's life, or to be more precise, another girl. When Lucas met Toole's niece, Becky Powell, the girl was only ten years old. Lucas took a paternal interest in her, and as Becky got older, they became common-law husband and wife. After escaping from a juvenile detention home in 1981, Becky Powell became the road companion of Lucas and Toole and may have been an accessory in their killings.

After drifting across the Southwest, Lucas and Powell found a temporary home at the All People's House of Prayer, a fundamentalist religious commune in Stoneburg, Texas. While there, Powell experienced a religious awakening and came to the decision that she must return to Florida, serve her juvenile detention time, and live an honest life. Lucas was not pleased, but still he agreed to hitchhike with her back to her home state. Their life together came to an end one night soon after their trip began. While camping out, they got into an argument, and Powell got so infuriated that she slapped Lucas's face. Lucas's response was to get his knife and thrust it through her heart. Then he carved up his fourteen-year-old spouse and buried the pieces.

Lucas killed again three weeks later, and once more his victim was someone close to him: Kate Rich, a woman whom Lucas and Becky Powell had befriended. After stabbing the old woman, he sliced an upside-down cross between her breasts and sexually violated her corpse. Nine months after Rich's death, local police arrested Lucas, but not on murder charges. He was jailed for possession of a handgun. As it turned out, this minor arrest led to the discovery of not only one but hundreds of murders.

When Lucas decided to confess, he started a process that would last eighteen months. In that time he admitted not only to 360 murders committed by himself, but to more than a hundred others carried out with the help of Ottis Toole. The tally has fluctuated, however. Many of Lucas's murder confessions were corroborated by police, but then he clearly lied about many of his other supposed killings. He further compromised his reliability when he started telling stories about bringing poison to Guyana for the Jonestown massacre.

Lucas was convicted of just ten murders, including the killings of Becky Powell and Kate Rich, and was sentenced to death by lethal injection. Over the years, police investigators have put Lucas's murder total as low as 69, and as high as 81 and 199. A recent book on Lucas by Joel Norris, on the other hand, opts for the number 157. As if this were not confusing enough, Lucas made a complete turnabout in 1985 and claimed he had only murdered his mother, Powell, and Rich. Before long, he went even further, denying that he had killed anyone other than his mother.

The extent of Henry Lee Lucas's homicidal career is still a matter of speculation as he waits on death row.

ARTHUR GARY BISHOP
1951–1988

The Arthur Bishop case serves as one of those recurring, and terrifying, reminders of why parents warn their children never to talk to strangers—*any* strangers. Even without proper instruction a child might instinctively shy away from someone he or she didn't know if the person were some obviously wild-eyed maniac. But children must be taught stringent rules in order for them to avoid an apparently normal, helpful stranger, as well—someone, say, who has devoted himself to being a Big Brother or who is perhaps so devoutly religious that he has even gone abroad to preach Christian beliefs. Arthur Bishop was that sort of person—he'd done both of these things. But he was also a killer,

committing crimes so hideous that they would seem to have sprung from a parent's nightmare.

The details of the story that would horrify the state of Utah first came to light in the summer of 1983. The Salt Lake City police went to the home of a young accountant named Roger Downs to ask some questions about a missing boy, thirteen-year-old Graeme Cunningham, who had dropped out of sight just a few days earlier. The reasons for seeing Roger Downs about the disappearance were routine; the Cunningham boy had been expected to go on a camping trip with Downs a week after his disappearance, and the police were simply following up on this information. But it didn't take long for them to surmise that the questioning was not routine for Downs. The clean-cut young accountant acted as if he wanted to tell the police something. Before long, he did. Admitting that his real name was Arthur Bishop, he told the police about five dead boys, one of which was Graeme Cunningham.

The thirty-three-year-old Bishop said that he had killed the boys, who ranged in age from four to thirteen, over a four-year period. Capitalizing on his conspicuously unsuspicious appearance, Bishop had managed to abduct boys from the most wide-open places. He had snatched one of the boys from his own front yard; another had been taken from a grocery store, where the child was shopping with his grandfather. Bishop took each victim to an isolated spot, where he raped the boys, then killed them in various ways, either by strangulation, shooting, drowning, or bludgeoning (police would later find a bloody hammer in Bishop's home).

Bishop took the police to the graves of his victims, located south of Salt Lake City. An examination of the corpses gave the investigators more information, some of which belied what Bishop was telling them. Bishop, who had also confessed to being a serial rapist of many more than five boys, had said his reason for killing had been to keep these particular boys from talking about his sexual abuse of them. But the physical evidence gleaned from the corpses' condition made it clear that some of the victims had also been mutilated, indicating that violence had been an end in itself for Bishop. Eventually, the killer would also confess that he had fondled the dead bodies.

Bishop was arrested on July 23, 1983, and was arraigned on first-degree murder charges four days later.

As would be expected, news of the case was absolutely devastating to the people of Utah, an unusually law-abiding state. The savagery of the crimes was shocking enough. Added to that was the unnerving fact that the perpetrator, the product of a righteous Mormon family, had succeeded in projecting such a trustworthy persona for so long. At the time, the newspapers made much of the fact that as a boy Arthur Bishop had been an Eagle Scout (like, incidentally, other mass murderers such as Charles Whitman and Richard Angelo) and that he had also been a good student and a faithful churchgoer. He had even maintained his moral course after high school by shipping out to the Philippines as a Mormon missionary. Later he had continued to pursue Mormon values of industriousness by distinguishing himself in business college. But as the 1983 investigation of the case continued, the police soon learned that the troubling undercurrents had not been too far below the surface—and had begun to overflow in the late seventies.

In his late twenties at that time, and working as an accountant, Bishop had begun to covet his employers' wealth; he was convicted in one case of embezzlement and was suspected in another. This behavior, in turn, led to a more profound sort of trouble—his excommunication from the Mormon faith. With this sacred tie severed, Bishop descended into a secret world. He remained in Salt Lake City, but he lived under aliases. Not only did he succeed in eluding police after his embezzlement conviction (he was supposed to repay the money), but he also cut himself off completely from his family. Try as they might, they could not locate him. For all intents and purposes Arthur Bishop ceased to exist. The person who took his place became more and more obsessed by dark passions. Even his choice of philanthropic activities—being a Big Brother to fatherless boys—had a sinister purpose: it was an easy way to cultivate the trust of potential victims. His first child-murder was committed in October 1979.

After this crime Bishop's compulsion to kill was so overpowering that he started butchering puppies as a way of reliving the murderous experience. At his trial Bishop was described by his lawyer as a man "out of control" who desperately wanted to be stopped. His willingness to confess seemed to bear this out. So did one of his more bizarre acts: soon after killing Graeme Cunningham, his final victim, Bishop went to see the boy's mother. "I wanted to help her," he later said. "I just didn't know how to tell her that I killed her child."

Convicted of five counts of murder in March 1984, Bishop was sentenced to die. The Utah legal code gave him a choice: death by firing squad or death by lethal injection. He chose injection. For four years his sentence was argued in court, then Bishop decided not to appeal anymore. He believed the time had come to face his sentence. "With great sadness and remorse," he said in his final statement, "I realize that I allowed myself to be misled by Satan." He died of lethal injection on June 10, 1988.

THE GREEN RIVER KILLER
1982–1984

In 1982, just eight years after suffering Ted Bundy's first murderous onslaught, the state of Washington was once again faced with a relentless series of killings. For two years someone littered the Seattle area and surrounding King County with the bodies of young women. The closest the police came to a solution of the case was the extensive investigation of a suspect five years after the last murder was committed.

The unknown murderer got his name from the dumping ground used for the first five victims. On July 15, 1982, the body of a sixteen-year-old girl was found in the Green River, which courses along the

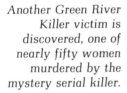

Another Green River Killer victim is discovered, one of nearly fifty women murdered by the mystery serial killer.

western and southern perimeter of King County. The police pulled another female corpse out of the river on August 12 and, propelling the horror a quantum leap forward, discovered three more bodies there on a single day later in the month. "The Green River Killer" quickly established himself as a frighteningly fast-working murder machine.

Over the years, police found that keeping track of both the number of victims and the order in which they were killed was a difficult process. Not only was the murderer working quickly, but he was disposing of his victims so efficiently that many weren't uncovered until months after their disappearance. In the case of fifteen-year-old

Debra Estes, who vanished in September 1982, the body wasn't found until nearly six years later. A profile of the Green River Killer's preferred target, however, was easy to determine. The murderer was picking out young women who could be easily isolated and who were not likely to be tracked down immediately after dropping out of sight. At first the victims were exclusively prostitutes, but then they also started to include runaways and other transients. They were either strangled or stabbed. Many times, though, no specific murder method was determined; after months, or years, of decomposition, a victim's remains were not likely to offer many clues as to the cause of death.

The murder spree reached especially grisly heights in May 1983, when three young women were murdered in as many days. Then, a few months later, the killings came to a stop. No suspects had been arrested, but perhaps, the people of King County hoped, the murders had finally come to a mysterious conclusion, as other unsolved serial-murder cases had in the past.

The respite lasted only until February 1984, when the corpse of a nineteen-year-old prostitute was discovered. The killing continued.

When the murders actually did come to an end later that year, twenty-four victims were attributed to the Green River Killer. As the police followed up on suspicious cases of missing persons, they were forced to add more victims to their list. By May 1986 the total was thirty-five. But still more skeletal remains were uncovered. The apparently final, definitive number given in 1989 was an astounding forty-nine women killed.

In the course of their exhaustive investigation, the police spent $15 million. They were able to determine that the killer was probably a white man in his late twenties or early thirties, and they believed he posed as a policeman in order to either win the confidence of or intimidate his victims.

At the end of 1988, phone callers to the TV show "Manhunt" implicated a young Washington man as the culprit the authorities were looking for. The man's name was William Jay Stevens II. He was a thirty-eight-year-old law student who also happened to be a convicted thief. While Stevens was in jail on other charges, the police investigated the possibility of his being the Green River Killer. A search of Stevens's home revealed that he collected police paraphernalia. Implicating him further were credit card receipts that indicated he was in the vicinity of some of the Green River Killer's known crimes. By the summer of 1989, the police announced that Stevens was a serious suspect. But in the end they decided that Stevens was not the killer. He was officially eliminated as a suspect in November 1989.

While authorities made no further progress in King County, Washington, some law enforcement officials formulated an especially unsettling explanation for the halt in the Green River killings. In June 1985, around a year after the last of the King County murders, another string of murders began in San Diego, California. All of the victims—there were at least ten of them—were young women, and most of them were strangled. Theorists speculate that these murders were the work of the same man responsible for the killings in Washington.

The culprit in the San Diego case was never caught.

CHRISTOPHER BERNARD WILDER
1945–1984

In the spring of 1984, America was forced to come to grips with an especially frightening form of serial-murder menace: the nomad killer, the multiple murderer who roams the interstate highways and is gone from a murder scene before the homicide can be connected to similar crimes. This law enforcement problem was brought into stark focus in April 1984 by two cases. In that month, Henry Lee Lucas, the drifter responsible for perhaps more than a hundred deaths, was convicted of murder in Texas, while the horrifying murder spree of Christopher Wilder, which stretched from one end of the country to the other, was just coming to an end.

Not only did these two cases dramatize the great danger of this type of murderer, they also demonstrated how strikingly different these killers could be, making it clear that the public couldn't complacently be on guard against just one kind of individual. Henry Lee Lucas was a physically scarred, working-class wanderer who lived from hand to mouth, someone who would be likely to fit the common conception of a dangerous loner. Christopher Wilder, on the other hand, was a wealthy

young man who lived the life of a playboy, complete with speedboat, high-priced seaside home, and swanky cars. He sometimes raced his Porsche in competitions. When he died, he left an estate estimated at somewhere between $449,000 and $1.8 million. He also left a legacy of torture and murder that included at least eight murders and disappearances.

Before he turned homicidal, Christopher Wilder had been arrested several times for sex offenses, in his native Australia as well as the United States. He managed to avoid prison sentences in all cases. In one instance he was acquitted, in another the complainant failed to testify, and in the rest of the cases he pleaded to lesser charges and got off with probation. None of his trouble with the law prevented him from making a good living. Based in Boynton Beach, a Florida town situated between Palm Beach and Miami, he established himself as a shrewd real estate investor and in 1979 cofounded two contracting companies, Sawtel Electric and Sawtel Construction.

His waterside house had its own pier, a sauna in the master bedroom, and a photo studio. His sideline in photography was a way to meet attractive young women: he smooth-talked them into posing for him.

It has been suggested that Wilder's murderous impulses were set off early in 1984 when a beautiful young woman rejected his marriage proposal. Soon after that, on February 26, 1984, his string of killings began. The thirty-eight-year-old Wilder was racing in the Miami Grand Prix, and while there, he came upon Rosario Gonzalez, a model whom he had previously persuaded to pose for a paperback book cover (not surprisingly, the photo was never published). Gonzalez left the race with Wilder and was never seen again.

Around a week later, Elizabeth Kenyon, the woman who had

refused to marry Wilder, was seen with him at a Coral Gables gas station. She, too, disappeared. When police began to suspect him, Wilder took $50,000 out of his bank account and left Boynton Beach behind. His cross-country journey of death had begun.

Wilder traveled north to Georgia, then wandered west, passing through Texas and Oklahoma, then continuing on to California. Murdering along the way, he found his victims in areas unfamiliar to him and wasn't able to conceal the bodies as well as he had in Boynton Beach. Corpses were found, and they revealed the ferocity of Wilder's spree.

Even after the murders were brought to a stop, the FBI was unwilling to divulge the full gory details for fear of copycat crimes, but the media was informed that Wilder's attacks involved multiple rapes and torture before the victims were stabbed to death. The means of torture was usually an electric prod. In the case of one abductee who managed to escape, Wilder sealed her eyelids shut with glue. The killer found most of his victims in shopping malls, convincing the young women that he could give them a big break in the modeling business. When they didn't go along willingly, he would force them into his car.

By April 5, when the FBI announced they were on Wilder's trail, three deaths were verified and four young women were still missing. Since the country was in a state of alert, Wilder needed help finding new victims. He abducted a sixteen-year-old named Tina Marie Risico and forced her to become his accomplice.

In Merrillville, Indiana, a teenager let Risico talk her into modeling together for a photo session, and by the time the girl reached Wilder's car she was trapped. The killer pulled her inside. For two days he raped and tortured her, then left her suffering from stab wounds outside the western New York town of Penn Yan. She lived, and was able to inform police that Wilder was now in the Northeast. The authorities taking part in the nationwide manhunt were beginning to close in.

After fatally shooting a woman in order to steal her car, Wilder took Risico to Boston and put her on a plane back to her California home. Since Wilder didn't live to explain his actions, the reasons behind his release of Risico are a mystery. The next day, the search for Wilder ended in the New Hampshire town of Colebrook.

At a gas station, two state policemen identified the car Wilder had stolen. When the killer grabbed a .357 magnum out of his glove compartment, state trooper Leo Jellison grappled with him, and Wilder's gun went off twice. Jellison was wounded; Wilder was shot fatally through the heart. Law enforcement officials have speculated that he might have killed himself intentionally.

RICKY KASSO

1967–1984

When the news about the murder of seventeen-year-old Gary Lauwers first broke, a rash of articles appeared, speculating on the growth of organized, bloodthirsty Satan cults taking hold of suburban youth. Early accounts of the killing included stories of a barbaric human sacrifice, complete with a circle of chanting devil worshipers and ritual mutilation—all of which was carried out just a ten-minute walk away from Main Street in a picture-postcard Long Island town. As investigators gathered more information, they came to believe that the incident was actually not quite so bizarre, that the horror-film trappings of the case had been exaggerated in the initial reports. But for all that, the murder was no less brutal and senseless.

The police of Northport, Long Island, first became aware of the crime on July 2, 1984, when an anonymous phone caller directed them to a part of town known as the Aztakea Woods. There, in a shallow grave, they found the remains of Gary Lauwers, already over two weeks dead. A medical examiner's report would later establish that the teenager had been stabbed with a pocketknife at least thirty-two times, twenty-two times in the face. The actual total of stab wounds might have been more, but the advanced decomposition of the flesh on Lauwers's torso made it impossible to say for certain.

Tracking down the teenagers who had been seen with Lauwers shortly before he disappeared on June 16, the police focused their attention on seventeen-year-old Ricky Kasso and eighteen-year-old James Troiano. They were both high school dropouts and known heavy drug users who lived on the streets, sleeping wherever they could—in their car, in the park, in friends' houses. Troiano had a record of burglary arrests. Kasso's recent brush with the police was more unusual: he was currently facing a charge of grave robbing. In April he had dug up a 19th-century grave from which he had stolen a skull and the skeletal remains of a hand. He had intended for them to be used in some sort of Satanic rite.

Soon after they were taken into custody, both boys confessed to the Gary Lauwers murder. Kasso admitted to the stabbing of Lauwers, and Troiano told police he had helped by holding the victim in place.

After the arrest of Kasso and Troiano on July 6, the authorities made public the ritual-murder theory. The two suspects were linked to a local Satanic group known as the Knights of the Black Circle, which had as many as twenty members and had already become known for stealing pets for animal sacrifices. The murder of Gary Lauwers was characterized as the logical, if horrific, culmination of the group's activities, a human sacrifice witnessed by several teenagers who chanted along with Kasso's knife thrusts. As part of the demonic mutilation, Kasso gouged out Lauwers's eyes.

Kasso might have been able to shed more light on the background to the murder, but he eliminated any chance of that when he hanged himself in his cell in the early hours of July 7.

By the time James Troiano went on trial for second-degree murder at the beginning of the next year, the authorities had revised their opinion of the case. They learned that the Knights of the Black Circle had been virtually a thing of the past by the time the murder occurred, and in any case, Kasso had never been closely associated with them. Investigators also verified that, instead of a large group of devil worshipers at the scene of the crime, there had been only one witness, a friend of Kasso and Troiano by the name of Albert Quinones. Devil worship had been a factor in the murder—Kasso had certainly dabbled in heavy-metal–style Satanism—but much more important was the influence of drugs.

According to the corrected version of events, the antagonism that eventually triggered the murder began in April 1984 when Gary Lauwers stole ten bags of angel dust from Kasso. He never paid Kasso back. Kasso, in turn, spent two months brooding about the rip-off and then, on the night of June 16, decided to teach Lauwers a lesson.

Lauwers was in the woods outside town that night with Kasso, Troiano, and Quinones. They were all tripping on mescaline. Kasso started to harass Lauwers, then started beating him. Soon he was out of control. He went after Lauwers with his pocketknife.

Kasso stabbed him over and over again. He kept barking at Lauwers, "Say you love Satan!" Lauwers responded with "No, I love my mother!" The orgy of stabbing continued. Kasso apparently cut out Lauwers's eyes during the frenzied slashing of Lauwers's face. When it was all over, Kasso left the body lying deeper in the woods, covered with leaves. According to Kasso's confession he then heard the screech of a crow, which, in his mescaline-driven mind, was Satan's way of saying that the murder was a good thing.

Kasso bragged about the killing to friends and even took some of them to see the body. After two weeks he decided the time had come to shovel some dirt over the foul-smelling remains. The anonymous call to the police that started the investigation came from a teenager who had overheard others talk about Kasso's boasting.

At his trial James Troiano retracted his confession. His lawyer argued that the defendant's admission had merely been an attempt to fill in gaps of memory shrouded in a hallucinogen-induced haze. Troiano, he maintained, was only a witness to the killing, not an accomplice. The jury agreed with him and pronounced Troiano not guilty.

JAMES OLIVER HUBERTY
1943–1984

On Tuesday, July 17, 1984, Etna Huberty persuaded her husband, James, to call a mental health clinic. For some time he had been deeply despondent. Even when employed, the forty-one-year-old James Huberty was known as a gloomy character, but since he had been fired as a security guard in early July, he had seemed overwhelmed by the anger that had been festering within him for so long. He placed a call to the clinic in his town of San Ysidro, California, and was told that someone would get back to him about making an appointment for counseling. Huberty waited. The call never came.

The next morning, James Huberty was busy in traffic court, set- tling a traffic violation. After- ward, he met his wife and four- teen-year-old daughter for lunch at a McDonald's across the street from the courthouse. If there is any benefit to being unemployed, it is the opportunity to spend more time with one's family, and on this afternoon Huberty at- tempted to take advantage of his free time by going with his wife and daughter to the nearby San Diego Zoo. His mind, though, was not on the excursion. He was obviously brooding. When he got around to talking about the clinic's failure to return his call the day before, he told his wife, "Society's had their chance."

After the family returned to their apartment later that afternoon, James decided to go out and went into the bedroom to kiss his wife good-bye. Etna wanted to know if he needed money. James said it wasn't necessary. He also said something else.

During his recent bout of depression, Huberty had been prone to saying "wild things," as Etna later put it. For this reason she naturally didn't give his words much thought when, on his way out, he said, "I'm going hunting—hunting humans."

Huberty didn't go far. He drove a half-block to a McDonald's—not the one in which he had had lunch—and parked the car. Around four o'clock he entered the restaurant—with a semi-automatic rifle slung from one shoulder, a 12-gauge shotgun slung from the other, and a semi-automatic pistol tucked in his belt. Ten minutes later, twenty of the people inside were dead. Most of the victims were children and teenagers.

Huberty unleashed his barrage after issuing the senseless order "Everybody get down on the floor or I'll kill somebody." He shot at people as they tried to comply with the order and as they ran for the exits and as they unwittingly approached the restaurant from the street.

When the police surrounded the fast-food restaurant and took stock of the situation, they called in a SWAT team. Still no move could be made. The SWAT officers took position, but they didn't know enough about what was going on inside the McDonald's. Considering the amount of gunfire coming from the restaurant, it was possible that more than one gunman was involved. Another consideration was whether any hostages had been taken.

Huberty did not actually display any great concern about fending off the law. He was there simply to shoot and kill. After the first ten minutes, the fire eased up somewhat, but he still continued to shoot sporadically for the next hour. That was how long the SWAT team waited. The breakthrough came when one of the McDonald's employees escaped through a back door. The employee was able to inform the police that only one gunman was involved and no hostages had been taken. The SWAT sharpshooters were now free to line up their target and shoot. The first four rounds hit nothing. Then an officer perched atop the adjacent post-office roof locked Huberty in his sights and squeezed the trigger. The round smashed through Huberty's chest. He dropped to the floor, dead. At 5:17 the shooting-spree horror was over.

Inside and just outside the restaurant were twenty dead bodies and twenty wounded. Soon, another one of the wounded would die. At that time, the incident was the worst mass shooting in American history. One policeman on the scene had to be relieved because he was so sickened by the carnage he saw.

In trying to construct a psychological portrait of the man responsible for the massacre, experts pointed to the divorce of Huberty's parents when he was in grade school and recent difficulties in finding work, and gleaned further information about him from associates and friends. Huberty's employment troubles began in his native Ohio, where he had lost a good job as a welder when his plant shut down. His move with his family to California in December 1983 seemed to have opened up new opportunities; then he lost his job as a security guard. Friends and acquaintances described Huberty as a loner and as a man "full of unfocused anger." The weapons he had used in the attack were part of the gun collection that the sullen Huberty had been assembling over the years.

Unfortunately, this profile, though consistent with other killers of this type, may not be very useful. As psychiatrists and sociologists point out, the sort of anger that is virulent enough to lead to a paroxysm of mass murder is difficult, if not impossible, to identify before the actual explosion takes place.

LEONARD LAKE
1946–1985

Leonard Lake was a survivalist. After four years in the U.S. Marine Corps—two of which were spent in psychiatric care—he settled in his native northern California and became increasingly obsessed with the idea of an impending apocalypse. He became convinced that a nuclear holocaust would reduce the world to a savage state where only the fittest, and the most prepared, would survive. He was determined to be one of those who would persevere.

In the 1970s, while working as an elementary school teacher and performing volunteer community service, he collected weapons and made plans for building his own personal refuge in the woods that would provide him with everything he needed while the rest of the world crumbled. Lake, the future guerrilla survivalist in a devastated world, often obtained the things he wanted through illegal means. In 1980 he received a year's probation for attempting to steal construction materials.

Throughout this period Lake was also preoccupied with something else. He spent much of his spare time engaged in amateur pornography, his particular passion being the photographing of women in bondage. This interest was nothing new for Lake. He had started taking photos of naked girls when he was in his teens. Among his photographic subjects was his sister, with whom he also had an incestuous relationship. Lake's two obsessions—survivalism and deviant sex—would eventually dovetail, with horrifying results.

Lake's partner in some of his schemes was a young Chinese man named Charles Ng (pronounced "ing"). The two met in 1981, when Lake was thirty-five and Ng was twenty. They devoted themselves to putting together a private arsenal of automatic weapons. Their venture was temporarily derailed in 1982 when they were arrested for possession of illegal firearms. Lake jumped bail and hid out in Humboldt County, where he constructed a survivalist ranch. Two men who were invited there disappeared and were probably killed by Lake. One was his brother, the other a friend of his from the marines. Ng, meanwhile, plea-bargained a sentence of three years and was paroled after a year and a half.

Lake and Ng reunited in 1984 at Lake's new forest compound outside Wilseyville in Calaveras County. The place had a cabin, well stocked with automatic weapons, and a bunker made of cinderblock to serve as an emergency shelter. Lake now initiated a scheme that he gave the paramilitary name of Operation Miranda.

Lake believed in the necessity of sex slaves. Once the country was destroyed by nuclear war, he reasoned, there would be no women available to do his cooking, his cleaning, and to provide sexual service. Operation Miranda involved the collection of women before disaster struck. Lake, the pornographer, also believed in recording the sounds and pictures of his dealings with the women.

Lake stole a set of video equipment from a San Francisco photographer named Harvey Dubs. He also kidnapped Dubs, along with his wife, Deborah, and the couple's baby. At his Wilseyville compound Lake killed Dubs and the baby, and designated Deborah Dubs as his sex slave. But she wasn't kept for postapocalypse contingencies. She was raped, tortured, and murdered, all of which was recorded on videotape.

The same thing happened to a neighbor named Brenda O'Connor. As was the case with the Dubs family, the victim's husband and baby were murdered. Yet another woman whose torture and death were videotaped was Kathleen Allen, lover of one of Ng's friends. And there were other victims. Exactly how many is not known.

Lake was arrested in June 1985 on one of his provisioning expeditions; he was parked outside a San Francisco lumber outlet, while Ng was inside shoplifting a bench vise. Ng was spotted on his way out, and when police arrived, he left the vise in the trunk of the car and ran off. He managed to get away, but Lake did not. Police found a semi-automatic pistol fitted with a silencer in the car and took Lake into custody for illegal gun possession.

At the police station the officers had some difficulty identifying their suspect. Lake's driver's license bore the name of Robin Stapley, a Guardian Angel who had disappeared after being hired by Brenda O'Connor as a bodyguard, and the car was registered in the name of Paul Cosner, an auto dealer who had also vanished. Both are now believed to have been Lake murder victims. Fingerprinting of the suspect finally led the police to Lake's real name, but he had no intention of standing by for any further investigation. In true paramilitary fashion he swallowed a cyanide capsule to avoid imprisonment. He died a few days later.

A search of Lake's compound uncovered the remains of twelve people buried behind the cabin. Further investigation revealed that the murder total might have been as high as twenty-five. The police now became very interested in the Chinese man who had run away from the scene of Lake's arrest.

Charles Ng was found a month after Lake's death when he was arrested for shoplifting north of the border, in Calgary, Alberta. In September 1991, after a lengthy appeals process, he was extradited to California to face twelve charges of murder for his alleged participation in Leonard Lake's crimes.

DR. TEET HAERM
1953–

Since the release of the film *The Silence of the Lambs*, the character of Dr. Hannibal Lecter has come to personify the ultimate in serial-killing horror. A deranged psychiatrist with a taste for human flesh, he embodies a bizarre, and completely unsettling, combination of intellect, medical knowledge, and mind-boggling, savage violence. Serial murderers of this kind, who have coupled a high level of normal, professional achievement with a secret homicidal life, are rare indeed in the real world, but not altogether unheard of. Arguably, a real-life parallel to Hannibal the Cannibal is Swedish murderer Dr. Teet Haerm, whose case was largely undocumented in the United States until the 1992

The streets of Stockholm were the hunting grounds for Dr. Teet Haerm, the medical examiner turned serial murderer.

publication of Jay Robert Nash's *World Encyclopedia of 20th Century Murder*. Convicted in the late eighties, several years after Lecter was first created by novelist Thomas Harris, Haerm may not have been an eminent psychiatrist, but he did acquire considerable respect in Stockholm as a forensic pathologist. And if the testimony of his alleged accomplice is true, he was also capable of unspeakable murder.

In 1984 Dr. Haerm was a medical examiner held in high regard by the Stockholm police. His youthful, innocent looks underscored the young age at which he had distinguished himself. He was a man who had overcome personal tragedy—his wife had committed suicide two years before—to become a key participant in the investigation of many of the city's murder cases; he had also published articles in forensic medical journals and further established himself as an expert in his field. The police first started to suspect that there was a secret side to the thirty-one-year-old Haerm during the investigation of a series of grisly murders in the red-light district.

Three prostitutes had been found murdered and dismembered, and five others were missing. With no real clues to follow up, the police department cast a net of investigating officers into the city's vice district with instructions to question any prostitute they encountered, in the hope of hauling in some tidbit of information. The police waded through a mass of useless answers, but eventually something interesting emerged. They found they were coming upon a recurring observation about a man in a white Volkswagen cruising the district.

The car's license plate number was traced to the vehicle of Dr. Teet Haerm, who also happened to answer the general description of the man seen driving the car in question. He was taken into custody.

The police now took a closer look at their associate and discovered something disturbing. In a search of Haerm's house, they found a photograph of the man's deceased wife with a rope tightened around her throat. The woman was supposed to have hanged herself. Could she have been a murder victim instead?

Circumstantial evidence cast an aura of suspicion about Haerm, but not enough to warrant an indictment, let alone a conviction. He was set free. For a time it seemed that he might have been a deeply wronged man, as all the nasty allegations leveled against him subsequently prompted his dismissal from his job. Meanwhile, the police pursued the vice-district murder case, relying to a certain extent on autopsies that had been performed by none other than Dr. Haerm. The elusive compelling evidence against the ex-pathologist eventually emerged from an unexpected source.

One of Haerm's friends was another doctor named Thomas Allgren, who, as it turned out, shared many of Haerm's interests. What those interests were may never have come to the police's attention if it weren't for one of Allgren's more detestable proclivities: he was sexually molesting his four-year-old daughter. One thing Allgren was not, though, was a tight-lipped crook. He confessed to abusing his daughter soon after being confronted by social welfare workers, and once his tongue was loosened, he proceeded to talk about other things as well.

He first implicated his friend Haerm by mentioning that the man was with him when he molested his daughter. Allgren's next revelation was that he had helped the former medical examiner murder and butcher prostitutes. The more detailed the story got, the more horrendous it became. Allgren said that Haerm was determined to wipe out the sinful women of the streets; he also said that Haerm was fond of eating the prostitutes' flesh. As was the case with the molestation charge against Allgren, a little girl figured into a story that emerged about the red-light murders. This time, the girl was Haerm's five-year-old daughter: she witnessed the power-saw beheading of one of the prostitutes.

In all, Haerm was charged with the murder of seven prostitutes, his wife, and a female student found strangled and mutilated in 1986 in Copenhagen, across the Ore Sound from Sweden's west coast. He was ultimately convicted in 1988 of murdering prostitute Catrine da Costa, the case for which the prosecution assembled its best evidence. Allgren pleaded guilty to the same crime. Both men received life sentences.

GARY HEIDNIK
1943–

Gary Heidnik has been many things in his life: a soldier, a practical nurse, a landlord, a church minister, and a stock speculator. The first of these ventures, his enlistment in the U.S. Army in the early sixties, was not his most successful, though it certainly was in keeping with his future experiences. His stint ended after two years with a discharge due to mental disability. From then on, his various jobs and enterprises would, by necessity, be pursued during those periods between suicide attempts and periodic stays at Pennsylvania mental institutions.

Heidnik's career as a nurse in Philadelphia was reasonably successful, but it was also short-lived. Grander plans seemed to lead him on to other things. The grandest was the founding of his own church, the United Church of the Ministries of God, which, not surprisingly, resulted in his self-appointment as bishop. He also began to play the

stock market. Showing the ability that his keen mind possessed—he has an IQ of 130—
Heidnik was able to build a port-
folio of investments that would
eventually amount to half a million dollars.

But material wealth was not
enough for Gary Heidnik. Bizarre
notions kept brewing in his
mind, obsessions that wouldn't
let him be. His insanity might
have originally been driven by a
desperate childhood in which he
was psychologically dominated
by a cruel disciplinarian of a
father and an alcoholic mother.

As an alternate explanation, Heidnik claimed at one time that his
sadistic impulses were triggered by mind-scrambling LSD experiments
to which the army subjected him in the early sixties. Whatever the
reason, by 1986 Heidnik's psychological demons were telling him to
assemble a harem of ten women and set himself up as a veritable
patriarch who would propagate a small tribe of offspring.

Heidnik had already become a practiced womanizer—of sorts. He
preferred women who were black and retarded, and he had served
prison time in the late seventies for abducting just such a woman from
a mental institution and subjecting her to rape and sodomy. But not all
his women fit into this category. He married a mentally competent
Filipino woman in 1985, for instance. After being assaulted and forced
to watch Heidnik have sex with prostitutes, she left him after just three
months. Heidnik's plan for a harem was designed to preclude the
possibility of any other woman leaving him.

In all, Heidnik kidnapped six women and imprisoned them in the
basement of his Philadelphia house. For four months, despite all the
anguished cries that must have emanated from his basement, no discovery was made of what went on in the Heidnik place. Only when one of
his captives managed to escape did the police get word. And even then
they found it hard to believe the fantastic story they were told of torture
and murder. Just the same, they secured a search warrant and entered

Heidnik's house the next morning, March 25, 1987.

Tabloid newspapers are known for headlines that sensationalize and exaggerate the truth. But in this case, the tabloid label of "Philadelphia Torture Dungeon" was an exact description of Heidnik's cellar.

In the freezer the police found a human forearm, while in the kitchen stove was a roasted human rib. Both parts, it turned out, belonged to Sara Lindsay, who had died after being left to hang by her wrists for a week. Heidnik had carved up her corpse with a power saw, then food-processed her flesh, mixed it with dog food, and forced the other captive women to eat it. Those other women were still in the basement, either completely naked or naked from the waist down, two of them chained to pipes, the other trapped in a pit. Their hellish appearance was testimony to their daily treatment of torture, beatings, and rape.

One of Heidnik's six captives could not be found in the Philadelphia Torture Dungeon. That woman, the police found out, was Deborah Dudley. She had not been submissive enough for Heidnik's tastes. He punished the chained woman by putting her in a pit filled with water, then dropping in a live electrical wire. The woman was electrocuted when the wire came into contact with her chains. Her body was then taken across the state line into New Jersey and dumped in a forest.

Two of the eighteen counts of which Heidnik was eventually convicted were for first-degree murder. He is now on death row, waiting out the lengthy appeal of his death sentence. He has already made two suicide attempts since his arrest for murder.

RICHARD ANGELO

1964–

"The Angel of Death"

There is an emergency in the intensive care unit, and the male nurse comes running. With luck he'll be the first one on the scene. At the patient's bedside, while the patient labors for breath and the last seconds of life tick away, the nurse puts all his training to use. The situation doesn't improve. More life-saving measures are taken. Then, finally, the patient's breathing comes more easily, and soon he is out of danger completely. The quick-thinking nurse has brought a fellow human being back from death's door. He is a hero.

Richard Angelo, a registered nurse at Good Samaritan Hospital on Long Island, New York, wanted desperately to live this scenario. A former Eagle Scout and volunteer fireman, he was determined to serve humanity. All he needed was the opportunity. And to that end he did everything he could to make sure the opportunity would occur. If he rescued enough patients, Angelo must have reasoned, he would be considered an invaluable employee at his hospital. But things did not work out as planned.

Angelo's first experiment in artificially arranged heroism was conducted with the unwitting participation of John Stanley Fisher, in September 1987. A stroke victim whose condition had stabilized, Fisher was in the intensive care unit when twenty-three-year-old Angelo came to him in the middle of the night and injected something into Fisher's intravenous tube. Soon after that the patient was in critical condition. Here was an opportunity for Angelo, but it turned out to be a lost one. John Stanley Fisher died that night before he could be rescued. Angelo, however, was not discouraged from further attempts.

The number of times Angelo administered his deadly prescriptions in the six months he worked at Good Samaritan is not clear. We do have some idea, though, of how many times he failed. In September and October 1987, at least three patients in addition to Fisher died under suspicious circumstances. None of them seemed to be facing immediate life-threatening disorders at the time. One was recovering from pulmonary disease, one had just undergone a successful gall bladder operation, and another was on his way to prostate surgery. All died suddenly after respiratory or cardiac arrest. The drug that triggered these crises was usually either Pavulon or Anectine, both of which can produce muscle paralysis, which in turn can halt breathing. Some investigators believed there were more deaths of this kind that were not as conclusively established by evidence. In all, Angelo may have sent over ten patients to their deaths in his quest for recognition.

A picture of what Angelo's ministrations were like comes from the testimony of Good Samaritan patient Gerolamo Kucich. A visitor from Yugoslavia, Kucich was in the hospital on October 11, 1987, recovering from heart problems. Seeing a bearded man in a white hospital coat at his bedside, Kucich thought he was about to be treated by a doctor. The man assured Kucich that he would soon feel better, then injected Pavulon into the patient's IV tube. Left alone, Kucich soon had difficulty breathing. The condition worsened rapidly. He flopped around on the bed, gasping for air. The 75-year-old Kucich was so terrified that he called on his mother and father to somehow deliver him from encroaching death. Fortunately, he also managed to press the nurse call button. Help arrived in time. Among the hospital personnel who responded was Angelo, who used a hand-held respirator to aid in reviving the patient.

Kucich told his story about the bearded man in the white coat to hospital authorities. Masterful deduction was not needed to figure out who Kucich was talking about: Angelo was the only bearded male nurse on duty at the time Kucich's condition became critical. But hospital officials proceeded cautiously, putting Angelo on suspension until physical evidence could be gathered. They waited to inform the police until a urine sample revealed that Pavulon had been injected into Kucich.

Angelo was arrested in November after vials of Pavulon and Anectine were found during a search of his apartment. He confessed to murder almost immediately. Two years later, a jury found him responsible for the deaths of four patients, convicting him of two counts of second-degree murder, one count of manslaughter, and one count of criminally negligent homicide. Angelo received the maximum sentence allowed by law; his dreams of heroism brought him a prison term of sixty-one years to life.

ADOLFO DE JESUS CONSTANZO
1962–1989

"The Godfather of Matamoros"

On April 9, 1989, a young man named Serafin Hernandez Rivera swerved his car around a roadblock set up by Mexican police. The evasive maneuver triggered a high-speed chase that eventually came to an end when the *federales* ran their man down at a cattle ranch outside the Mexican border town of Matamoros.

Whatever Rancho Santa Elena was being used for, it was no longer the raising of cattle; the dilapidated spread clearly had not been used for agriculture for some time. Since the roadblock had been instituted as a routine measure in the police's campaign against border drug smuggling, the *federales* were inclined to assume that the ranch was a drug-

trafficking outpost and that the evasive Hernandez was involved in its operations. The marijuana discovered in Hernandez's car bore out the second assumption; more marijuana found on the ranch, in the amount of thirty kilos, bore out the first. Hernandez was arrested, along with three other men found on the ranch, one of them Hernandez's uncle Elio Hernandez Rivera, the chief of the drug ring. But then the search uncovered something else, something that prompted the police to call off any further investigation for that day.

Inside a tin-roofed shack, and just outside it, were four caldrons, melted candles, cigar butts, and empty bottles. As far as the *federales* were concerned, these items dictated only one reasonable course of action: no further steps could be taken until they brought in a sort of medicine man known as a *curandero*, a person who could rid the shack of evil spirits. Some form of black magic had obviously been practiced at the Rancho Santa Elena.

While the *curandero* did his work with garlic and peppers and white candles, the *federales* convinced their four prisoners to talk. The suspects from Rancho Santa Elena told a story of drug smuggling and occult worship that involved the sacrifice of both animals and human beings. They also showed the police where the bodies were buried outside the ranch shack.

The first to be exhumed was twenty-one-year-old Mark Kilroy, a Texas college student who had been missing for the last month. He had last been seen while on spring break in Matamoros on March 13. According to the *federales'* prisoners, the young American had been hauled off the street and onto a pickup truck and driven to Rancho Santa Elena. There, after twelve hours of captivity, he was killed with a machete. The Santa Elena drug smugglers then removed his brain, which was boiled in blood to make a satanic brew. The Santa Elena cult believed they derived strength and protection from drinking such things.

Mark Kilroy's body was the first to be uncovered by the Mexican police, but it was far from the last.

When the gruesome procedure was finally completed, fifteen bodies were found, all of them male, two of them as young as fourteen years old, most of them mutilated in some way as part of the cult's black-magic rituals. In addition to revealing the location of the corpses, the police interrogation of the four suspects also drew out information about the guiding force behind the Matamoros cult, a Cuban-American by the name of Adolfo de Jesus Constanzo.

Raised in Miami, Constanzo grew up in a household where the religious beliefs of Santeria were practiced. A sort of Hispanic equivalent of the French West Indian voodoo, Santeria is a Caribbean adaptation of African religion that has acquired certain Roman Catholic trappings. One of its features is animal sacrifice. By the time Constanzo moved to Mexico City in the mideighties, he was also a student of Palo Mayombe, another offshoot of African beliefs, but one with a more sinister reputation.

Not a great deal is known about Constanzo, but one fact clearly emerges from the various descriptions of him: he was a charismatic figure, reputed to have great spiritual powers. It was this reputation that led Elio Hernandez Rivera to seek him out when Hernandez's marijuana-smuggling business fell on hard times in 1988. He wanted to know what Constanzo could do to help.

Constanzo's solution to Hernandez's difficulties with the *federales* and rival gangsters was the implementation of black magic. As Hernandez's high priest, Constanzo set out to instill discipline in the gang and to provide protection for their efforts through occult practices. He became known as *El Padrino*, or the Godfather. The religion Constanzo imparted to Hernandez's men did not conform exactly to any known creed. It was Constanzo's own creation, part Palo Mayombe, part Santeria, part voodoo, part Aztec Santismo, part satanism. Whatever one might call it, it required human sacrifice, mutilation, the ripping out of hearts, and the boiling of brains.

Sometimes Constanzo's drug-smuggler cult would kill drug-business competitors or troublesome lawmen, but their targets could also seem quite random. Just about anyone would do for the cult's mystical purposes. The cultists were known to kidnap fellow Mexicans from the streets of Matamoros and from the surrounding countryside. On the night of March 13, 1989, Constanzo was reported to have said to his followers that they should "go out and bring in an Anglo male." Mark Kilroy happened to have been the Anglo that was snatched. According to the four suspects questioned by the police, Constanzo himself had been the one to deliver the fatal machete stroke that began the night's bloody ritual.

After gleaning everything they could from their prisoners, Mexican police were able to track Constanzo to Mexico City where he was holed up in a building with six members of the gang. The police surrounded the place, but they never had the chance to put "the Godfather of the Matamoros" under arrest. Before they could reach him, Constanzo ordered one of his men to kill him. Police found Constanzo already machine-gunned to death.

JEFFREY DAHMER

1960–

"The Milwaukee Monster"

The all-too-crowded parade of serial killers over the past twenty years has blunted our sensibilities to a certain extent. Each new report of senseless murder may get our attention and may even inspire some sort of public outcry, but it takes something wildly horrific to really shock us anymore. The atrocities committed in Milwaukee by Jeffrey Dahmer provoked just such a response.

The real-life nightmare sprang into the public consciousness in July 1991, when policemen came upon a young man named Tracy Edwards running down the street with handcuffs attached to one wrist. Edwards told the officers of his escape from a murder attempt and directed them

 to apartment 213 in the nearby Oxford Apartments. There they found Jeffrey Dahmer, a tall, empty-eyed man in his early thirties, living in what amounted to a museum of horrors.

Preserved in the freezer and refrigerator were human heads, intestines, kidneys, lungs, livers, and a heart. Squirreled away around the rest of the apartment were other ghastly mementos: rotting hands, genitalia, bones— including skulls, some complete skeletons, and small, fragmented bits. Polaroid snapshots of mutilated bodies provided more evidence of what had happened to previous visitors to apartment 213, young men who had been subjected to the tools of Dahmer's trade that the police now uncovered: chloroform, to subdue the victims; electric saws, to carve the bodies up; a barrel of acid, to burn away the flesh; formaldehyde, to save certain pieces for Dahmer's ghoulish collection. Once they had a chance to sift through it all, the police determined that the apartment contained the remains of eleven young men. But Dahmer did not have souvenirs of all his victims in that apartment. His confession would eventually put the murder total at seventeen.

Although most of the murders had occurred within the previous couple of years, Dahmer's first killing, it turned out, dated back thirteen years, to 1978. He was only eighteen at the time. By then he was already well rehearsed for the role of slayer and mutilator.

Jeffrey Dahmer grew up in a household racked by fierce marital discord. While his parents were fighting each other, they paid little attention to their son Jeffrey, which meant they neglected Dahmer a great deal of the time. Dahmer was also a victim of sexual abuse, molested by a male neighbor when he was only eight years old.

One of Dahmer's favorite pastimes while growing up was the butchering of animals. Many ended up in the pet cemetery he kept alongside his house. Others were staked to trees in the woods behind the Dahmer property.

The gruesome craft Dahmer practiced for so long on helpless animals was directed toward a fellow human being soon after his parents' divorce. Eighteen-year-old Dahmer was living alone in the family house at the time—neither divorced parent had taken him along when they moved out—and Dahmer was clearly in need of some kind of company. He settled on a nineteen-year-old hitchhiker named Steven Hicks, who went back to the house with Dahmer for some casual sex. At least, the sex was supposed to have been casual as far as Hicks was concerned. When the young man said he would be on his way, Dahmer would not let himself be abandoned again. He took a barbell and smashed it into the back of Hicks's skull, then strangled the young man to finish the job. When Dahmer was through disposing of the body, Hicks's bone fragments were dispersed along the slope of a nearby ravine.

After this first murder Dahmer made some attempt at normalcy, trying college for a while (he lasted only a few months) and signing on for a six-year hitch in the army (the army had enough of his excessive drinking after two years and discharged him). By 1985 he was living with his grandmother in a Milwaukee suburb and was working at the Ambrosia Chocolate Factory. But now, seven years after the murder of Steven Hicks, the lull would come to an end as a storm of deranged impulses broke loose.

Dahmer would pick up gay men, usually bringing them back to his grandmother's house, and then he would drug his victims; often the procedure entailed spiking coffee or alcoholic drinks with sleeping pills. Once the victim was unconscious, strangulation would be easy. Sexual assault of the corpse would often follow. Then came dismemberment.

At first the killings were sporadic, but after Dahmer moved into his own place at the Oxford Apartments in Milwaukee, they became steadily more frequent. In the ten months preceding his arrest, Dahmer averaged a murder every thirty days.

Opportunities to stop the slaughter came and went. The most outrageous and most-often-cited example of a missed, or rather ignored, opportunity came in 1991 when a naked, bleeding fourteen-year-old boy was spotted running down an alley, followed close behind by Dahmer. Police arrived on the scene, but they disregarded the compelling evidence before their eyes and believed Dahmer's story that he and the boy were merely having a lovers' spat. The officers moved on. The boy ended up as part of Dahmer's collection of body parts. When police finally responded appropriately to would-be victim Tracy Edwards in July 1991, Dahmer's arrest was long overdue.

At his trial, Dahmer was judged to be legally sane, legally responsible for his atrocious acts. He was given fifteen consecutive life sentences, which meant that he would be eligible for parole in 936 years.

ANDREI CHIKATILO
1936–
"The Mad Beast"

According to traditional communist dogma, crime is a capitalist phenomenon not to be found in a true people's republic like the Soviet Union. As was the case with other official Communist party myths, this notion has been shattered since the tearing down of the iron curtain. Revelations about Andrei Chikatilo in particular have shown that the former Soviet Union not only had its share of crime but also could be plagued by the most hideous crimes imaginable. A good case can be made for the news media's assertion that Chikatilo is the worst serial killer in modern times. Not only was the violence of his killings as savage as any previous mass murder case, but he indulged his sadistic passions for as many as twelve years, in which time he killed a staggering total of at least fifty-two victims.

In his confession, Chikatilo said that his homicidal madness had its beginning at a time when another form of madness held sway, namely Stalin's forced collectivization of the 1930s. This brutal policy created devastating famine in such areas as Chikatilo's native Ukraine. The widespread hardship was apparently especially horrific for the Chikatilo family; Andrei Chikatilo has alleged that his brother was eaten by peasants who had been driven insane with hunger. The stories Andrei's mother told him about this atrocity must have had a profound effect on him.

The importance of Soviet policies in the formation of Chikatilo's deranged psyche is a matter of conjecture, but it is quite clear that Communist party practices did play a role in making it easier for the adult Chikatilo to find victims. Soviet authorities didn't allow any information about the murders to appear in the state-controlled media. To allow the killings to be reported would, after all, have been tantamount to admitting that serious crime could exist in a Marxist-Leninist society, and that was an admission that Soviet authorities would not make. As a result, Soviet citizens were not on their guard against the serial-killer menace in their midst. Chikatilo could lure his unsuspecting victims quite easily.

The murders began in 1978 when Chikatilo was forty-two. By that time Chikatilo, a seemingly meek family man, the father of two children, had been dismissed from a job as a school dormitory supervisor due to allegations that he had sexually molested students. Now employed as a factory supply clerk, he started searching for victims who would satisfy much more terrifying impulses. In the industrial city of Rostov-on-Don in southern Russia, he would strike up conversations with boys, girls, or young women at such places as bus stops and train stations, and convince many of them to walk away with him. Sometimes he would offer them a car ride or a free meal; sometimes he would ask them to do him a favor. The walk with Chikatilo would end in a stretch of woods out of public view.

Once he began his attack, Chikatilo turned into a berserk creature, a "mad beast" as he later described himself in court. He used a rope to bind his victim's hands, a knife to slash, and his bare hands to tear at clothes and flesh. During the course of an attack, he would mutilate genitalia, gouge out eyes, and rip the victim's torso open. He would also devour flesh, as starvation-crazed peasants allegedly did to his brother.

For years young people continued to walk away willingly with Chikatilo. The killing grounds began to range beyond Rostov as Chikatilo went on state-approved business trips to Moscow, Leningrad, and parts of the Ukraine and Uzbekistan. Even after eight butchered bodies were uncovered in August 1984 alone, officials still refrained from releasing any information to the public. Had they known about the string of murders, many children and young women might have backed off from Chikatilo's come-on; they also might have passed along valuable information to the police about the man who had approached them.

In 1984, at the height of the grisly murder spree, the police placed Chikatilo in custody, believing him to be a prime suspect in the killings. But he slipped through the law's grasp; officials released him when they were unable to produce any physical evidence of his involvement in the murders.

Despite the close call with the police, Chikatilo continued his depravity, always finding new victims. After six more years of secret investigation, encompassing some 25,000 suspects, the police pulled in Chikatilo once again, having established his presence near a recent killing. Chikatilo's confession soon made it clear that the police had the right man.

At his trial, this Russian grandfather was charged with fifty-two murders, although Chikatilo's statements suggest that the total might have been higher. While in court, he was placed in a steel cage to protect him from his victims' relatives, but by the end of the trial he was never in the room for more than a few minutes at a time: his bizarre outbursts forced the presiding judge to evict him over and over again. Chikatilo would tear off his clothes, shout curses at the judge, rattle on about his fight against Assyrian mafia, and announce that he was pregnant and lactating. Judge Leonid Akubzhanov maintained that these outbursts were nothing more than calculated theatrics designed to win an insanity plea. On October 15, 1992, he sentenced Chikatilo to death. An appeal of the verdict is now pending. Should the appeal fail, Chikatilo will be executed with a bullet to the back of the head.

BIBLIOGRAPHY

In addition to magazines and newspapers, the following books were consulted in the research for *Human Monsters*:

Altman, Jack, and Marvin Ziporyn. *Speck: The Untold Story of a Mass Murderer.* Delavan, WI: Hallberg Publishing, 1984.

Bland, James. *True Crime Diary.* London: Futura Publications, 1987.

Bugliosi, Vincent, and Curt Gentry. *Helter Skelter.* New York: Norton, 1974.

Cahill, Tim. *Buried Dreams.* New York: Bantam Books, 1986.

Churchill, Allen. *A Pictorial History of American Crime, 1849–1929.* New York: Holt, Rinehart & Winston, 1964.

Cray, Ed. *Burden of Proof: The Case of Juan Corona.* New York: Macmillan Publishing, 1973.

Crockett, Art, ed. *Serial Murderers.* New York: Pinnacle Books, 1991.

Duke, Thomas S. *Celebrated Criminal Cases of America.* San Francisco: James H. Barry, 1910.

Fido, Martin. *Murder Guide to London.* Chicago: Academy Chicago Publishers, 1986.

Fowler, Will. *Reporters.* Malibu, CA: Roundtable Publishing, 1991.

Frank, Gerold. *The Boston Strangler.* New York: New American Library, 1967.

Gaute, J. H. H., and Robin Odell. *The New Murderers' Who's Who.* New York: Dorset Press, 1991.

Gribble, Leonard. *Sisters of Cain.* London: John Long, 1972.

Griffiths, Major Arthur. *Mysteries of Police and Crime.* London: Cassell and Co., 1898.

Heppenstall, Rayner. *French Crime in the Romantic Age.* London: H. Hamilton, 1970.

Jones, Ann. *Women Who Kill*. New York: Holt, Rinehart & Winston, 1980.

Jones, Richard Glyn, ed. *The Mammoth Book of Murder*. New York: Carroll & Graf Publishers, 1989.

————, ed. *Still Unsolved*. New York: Lyle Stuart, 1990.

Kent, Arthur. *Deadly Medicine*. New York: Taplinger, 1974.

Klausner, Lawrence D. *Son of Sam*. New York: McGraw-Hill, 1981.

Krafft-Ebing, Richard von. *Psychopathia Sexualis*. New York: G. P. Putnam's Sons, 1965.

Levin, Jack, and James Alan Fox. *Mass Murder*. New York: Plenum Press, 1985.

Lincoln, Victoria. *A Private Disgrace: Lizzie Borden by Daylight*. New York: G. P. Putnam's Sons, 1967.

Lucas, Norman. *The Sex Killers*. London: W. H. Allen & Co., 1974.

Lunde, Donald T. *Murder and Madness*. San Francisco: San Francisco Book Company, 1976.

McNally, Raymond T., and Radu Florescu. *In Search of Dracula*. New York: Galahad Books, 1972.

Maeder, Thomas. *The Unspeakable Crimes of Dr. Petiot*. Boston: Atlantic, Little, Brown, 1980.

Maine, C. E. *The Bizarre and the Bloody*. New York: Hart Publishing Company, 1972.

Markman, Ronald, M.D., and Dominick Bosco. *Alone with the Devil*. New York: Bantam Books, 1990.

Masters, Brian. *Killing for Company*. New York: Stein & Day, 1986.

Millett, Kate. *The Basement*. New York: Simon & Schuster, 1979.

Mitchell, Edwin Valentine, ed. *The Newgate Calendar*. Garden City, NY: Garden City Publishing, 1926.

Morley, Jackson, ed. *Crimes and Punishment*. London: BPC Publishing, 1973.

Nash, Jay Robert. *Almanac of World Crime*. New York: Doubleday, 1981.

――――. *Bloodletters and Badmen*. New York: Evans, 1973.

――――. *Look for the Woman*. New York: Evans, 1981.

――――. *Murder, America*. New York: Simon & Schuster, 1980.

――――. *World Encyclopedia of 20th Century Murder*. New York: Paragon House, 1992.

Newton, Michael. *Hunting Humans*. Port Townsend, WA: Loompanics Unlimited, 1990.

Nickel, Steven. *Torso*. Winston-Salem, NC: John F. Blair, 1989.

Norris, Joel. *Serial Killers*. New York: Doubleday, 1988.

O'Brien, Darcy. *Two of a Kind: The Hillside Stranglers*. New York: New American Library, 1985.

Otten, Charlotte T., ed. *A Lycanthropy Reader: Werewolves in Western Culture*. Syracuse, NY: Syracuse University Press, 1986.

Pinkerton, Matthew Worth. *Murder in All Ages*. Chicago: A. E. Pinkerton & Co., 1898.

Rule, Ann. *The Stranger beside Me*. New York: New American Library, 1980.

Rumbelow, Donald. *Jack the Ripper: The Complete Casebook*. Chicago: Contemporary Books, 1988.

St. Clair, David. *Say You Love Satan*. New York: Dell Publishing, 1987.

Schechter, Harold. *Deranged*. New York: Pocket Books, 1990.

――――. *Deviant*. New York: Pocket Books, 1989.

Schwartz, Ted. *The Hillside Strangler*. New York: Doubleday, 1981.

Sifakis, Carl. *The Encyclopedia of American Crime*. New York: Facts on File, 1982.

Stolper, Gustav, Karl Hauser, and Knut Borchardt. *The German Economy: 1870 to the Present*. New York: Harcourt, Brace & World, 1967.

Summers, Montague. *The Werewolf*. London: K. Paul, Trench, Trubner & Co., 1933.

Tannahill, Reay. *Flesh and Blood*. New York: Stein & Day, 1975.

Thorwald, Jurgen. *The Century of the Detective*. New York: Harcourt, Brace & World, 1964.

Williams, Emlyn. *Beyond Belief*. New York: Random House, 1967.

Wilson, Colin. *Criminal History of Mankind*. London: Granada, 1984.

———. *The Mammoth Book of True Crime 2*. New York: Carroll & Graf Publishers, 1990.

———, and Patricia Pitman. *Encyclopedia of Murder*. New York: G. P. Putnam's Sons, 1961.

———, and Donald Seaman. *Encyclopedia of Modern Murder*. New York: G. P. Putnam's Sons, 1985.

———, and Donald Seaman. *The Serial Killers*. New York: Carol Publishing Group, 1991.

Wolf, Leonard. *Bluebeard*. New York: C. N. Potter, 1980.

INDEX